Film and Constitutional Controversy

In modern-day Hong Kong, major constitutional controversies have caused people to demonstrate on the streets, immigrate to other countries, occupy major thoroughfares, and even engage in violence. These controversies have such great resonance because they put pressure on a cultural identity made possible by, and inseparable from, the 'One Country, Two Systems' framework. Hong Kong is also a city synonymous with film, ranging from commercial gangster movies to the art cinema of Wong Kar-wai. This book argues that while the importance of constitutional controversies for the process of self-formation may not be readily discernible in court judgments and legislative enactments, it is registered in the diverse modes of expression found in Hong Kong cinema. It contends that film gives form to the ways in which Hong Kong identity is articulated, placed under stress, bolstered, and transformed in light of disputes about the nature and meaning of the city's constitutional documents.

Marco Wan is Associate Professor of Law and Director of the Law and Literary Studies Programme at the University of Hong Kong. He is trained in both legal and literary/cultural studies, and his research focuses on law and film, law and literature, and the ways in which perspectives from the humanities shed light on the legal regulation of gender and sexuality. His first book, *Masculinity and the Trials of Modern Fiction* (2017), was awarded the Penny Pether Prize from the Law, Literature, and Humanities Association of Australasia. He is Managing Editor of *Law & Literature*.

Law in Context

Series editors
Professor Kenneth Armstrong *University of Cambridge*
Professor Maksymilian Del Mar *Queen Mary, University of London*
Professor Sally Sheldon *University of Kent*

Editorial advisory board
Professor Bronwen Morgan *University of New South Wales*
Emeritus Professor William Twining *University College London*

Since 1970, the Law in Context series has been at the forefront of a movement to broaden the study of law. The series is a vehicle for the publication of innovative monographs and texts that treat law and legal phenomena critically in their cultural, social, political, technological, environmental and economic contexts. A contextual approach involves treating legal subjects broadly, using materials from other humanities and social sciences, and from any other discipline that helps to explain the operation in practice of the particular legal field or legal phenomena under investigation. It is intended that this orientation is at once more stimulating and more revealing than the bare exposition of legal rules. The series includes original research monographs, coursebooks and textbooks that foreground contextual approaches and methods. The series includes and welcomes books on the study of law in all its contexts, including domestic legal systems, European and international law, transnational and global legal processes, and comparative law.

Books in the Series

Lewis: *Choice and the Legal Order: Rising above Politics*

Likosky: *Law, Infrastructure and Human Rights*

Likosky: *Transnational Legal Processes: Globalisation and Power Disparities*

Lixinski: *Legalized Identities*

Loughnan: *Self, Others and the State: Relations of Criminal Responsibility*

Lunney: *A History of Australian Tort Law 1901–1945: England's Obedient Servant?*

Maughan & Webb: *Lawyering Skills and the Legal Process, 2nd Edition*

McGlynn: *Families and the European Union: Law, Politics and Pluralism*

Mertens: *A Philosophical Introduction to Human Rights*

Moffat: *Trusts Law: Text and Materials*

Monti: *EC Competition Law*

Morgan: *Contract Law Minimalism: A Formalist Restatement of Commercial Contract Law*

Morgan & Yeung: *An Introduction to Law and Regulation: Text and Materials*

Nicola & Davies: *EU Law Stories: Contextual and Critical Histories of European Jurisprudence*

Norrie: *Crime, Reason and History: A Critical Introduction to Criminal Law, 3rd Edition*

O'Dair: *Legal Ethics: Text and Materials*

Oliver: *Common Values and the Public–Private Divide*

Oliver & Drewry: *The Law and Parliament*

Palmer & Roberts: *Dispute Processes: ADR and the Primary Forms of Decision-Making, 1st Edition*

Palmer & Roberts: *Dispute Processes: ADR and the Primary Forms of Decision-Making, 3rd Edition*

Picciotto: *International Business Taxation*

Probert: *The Changing Legal Regulation of Cohabitation, 1600–2010: From Fornicators to Family, 1600–2010*

Radi: *Rules and Practices of International Investment Law and Arbitration*

Reed: *Internet Law: Text and Materials*

Richardson: *Law, Process and Custody*

Roberts & Palmer: *Dispute Processes: ADR and the Primary Forms of Decision-Making, 2nd Edition*

Rowbottom: *Democracy Distorted: Wealth, Influence and Democratic Politics*

Sauter: *Public Services in EU Law*

Scott & Black: *Cranston's Consumers and the Law*

Seneviratne: *Ombudsmen: Public Services and Administrative Justice*

Seppänen: *Ideological Conflict and the Rule of Law in Contemporary China: Useful Paradoxes*

Siems: *Comparative Law, 2nd Edition*

Stapleton: *Product Liability*

Stewart: *Gender, Law and Justice in a Global Market*

Tamanaha: *Law as a Means to an End: Threat to the Rule of Law*

Turpin & Tomkins: *British Government and the Constitution: Text and Materials, 7th Edition*

Twining: *General Jurisprudence: Understanding Law from a Global Perspective*

Twining: *Globalisation and Legal Theory*

Twining: *Human Rights, Southern Voices: Francis Deng, Abdullahi An-Na'im, Yash Ghai and Upendra Baxi*

Twining: *Jurist in Context: A Memoir*

Twining: *Karl Llewellyn and the Realist Movement, 2nd Edition*

Twining: *Rethinking Evidence: Exploratory Essays, 2nd Edition*

Twining & Miers: *How to Do Things with Rules, 5th Edition*

Wan: Film and Constitutional Controversy

Ward: *A Critical Introduction to European Law, 3rd Edition*

Ward: *Law, Text, Terror*

Ward: *Shakespeare and Legal Imagination*

Wells & Quick: *Lacey, Wells and Quick: Reconstructing Criminal Law: Text and Materials, 4th Edition*

Zander: *Cases and Materials on the English Legal System, 10th Edition*

Zander: *The Law-Making Process, 6th Edition*

International Journal of Law in Context: A Global Forum for Interdisciplinary Legal Studies

The *International Journal of Law in Context* is the companion journal to the Law in Context book series and provides a forum for interdisciplinary legal studies and offers intellectual space for ground-breaking critical research. It publishes contextual work about law and its relationship with other disciplines including but not limited to science, literature, humanities, philosophy, sociology, psychology, ethics, history and geography. More information about the journal and how to submit an article can be found at http://journals.cambridge.org/ijc.

Film and Constitutional Controversy

Visualizing Hong Kong Identity in the Age of "One Country, Two Systems"

MARCO WAN

The University of Hong Kong

CAMBRIDGE
UNIVERSITY PRESS

CAMBRIDGE
UNIVERSITY PRESS

University Printing House, Cambridge CB2 8BS, United Kingdom

One Liberty Plaza, 20th Floor, New York, NY 10006, USA

477 Williamstown Road, Port Melbourne, VIC 3207, Australia

314–321, 3rd Floor, Plot 3, Splendor Forum, Jasola District Centre,
New Delhi – 110025, India

79 Anson Road, #06–04/06, Singapore 079906

Cambridge University Press is part of the University of Cambridge.

It furthers the University's mission by disseminating knowledge in the pursuit of
education, learning, and research at the highest international levels of excellence.

www.cambridge.org
Information on this title: www.cambridge.org/9781108495776
DOI: 10.1017/9781108863025

© Marco Wan 2020

First published 2020

A catalogue record for this publication is available from the British Library.

ISBN 978-1-108-49577-6 Hardback
ISBN 978-1-108-79776-4 Paperback

Cambridge University Press has no responsibility for the persistence or accuracy of
URLs for external or third-party internet websites referred to in this publication
and does not guarantee that any content on such websites is, or will remain,
accurate or appropriate.

To all those who care about Hong Kong.

Contents

Acknowledgments

This book brings together two of my great passions – constitutional law and film – and it is a pleasure to thank the people working within, and across, each of the two areas who have inspired me in the project. I am grateful to Peter Goodrich for inviting me to the *In Flagrante Depicto* symposium at the Benjamin N. Cardozo School of Law in New York, during which I first began thinking about law and film. His work continues to inspire. Gina Marchetti, with whom I co-taught a course on law and cinema at the University of Hong Kong (HKU), has generously shared her vast knowledge of East Asian film with me over the years, and I feel fortunate to have her as an interlocutor. Scott Veitch is a model of clear thinking, and his probing questions helped make the argument here sharper. I have also learned much from the work of Alison Conner, William P. MacNeil, and Desmond Manderson.

Joe Ng and Gemma Smith at Cambridge University Press have been wonderfully helpful editors. Cora Chan, Rey Chow, Sarah Cooper, Christopher Munn, and Michael Palmer read parts of the manuscript and gave many insightful comments. Andrew Counter once again read every word I wrote with love and care. Alision Lam provided helpful research assistance. I have also benefited from conversations with Russell Boaz, Jenny Chamarette, Johannes Chan, Albert Chen, Chu Yiu-wai, Christian Delage, Chris Hutton, Derek Lam, Li Cheuk-to, Daniel Matthews, Margaret Ng, Michael Ng, Helen Siu, Emma Wilson, John Wong, and Herman Yau.

Part of the book was written during a fellowship at the Käte Hamburger Center for Advanced Study in the Humanities "Law as Culture" in Bonn, Germany, and I would like to thank the director, staff, and fellows there for their warm hospitality. A version of Chapter 2 appeared in 31(4) *Cardozo Law Review* (2010), and a version of Chapter 4 appeared in *Law and Language*, edited by Michael Freedom and Fiona Smith (Oxford: Oxford University Press, 2010). I thank the publishers for permission to reproduce the material here. I also acknowledge with gratitude support from the General Research Fund (GRF) of the Hong Kong University Grants Committee.

Abbreviations

CEDAW   Convention on the Elimination of All Forms of Discrimination against Women
CEPA   Mainland and Hong Kong Closer Economic Partnership Arrangement
ICAC   Independent Commission against Corruption
ICCPR   International Covenant on Civil and Political Rights
NGO   nongovernmental organization
NPCSC   Standing Committee of the National People's Congress
PLA   People's Liberation Army
PRC   People's Republic of China
SARS   Severe Acute Respiratory Syndrome

Introduction[*]

In early 2016, a film that had been sold out at cinemas in Hong Kong was abruptly taken off screens. *Ten Years* (十年; 2015) comprises a series of short films collectively depicting a dystopian future in which Hong Kong's freedoms are taken away by China. These shorts center on, respectively, a shop owner who gets reprehended by youth scouts reminiscent of Chinese Red Guards from the Cultural Revolution; a self-immolator whose tragic act evokes similar practices in Tibet; a couple who tries to preserve the Hong Kong that they know through macabre attempts at turning themselves and the things around them into biospecimens; and a taxi driver facing economic and psychological hardship because of a language policy favoring Mandarin, China's official language, rather than Cantonese, the dialect spoken in Hong Kong and the taxi driver's mother tongue. The film also includes a segment in which Hong Kong officials and their mainland Chinese counterparts stage a terrorist attack in order to forge the public support they need to pass laws relating to national security, an issue that has led in real life to intense anxiety about the potential curtailment of local rights and freedoms in Hong Kong. The sudden end to the cinematic lifespan of *Ten Years* coincided with an attack on the film by the state-run media in mainland China, as epitomized by the opinion piece in the *Global Times* which denounced it as "a virus of the mind" and as "absurd."[1] While the artistic achievement of the film is a matter of debate, the chilling effect on expression of such denunciations was undeniable[2]: as a long-time film critic notes, while "no exhibitor would admit to censorship or direct pressure from China," it was unprecedented for a film which sold "to full houses at every single screening" to have its run terminated in such

[*] This book was completed on January 31st, 2020, and I discuss constitutional developments and relevant cinematic productions up to that date in the following pages. All translations from Chinese sources are my own unless otherwise indicated.

[1] Illaria Maria Sala, "Ten Years – the Terrifying Vision of Hong Kong that Beijing Wants Obscured," *The Guardian*, March 11th, 2016.

[2] See, for instance, different assessments of the film in "Priscilla Leung Watches *Ten Years*: Story UnFair to Central Government," *Ming Pao Daily News*, January 21st, 2016 and Yat Kwong, "*Ten Years*," *Ming Pao Daily News*, November 20th, 2015.

a manner.[3] In response to the discontinuation of *Ten Years* at the cinemas, civic activists in Hong Kong organized free local screenings at community centers and open-air venues to ensure continued access for viewers, and the film directors often joined the audience for post-screening discussions.[4] *Ten Years* ended up winning Best Picture at the Hong Kong Film Awards.

Ten Years and its aftermath constitute a point of entry into the nexus of constitutional law, film, and identity which I will explore in this book. Hong Kong is a city synonymous with film: from the martial arts movies starring Bruce Lee to the arthouse cinema of Wong Kar-wai, and from the stylized gun fights choreographed by John Woo to the more recent independent documentaries by younger local filmmakers showcased at film festivals around the world, Hong Kong's prolific and varied cinematic productions constitute an industry that puts it firmly on the global cultural map. Even with the advent of new media in the late twentieth and early twenty-first centuries, film remains a highly popular form of entertainment among Hong Kongers. As one of Hong Kong's most dominant cultural forms, it addresses many of the territory's most salient social, cultural, and, as I will show, legal issues.

Ten Years itself engages with a critical problem in the territory, that of a growing identity crisis in a community constantly on guard against being subsumed by mainland China. More importantly for my purposes, the film suggests that in Hong Kong, questions of identity are often intertwined with issues of law, an intertwining which has so far been rarely explored on its own terms in the vast scholarship on either Hong Kong law or Hong Kong cinema: in the shorts, anxieties about a fading sense of selfhood are variously tied to the rise of surveillance and the decline of privacy, the implementation of censorship and self-censorship, a restriction of language rights, and the use of national security as a pretext for expanding government control. The circumstances surrounding the film's reception are also significant: it could still be viewed in Hong Kong, albeit in less conventional locations, and the awards ceremony still aired on primetime television in the city even though its broadcast was canceled in the mainland as a result of the Best Picture nomination.[5] These differences indicate that guarantees of rights and liberties such as artistic freedom and freedom of information underpin the existence of a distinct community of film viewers, directors, and producers from the rest of the country, a community whose boundaries are, as we shall we, becoming increasingly blurred as Hong Kong becomes more integrated with the mainland.

In the following pages, I argue that film can be approached as a set of images capturing the ways in which a selfhood interwoven with law is

---

[3] Sala, "Ten Years."

[4] See Karen Fang, "Cinema Censorship and Media Citizenship in the Hong Kong Film *Ten Years*," 16(2) *Surveillance & Society* (2018), 142–157.

[5] Alan Wong, "China News Blackout as *Ten Years* Takes Hong Kong Best Film Award," *New York Times*, April 4th, 2016.

articulated, placed under stress, bolstered, and transformed amid a number of constitutional controversies, first when Hong Kong transitioned from British colony to Chinese Special Administrative Region and then in the postcolonial period during which it became increasingly integrated into the Chinese nation. By "constitutional controversies," I refer to disagreements about the status and meaning of a corpus of legal texts – primarily the Basic Law, Hong Kong's post-handover constitutional document, but also associated texts such as the Sino-British Joint Declaration and the Bill of Rights Ordinance – that sparked heated debates, intense conflict, and grave concerns in Hong Kong society. These controversies reverberated not only among lawyers, judges, and lawmakers but among Hong Kong residents more broadly, causing many of them to march in the streets, occupy major commercial districts, and even engage in violence. I posit that while such reverberations are rarely picked up in more doctrinal discussions of constitutional interpretation focusing on, say, the application of the proportionality test, they are registered in some of the cinematic images that appeared at the same historical moment as the controversies. Filmmakers engage with such constitutional events with varying levels of awareness: sometimes, they explicitly select a contentious issue as the subject of their work, but often a film captures the mood or the *mentalité* of the city without the filmmaker consciously intending for it to do so. I therefore include in the selection of films in this book fictional narratives that thematize the legal process, such as courtroom dramas, as well as films that more explicitly reference or more consciously reflect upon ongoing, real-life legal controversies, such as documentaries. My investigation will proceed broadly chronologically from the 1980s to our own time.

Hong Kong is a liberal jurisdiction nestled within China's one-party socialist regime. Its over-arching constitutional principle is known as "One Country, Two Systems." First put forward by Deng Xiaoping, who emerged as China's paramount leader in the late 1970s and remained influential in Chinese politics until his death in 1997, it aims to ensure that the city's capitalist economic system, established during its time as a British colony, would remain unchanged for fifty years after China regained sovereignty and that China's socialist system and policies would not be implemented within that period. The principle also guarantees a separate political system and legal framework for Hong Kong. In the Sino-British Joint Declaration, the 1984 agreement signed between the British and Chinese governments which stipulated that the transfer of sovereignty would occur on July 1st, 1997, the principle of "One Country, Two Systems" is encapsulated in China's promise to designate Hong Kong as a "Special Administrative Region" that will "enjoy a high degree of autonomy" from the Central People's Government. The promises in the Declaration are given form in the Basic Law: while Article 1 states that Hong Kong is an "inalienable part" of China, the preamble reiterates the

"One Country, Two Systems" formula, and Article 2 enshrines Hong Kong's "high degree of autonomy." [6]

The constitutional document aims to strike a balance between acknowledging Chinese sovereignty and respecting the differences between Hong Kong and the rest of the country. Its significance is not only economic, legal, and political, but also cultural.[7] Article 5 underscores this point: it states that "the previous capitalist way of life shall remain unchanged for fifty years" and that "the socialist system and policies" of the mainland "shall not be practised in the Hong Kong Special Administrative Region."[8] The language here can be traced to Section 3(5) of the Joint Declaration, which states that the social and economic systems in Hong Kong will be preserved, "and so will the life-style."[9] The emphasis on "lifestyle" and "way of life" in the two documents underscores the imbrication of the constitutional guarantee and cultural identity: what the territory's highest law protects is not only a framework for trade and commerce but an entire way of living and an entire way of being. The "One Country, Two Systems" principle, as well as the Basic Law which enshrines it, forms the premise of a unique identity. In this light, challenges to the rights and freedoms guaranteed to Hong Kongers within their constitutionally demarcated economic, legal, and cultural spaces, whether real or imagined, often come to be regarded as nothing less than threats to that identity. It is precisely these threats, and the responses to them, that become visually registered in the films I examine.

In this Introduction, I will first provide, by way of background, a historical overview of the cultural processes which gave rise to a distinct Hong Kong identity. I then focus on the interweaving of law and identity: the second section traces how the construction of this identity became inseparable from law, and in particular from ideas about the rule of law, the common law, and human rights; and the third section reexamines the major constitutional controversies in post-handover Hong Kong in relation to their bearing on conceptions of self and community. In the fourth, I return to my discussion of Hong Kong cinema to consider how film operates as a medium engaging with the disputes about "One Country, Two Systems" that impacted upon

---

[6] Preamble, Article 1, and Article 2, *Basic Law of the Hong Kong Special Administrative Region of the People's Republic of China*.

[7] In his seminal work on the Basic Law, Yash Ghai argues that the emphasis of the constitutional document is economic, and not cultural (*Hong Kong's New Constitutional Order: The Resumption of Chinese Sovereignty and the Basic Law*, 2nd ed. (Hong Kong: Hong Kong University Press, 1999), pp. 184–185). The maintenance of Hong Kong's economic system is undoubtedly an important dimension of the Basic Law, but I differ from Ghai in my assessment of the cultural ramifications of Hong Kong's constitutional order.

[8] Article 5, *Basic Law of the Hong Kong Special Administrative Region of the People's Republic of China*.

[9] *Joint Declaration of the Government of the United Kingdom of Great Britain and Northern Ireland and the Government of the People's Republic of China on the Question of Hong Kong*.

Hong Kongers' sense of who they are and how they are situated in relation to mainland China.

Becoming Hong Kongese: A Brief History

Hong Kong as it exists today consists of three parts: Hong Kong island, which China permanently ceded to Britain in 1842 under the Treaty of Nanking; the Kowloon Peninsula, which it ceded to Britain in 1860 under the Convention of Peking; and the New Territories and a number of outlying islands, which it leased to Britain for ninety-nine years in 1898. As a number of historians have noted, people in Hong Kong did not begin to develop a sense of themselves as "Hong Kongers" until the middle of the twentieth century. For a long time, people who lived in Hong Kong were "sojourners, economic migrants or refugees" of Chinese ethnicity who "shared much more in common with their fellow countrymen living on the mainland of China" than with the expatriates in the colony.[10] This "sojourner mentality" began to change after the formation of the People's Republic in 1949: as Hugh Baker observes in an oft-cited article, the resultant "closing of the border between Hong Kong and China, and the very different political and economic situations on the two sides of it [. . .] led to the emergence of a new attitude on the part of the Chinese" living and working in the colony, who began to "look on Hong Kong as their permanent home."[11] This self-identification intensified in the 1960s and the 1970s, as the first postwar generation of people born in Hong Kong came of age; this was a generation that grew up in the British colony and had little firsthand experience of life in China. The contrast between the "political stability and economic freedom in Hong Kong" and the "repression and chaos" in China during the Great Leap Forward and the Cultural Revolution further consolidated emerging ideas of selfhood.[12]

Yet conditions in the colony were far from perfect, and vast inequalities led to serious riots in 1966. These riots were followed by further disturbances in 1967 which were directed by the clandestine Hong Kong branch of the Chinese Communist Party against "'the British imperialist capitalists'."[13] To gain public support in the aftermath of these events, the colonial government adopted policies to cultivate a sense of belonging in the people living in Hong Kong: it improved communication between the administration and the populace; built "New Towns" in the more sparsely populated New Territories to relieve overcrowding in the urban areas of Kowloon and

[10] Steve Tsang, *A Modern History of Hong Kong* (Hong Kong: Hong Kong University Press, 2004), p. 180.
[11] Hugh D. R. Baker, "Life in the Cities: The Emergence of Hong Kong Man," 95 *China Quarterly* (1983), 469–479 (478).
[12] John M. Carroll, *A Concise History of Hong Kong* (Hong Kong: Hong Kong University Press, 2007), p. 167.
[13] Tsang, *A Modern History of Hong Kong,* p. 185.

Hong Kong island; and expanded the budget for the arts to nurture Cantonese-language culture such as Cantonese opera and drama.[14] These policies contributed substantially to the consolidation of "Hong Kongers" as a community, and by the time the Sino-British Joint Declaration was signed in 1984, a distinct identity had coalesced in the city. Writing one year before the Declaration, Baker discerns a category known as "the Hong Kong Man" that is "sui generis": brought up at the confluence of both Western and Asian cultural traditions, this is a hybrid being who, while moving comfortably between the two cultures, "gives little credit to the Union Jack" and is "not necessarily happy at the prospect of the five-starred red flag presiding over his activities." Instead, "he belong[s] to Hong Kong" and is "intensely proud of it."[15] The cultural critic Ackbar Abbas makes a similar point when he observes, shortly before the 1997 handover, that "it is not true, as some might wish to believe, that if you scratch the surface of a Hong Kong person you will find a Chinese identity waiting to be reborn. The Hong Kong person is now a bird of a different feather, perhaps a kind of Maltese Falcon."[16]

Since the retrocession, academic and nonacademic commentators have identified an "identity crisis" gathering pace in Hong Kong.[17] One way of approaching this crisis is as a reaction to the feeling that the cultural hybridity or uniqueness inherent in Hong Kong identity is gradually being eroded as the city moves further away from its colonial past and becomes more deeply integrated with China. This integration takes place on multiple levels. In economic terms, one significant moment of integration came in 2003, when the local Hong Kong government and the Chinese government signed the Mainland and Hong Kong Closer Economic Partnership Arrangement (CEPA), a free trade arrangement which provided greater access to Chinese markets for Hong Kong businesses, and enabled mainland businesses to use Hong Kong as a springboard to the global market. It also adopted the Individual Visit Scheme, which allowed people from mainland China to visit Hong Kong on an individual basis, whereas before 2003 they could only visit the city on business or as part of a group tour. These measures were meant to boost the Hong Kong economy after the Severe Acute Respiratory Syndrome,

---

[14] Carroll, *A Concise History of Hong Kong*, pp. 168–172.

[15] Tsang, *A Modern History of Hong Kong*, p. 195.

[16] Ackbar Abbas, *Hong Kong: Culture and the Politics of Disappearance* (Hong Kong: Hong Kong University Press, 1997), p. 2.

[17] May Sin-mi Hon, "SAR Still Has an Identity Crisis – Anson Chan," *South China Morning Post*, December 29th, 2002; Chris Yeung, "What Identity Crisis?," *South China Morning Post*, May 23rd, 2005; Howard Y. F. Choy, "Schizophrenic Hong Kong: Postcolonial Identity Crisis in the *Infernal Affairs* Trilogy" 3 *transtext(e)s transcultures* (2007), 52–66; "Feeling Special – Hong Kong's Identity Crisis," *Economist*, June 4th, 2009; Manik Mehta, "Hong Kong's Identity Crisis," *South China Morning Post*, September 8th, 2012; Sebastian Veg, "Hong Kong's Enduring Identity Crisis," *Atlantic*, October 16th, 2013; Michael Chugani, "Identity Crisis is the Root of an Unhappy Hong Kong," *Hong Kong Economic Journal*, February 14th, 2019; Brian Y. S. Wong, "Hong Kong's Identity Crisis is One of its Own Making," *South China Morning Post*, May 8th, 2019.

or the SARS epidemic, pushed it into the doldrums, but they also "reshaped the cityscape to accommodate the needs of the Mainland tourists" as Hong Kong became more financially reliant on Chinese tourism and commerce. The rising number of travelers, coupled with the increasing number of people relocating to the city to live and work from the mainland, meant that more Mandarin could be heard on the streets, and reports of culture clashes between mainlanders and local Hong Kongers became increasingly frequent.[18]

At the level of education, the Hong Kong government's 2012 attempt at introducing Chinese civic education in local primary and secondary schools, in the form of a curriculum on "moral and national education," sparked widespread concerns that it was seeking to brainwash the city's children through a program that espoused the position and doctrines of the Communist Party.[19] Anxieties about blurred boundaries reached a peak in 2015 following the disappearance of five men affiliated with a Hong Kong bookstore which specialized in gossipy titles about the Chinese leadership. The booksellers variously disappeared from Thailand, Hong Kong, and the mainland, and subsequently reemerged in custody in mainland China.[20] They claimed on state media that they had left Hong Kong voluntarily, but the incident sparked fears in Hong Kong that they were illegally abducted by the Chinese authorities for selling books banned in the mainland.[21] One of them subsequently told reporters that he was kidnapped while crossing the border and warned that "it can happen to you too [. . .] This is not just about me. This is about the freedom of the Hong Kong people."[22] Three years later, the high-profile opening of the fifty-five kilometre Hong Kong-Zhuhai-Macau Bridge, a project much criticized in Hong Kong for its detrimental impact on local aquatic life as well as its massive budget overruns, provided a symbol of this uneasy but ever closer union.[23]

All of these developments combined to put transformative pressures on established conceptions of identity and gave rise to a sense among some people that their selfhood was under threat. In many Hong Kongers who grew up before the handover, there arose a feeling that their uniqueness as a group of people situated in that in-between space of being, in Baker's description, both

[18]   See, for instance, Editorial, "Stop Culture Clash Getting Out of Hand," *South China Morning Post*, January 26th, 2012; Vivienne Chow, "Anger at Mainland Visitors Escalates with 'Locust' Ad," *South China Morning Post*, February 1st, 2012; Marla Friedman, "Cultures Clash as Mainland Chinese Tourists Flood Hong Kong," *Huffington Post*, November 20th, 2013; Tanna Chong and Chris Luo, "'Pee-in-HK' Call Over Picture Furor: Mainlanders Launch Online Campaign to 'Familiarize' Hong Kongers with Humans' Natural Functions After Clash Over Public Urination", *South China Morning Post*, April 24th, 2014.

[19]   Alexis Lai, "'National Education' Raises Furor in Hong Kong," *CNN*, July 30th, 2012.

[20]   Philia Siu, Ng Kang-chung, and Owen Fung, "Bookseller Lam Wing-kee Reveals Explosive Details of His Mainland China Detention," *South China Morning Post*, June 16th, 2016.

[21]   John Kang, "The Missing Hong Kong Booksellers Saga Explained," *Forbes*, June 17th, 2016.

[22]   Siu, Ng, and Fung, "Explosive Details."

[23]   Kanis Leung, "World's Longest Sea Crossing Is Finally Finished, but Hong Kong-Zhuhai-Macau Bridge Has Come at a High Cost," *South China Morning Post*, October 19th, 2018.

"not British or western" and "not Chinese in the same way that citizens of the People's Republic of China are Chinese" was wearing away.[24] The younger generation does not necessarily know of or remember any cultural reality other than the one under Chinese sovereignty, but as *Financial Times* correspondent Ben Bland observes, they evince a strong anti-integration sensibility and their self-understanding is anchored in the idea of "not being a mainlander," even if many of them "find it difficult to define what it means to be a Hong Konger."[25] Local journalist Michael Chugani further notes that many young people feel like "their culture and way of life is dying a slow death" due to the deepening integration.[26] According to a 2019 survey by the *Economist*, almost nobody in Hong Kong under the age of thirty identifies as Chinese.[27]

Scholars of Hong Kong culture have sought an analytical register for articulating this amalgamated sense of loss, nostalgia, disorientation, and cultural besiegement. One of the key figures in the field is Abbas. Looking back at the 1980s and the 1990s, Abbas identifies a "politics of disappearance" at work in the city: according to him, "the uncomfortable possibility" that China would impose "an alien identity" on Hong Kong led to an anxious sense that the self as one knew it was about to disappear, and this ever-present possibility of disappearance is what triggered reflection on what Hong Kong identity means.[28] In the postcolonial era, the identity crisis is often considered the result of a resistance to the pressures of disappearance arising from what is variously described as "re-Sinicisation,"[29] "mainlandization,"[30] and even Chinese "recolonization."[31] Concerns about the deepening of such processes have led to the emergence of localist sentiments and calls for Hong Kong independence in some quarters, as evidenced by the establishment of localist political parties such as Hong Kong Indigenous and Youngspiration in 2015, as well as Demosistō and the Hong Kong National Party in 2016.[32]

Hong Kong identity, then, can be said to be a form of selfhood that is built upon the possibility, even the likelihood, of its own disappearance as the city

---

[24] Baker, "Life in the Cities," 478.

[25] Ben Bland, "China Tensions Give Hong Kong an Identity Crisis," *Financial Times*, June 29th, 2017.

[26] Chugani, "Identity Crisis Is the Root of an Unhappy Hong Kong.".

[27] "Almost Nobody in Hong Kong under 30 Identifies as 'Chinese'," *Economist*, August 26th, 2019.

[28] Abbas, *Hong Kong*, p. 4.

[29] Choy, "Schizophrenic Hong Kong: Postcolonial Identity Crisis in the *Infernal Affairs Trilogy*," p. 55.

[30] Carol A. G. Jones, *Lost in China? Law, Culture and Identity in Post-1997 Hong Kong* (Cambridge, Cambridge University Press, 2015), p. 10.

[31] Sonny Lo, "The Mainlandization and Recolonization of Hong Kong: A Triumph of Convergence over Divergence with Mainland China," *The Hong Kong Special Administrative Region in its First Decade*, edited by Joseph Y. S. Cheng (Hong Kong: City University Press, 2007), pp. 179–232.

[32] The Hong Kong National Party was subsequently banned on the grounds that it posed a threat to national security: Lily Kuo, "Hong Kong Bans Pro-independence Party as China Tightens Grip," *Guardian*, September 24th, 2018.

becomes increasingly fused with the rest of China. Disquiet and angst about the politics of disappearance first emerged when negotiations for the city's return to China began in the 1980s, ebbed and waned in the 1990s, and returned in the first decades of the twenty-first century as Hong Kong's political, economic, and cultural integration with the mainland gathered pace. Given Hong Kong's physical location, first as a colonial outpost adjacent to China and then as a special administrative region within it, as well the common ethnicity of most of its own inhabitants and those across the border, there is little in geographical or ethnic terms that grounds Hong Kongers' self-understanding as having a distinct identity vis-à-vis the rest of the country. Furthermore, China's rapid economic growth and competition from places such as Shanghai have threatened to undermine the city's unique role as an international financial center in the country. In these circumstances, the law emerged as a differentiating factor or part of a set of "alternative, symbolic, boundary-markers" between Hong Kong and the mainland, and became increasingly entrenched as a definitive part of the community's understanding of itself in the postcolonial era.[33] I will explore the multiple links between law and self-identification in the territory in the next two sections, before returning to my discussion of film.

I Have the Rule of Law, Therefore I am

An important aspect of the process of "becoming Hong Kongese," and one which sometimes gets insufficiently foregrounded, is the role of law.[34] China has a socialist legal system, in contrast to Hong Kong's liberal system characterized by the rule of law, commitment to human rights, and independence of the judiciary. China's record of protecting rights and freedoms remains heavily disputed: while the Chinese constitution contains a list of protected rights, in reality the government deems the exercise of these rights unacceptable if it challenges party rule.[35] The state's tight control of the Internet and mass media undermines the freedom of expression and of access to information,[36] and there have been documented instances of forced confessions and torture which compromise the right to a fair trial.[37] Legal scholar Eva Pils has underscored that human rights defenders in China are often portrayed as "enemies of the state" and subjected to travel bans, informal house arrest, detention, and even forced disappearances.[38] Judicial independence remains shaky: as Pils also

---

[33] Jones, *Lost in China?* p. 39.   [34] Carroll, *A Concise History of Hong Kong*, p. 167.

[35] Albert H. Y. Chen, *An Introduction to the Legal System of the People's Republic of China*, 5th ed. (Hong Kong: LexisNexus, 2019), p. 66.

[36] Human Rights Watch, *World Report 2019: China.*

[37] Human Rights Watch, "Tiger Chairs and Cell Bosses: Police Torture of Criminal Suspects in China" May 13th, 2015.

[38] Eva Pils, *Human Rights in China: A Social Practice in the Shadows of Authoritarianism* (Cambridge: Polity Press, 2018), p. 118. For a discussion of a more specific crackdown on human rights lawyers and its aftermath, see Hualing Fu and Han Zhu, "After the July 9 (709)

points out, "the judiciary's institutional design does not support independence from other authorities of the Party-State," such that while "judges are required to apply the law to facts," "they must also be loyal to the Party, according to their professional oath."[39]

Hong Kong's Basic Law provides for the continuation of a separate legal system based on the common law: unless they contravene the constitution, and subject to amendment by the legislature, "the laws previously in force in Hong Kong" prior to the handover, "that is, the common law, rules of equity, ordinances, subordinate legislation and customary law shall be maintained" (Article 8). It also guarantees that Hong Kong's courts will "exercise judicial power independently, free from interference" (Article 85), that the system of trial by jury will be preserved (Article 86), and that the Court of Final Appeal can "invite judges from other common law jurisdictions" to adjudicate cases (Article 82). Importantly, the Basic Law gives Hong Kongers human rights protections beyond those enjoyed in the mainland. For instance, Article 39 guarantees that the provisions of the International Covenant on Civil and Political Rights (ICCPR), the International Covenant on Economic, Social, and Cultural Rights (ICESCR), and international labour conventions that apply to Hong Kong will remain in force after the resumption of Chinese sovereignty. The constitutional document's extensive list of rights is complemented by a well-established mechanism of judicial review in the courts, and the Bill of Rights Ordinance further incorporates provisions of the ICCPR at the level of domestic legislation. The legal structure in Hong Kong under "One Country, Two Systems" allows for a way of life characterized by freedoms that are impermissible in the rest of the country.

In this context, the rights which Hong Kongers enjoy within their constitutional order become a firm marker of identity, and the idea of a separate legal system becomes a fundamental part of how people understand their distinctiveness from their Chinese counterparts across the border. Recognizing the inextricable connections between law and selfhood sheds light on why references to legal processes, figures, and conundrums appear across genres in Hong Kong film: from comedies to documentaries to gangster movies, law is an important part of the territory's set of cultural representations because it is an integral part of Hong Kongers' conception of themselves.[40]

Crackdown: The Future of human Rights Lawyering," 41(5) *Fordham International Law Journal* (2018), 1135–1165.

[39] Pils, *Human Rights in China*, p. 46.

[40] On constitutions and identity beyond the Hong Kong context, see Michel Rosenfeld, *The Identity of the Constitutional Subject: Selfhood, Citizenship, Culture, and Community* (Abingdon: Routledge, 2010) (the constitutional subject as (re)constructed through negation, metaphor, and metonymy) and Gary Jacobsohn, *Constitutional Identity* (Cambridge: Harvard University Press, 2010) (the identity of a constitution as an ongoing negotiation of the demands of continuity and change). As both authors point out, constitutional identity intersects with, but is analytically distinct from, other identities such as national, cultural, and religious

In addition to the overall constitutional framework, the idea of the rule of law has also become a core part of Hong Kong identity. The historian Steve Tsang observes that the inextricable link between identity and the rule of law first emerged in Hong Kong during the mid-to-late 1960s: according to Tsang, Hong Kongers' acute awareness of the "lawless horror" involving the confiscation of property, public humiliations, mass relocations, and imprisonment that was occurring in such close geographical proximity to their own city during the Cultural Revolution "made this Anglo-Saxon concept particularly attractive," so much so that "by the 1970s, Hong Kong people of all ethnic origins had embraced the concept of the rule of law." Socio-legal scholar Carol Jones adds that the colonial government's "exhortation of the merits of English rule of law was in part a reflection of the colonisers' sense of themselves as bringers of civilisation to the East, and part conscious strategy to establish a red line between life under British rule and life in what was then seen as a barbarous China."[41]

The irony is that, for a long time, the record of the British administration's adherence to the rule of law in Hong Kong was patchy at best: corruption was rampant and "permeated [...] the government";[42] a racial hierarchy was instituted through the enactment of anti-Chinese legislation;[43] unfair commercial advantages were given to British businesses;[44] and there existed an extensive censorship system targeting the Chinese press.[45] The implementation of the rule of law in a more meaningful sense did not take place until after the riots of the late 1960s, as part of the colonial administration's attempt to cultivate a sense of belonging: in the decade that followed those riots, the "promise [...] that everyone would be treated openly and equally on the fair field of law" dovetailed with a "frenzy of new legislation" to improve living and working conditions, an emphasis on procedural fairness, greater access to justice through increased legal aid, and a higher level of government accountability.[46] In the same period, the Independent Commission Against Corruption (ICAC) was established to combat corruption, local Chinese people reached the upper ranks of the civil service, and some of the British conglomerates started to include Chinese board members.[47] These trends continued and the situation vastly improved in the final decades of British rule, but, as we will see, memories of past injustice resurfaced in some of the

identities. My emphasis here is on the role of constitutional law in the construction of cultural identity, rather than on constitutional identity per se.

[41] Jones, *Lost in China?* p. 21.   [42] Carroll, *A Concise History of Hong Kong*, p. 174.

[43] Peter Wesley-Smith, "Anti-Chinese Legislation in Hong Kong," in *Precarious Balance: Hong Kong between China and Britain, 1842–1992*, edited by Ming K. Chan (Armonk: M. E. Sharp, 1994), pp. 91–107.

[44] Ming K. Chan, "The Legacy of the British Administration of Hong Kong: A View from Hong Kong," 151 *China Quarterly* (1997), 567–582 (575).

[45] Michael Ng, "When Silence Speaks: Press Censorship and Rule of Law in British Hong Kong, 1850s–1940s," 29(3) *Law & Literature* (2017), 425–456.

[46] Jones, *Lost in China?* p. 23.   [47] Tsang, *A Modern History of Hong Kong*, p. 192.

films from the final years of the colonial era, as Hong Kong society reflected upon Britain's legacy.

The association of Hong Kong identity and the rule of law further strengthened in the aftermath of the Tiananmen Square Incident in Beijing on June 4th, 1989, during which the Chinese government brutally suppressed students who had gathered in the city's main square to demand democratic reform. Images of army tanks moving in on student protestors shocked the world, but they had a particularly disturbing resonance in Hong Kong as people interpreted what happened in Beijing as a foreshadowing of what could happen in their own city after the handover. In an attempt to reassure the local population and to calm investors, the colonial government enacted a Bill of Rights designed to provide an additional source of law for rights protection. Jones contends that the events of 1989 made the contours of Hong Kong identity come into even sharper focus by bolstering Hong Kong's image as a "city of law" in contradiction to the public perception of China as a "city of tanks."[48]

The history of the rule of law discourse in Hong Kong further helps to explain why and how law became so tied to constructions of selfhood in the city: the rule of law, as a concept, a rhetorical trope, a policy, and an ideology, gained prominence in the cultural imagination from the second half of the 1960s as a way of differentiating Hong Kong from China, and hence an important part of the definition of a Hong Konger. This knotting together of law and identity continued after 1997. In 2004, the rule of law was identified as one of the city's "core values" in a campaign to defend such values amid growing unease that Hong Kong was losing the qualities that made it unique as a cosmopolitan financial hub.[49] Speaking at a 2012 forum on Hong Kong identity, a young local activist noted that "Hong Kong culture is basically a respect for the rule of law," and while it was possible to identify other elements of that culture, "in the end, it's the rule of law."[50] In a telephone survey conducted by the Chinese University of Hong Kong in 2014, 92.7 percent of the respondents identified the rule of law as one of the city's core values, and over a fifth of the respondents identified it as the single most important core value.[51] Jones pithily summarizes the imbrication of law and selfhood in the city by noting that "when Hong Kongers talk of their way of life, one of the first things they mention is the rule of law."[52]

Finally, the Basic Law promises Hong Kong a process of steady democratization after it emerges from over a century of colonial rule: Article 45 states

---

[48] Jones, *Lost in China?* p. 23.
[49] Ambrose Leung, "Push to Defend City's Core Values," *South China Morning Post,* June 7th, 2004.
[50] Vaudine England, "Hong Kong Suffers Identity Crisis as China's Influence Grows," *Guardian,* March 23rd, 2012.
[51] "The Chinese University of Hong Kong Releases Survey Findings on Views on Hong Kong's Core Values," Communications and Public Relations Office, October 30th, 2014.
[52] Jones, *Lost in China?* p. 20.

that the method for selecting the city's leader, or the Chief Executive, will ultimately be by "universal suffrage" and that the pace of democratization in the city will be determined "in light of the actual situation" and upon the principle of "gradual and orderly progress." A "nominating committee" will select the candidates that the populace will ultimately be able to vote for, but this committee must be "broadly representative" of Hong Kong society, and the entire selection process must be "in accordance with democratic procedures." Article 68 sets out the pace of democratizing the legislative branch based on identical considerations. The role of democratization in the construction of Hong Kong identity cannot be overstated: as a liberal jurisdiction within a one-party state, the promise of free and fair elections makes the city nothing short of extraordinary in contrast to the rest of the country where the Communist Party does not tolerate challenges to its authority. As we will see, the question of democratization will prove to be an unceasingly contentious one after 1997.

In sum, Hong Kong's postcolonial constitutional framework, defined by the continuation of the common law system, a commitment to the rule of law, human rights safeguards, and the promise of gradual but steady democratization, sets the city apart from other areas in China and hence forms the foundation for a sense of selfhood. For many Hong Kongers, the awareness that they live in a different, and unequivocally demarcated, legal space is a crucial part of what makes them think of themselves as a distinct community. If the contours of this space start to fade away, then the possibility of Hong Kong selfhood and community could also disappear.

Constitutional Controversies and the Politics of Disappearance

It is in the context of the politics of disappearance that the key constitutional controversies in postcolonial Hong Kong should be understood. Disagreements over the status of the Basic Law as the territory's highest law; challenges to the scope of fundamental rights its residents enjoy; the exercise of interpretative authority by political organs in Beijing over legal cases arising in Hong Kong; and calls to circumscribe the degree of autonomy the city has over its internal affairs have such great resonance because they jeopardize, or are perceived to jeopardize, the continued viability of the legal space carved out by "One Country, Two Systems" and strike at the core of Hong Kongers' sense of selfhood. These constitutional issues are controversial because they are experienced not as purely legal problems or run-of-the-mill political disputes but as challenges to a community's sense of its own cultural exceptionality. The far-reaching consequences these legal disputes have on the construction of identity are a major reason why questions of law find themselves registered in cultural products such as film.

As both a piece of Chinese legislation enacted by the National People's Congress and the Special Administrative Region's constitution, the exact status of the Basic Law has been a cause of some disagreement.[53] Within Hong Kong, it is often referred to as a "mini-constitution" in both scholarly and popular discussions, yet this designation does little to address the different points of view. The problem of the Basic Law's status is reflected in disputes over the ultimate authority to determine its meaning, one of the constitutional flash-points of the postcolonial era. Article 158 in the Basic Law states that "the power of interpretation [. . .] shall be vested in the Standing Committee of the National People's Congress [NPCSC]," which in effect means that the Standing Committee has the power of final interpretation, and that its interpretations are binding on the Hong Kong courts. However, while Beijing has the right of final interpretation it must exercise this right with restraint, as frequent interventions would undermine the judicial independence of the Hong Kong courts and create the impression of political interference.

Two years after the handover, a group of cases concerning the right of abode in Hong Kong of children who were either born in the mainland of Hong Kong permanent residents[54] or born in the mainland of parents who were not Hong Kong permanent residents at the time of their birth, and at least one of whose parents subsequently acquired permanent residency, came before the Court of Final Appeal.[55] In both instances, Hong Kong's highest court held that the children had the right of abode in Hong Kong. The local government became gravely worried about the potentially unmanageable influx of people into the city and sought an Interpretation of the relevant constitutional provisions from the Standing Committee in order to overturn the court's decision. This was done despite the fact that Article 158 does not expressly permit the executive branch to request an intervention from Beijing: it states that it is "the courts of the Region" which shall seek such an interpretation "through the Court of Final Appeal" if there arises a need to "interpret the provisions [. . .] concerning affairs which are the responsibility of the Central People's Government, or concerning the relationship between the Central Authorities and the Region," and "if such interpretation will affect the judgments on the cases." The Standing Committee issued an Interpretation that differed from the judgment from the Court of Final Appeal, and in *Lau Kong Yung v. Director of Immigration* the court accepted that the power of interpretation which the NPCSC has under Article 158(1) is "general and unqualified."[56] The right of abode controversy gave rise to serious concerns in the legal profession: 600 lawyers took part in a silent protest march against Beijing's Interpretation,[57] and the local Bar Association penned an open letter to the

---

[53] Ghai, pp. 222–223.   [54] *Ng Ka Ling & Others* v. *Director of Immigration* [1999] CFA 72.

[55] *Chan Kam Nga & Others* v. *Director of Immigration* [1999] HKCFA 16.

[56] *Lau Kong Yung* v. *Director of Immigration* [1999] HKCFA 5, p. 755 Paragraph D.

[57] Cliff Buddle, "Six Hundred Lawyers Join Silent Protest March," *South China Morning Post*, July 1st, 1999.

people of Hong Kong warning that the intervention would create "a black hole [...] in the legal system and the spirit of the rule of law" by allowing the government to obtain another outcome if it found the court's decisions inconvenient.[58]

The right of abode controversy forms the backdrop to the Standing Committee's Interpretations and Decisions concerning elections in the city. Between 2004 and 2014, it issued an Interpretation and a series of Decisions about the selection of the Chief Executive (under Article 45) and the members of the Legislative Council (under Article 68). While these were made within the constitutional framework of the Basic Law, they came to be regarded as further interventions to delay, postpone, and frustrate the efforts at democratization. Mounting discontent spilled over in 2014, when the Standing Committee issued a Decision stating that all candidates running for the position of the Chief Executive must not only have the endorsement of over half of a nominating committee composed mostly of pro-Beijing members but must be a patriot who "loves the country and loves Hong Kong."[59] The Decision was regarded as yet another intrusion into Hong Kong's autonomy, this time a naked attempt to control the election outcome so that only a candidate with views acceptable to the Communist Party can be chosen for office: as one commentator observed in the immediate aftermath of the Decision, "even pro-establishment figures and government officials look pained, and 'disappointment' was a common reaction."[60]

An interpretative dispute over the constitutional provision governing oath taking caused another uproar two years later. Article 104 of the Basic Law states that legislators, among other key figures in the political structure, "must, in accordance with law, swear to uphold the Basic Law of the Hong Kong Special Administrative Region of the People's Republic of China and swear allegiance to the Hong Kong Special Administrative Region of the People's Republic of China." Two newly elected legislators, Yau Wai-ching and Sixtus Leung Chung-hang, appeared at the podium with a blue banner bearing the words "Hong Kong is not China" and mispronounced the word "China" in a way which made it resemble a derogatory term used to refer to the country by Japan during World War II. Another four candidates varied the oath by, among other things, variously adding additional words, taking long pauses between words, and turning their statements into questions. The Hong Kong

---

[58]   Hong Kong Bar Association, "An Open Letter to the Citizens of Hong Kong on the Right of Abode Case," in *Hong Kong's Constitutional Debate: Conflict Over Interpretation*, edited by Johannes Chan, Hualing Fu, and Yash Ghai (Hong Kong: Hong Kong University Press, 2000), pp. 383–386 (384).

[59]   *Decision of the Standing Committee of the National People's Congress on Issues Relating to the Selection of the Chief Executive of the Hong Kong Special Administrative Region by Universal Suffrage and on the Method for Forming the Legislative Council of the Hong Kong Special Administrative Region in the Year 2016 (August 31st, 2014).*

[60]   Emily, "Who Can Smile At the Impasse of Political Reform," *Ming Pao Daily News*, September 1st, 2014.

government initiated disqualification proceedings in the court against Yau and Leung. Before the court handed down its judgment, however, the Standing Committee issued an interpretation of Article 104 which in effect ensured that the pair would be disqualified.[61] The manner in which the oaths were taken was indeed problematic, and it is arguable that the local courts would have invalidated them on their own. Indeed, the Court of First Instance held against Yau and Leung without relying on the Interpretation.[62] However, the Court of Appeal in the same case held against them on the grounds that the Standing Committee Decision was binding on the court.[63] The government then initiated proceedings against the other four legislators, and the court once again relied on the Interpretation and disqualified them all.[64] The timing of the Interpretation made it seem like a "most disturbing and unwarranted" tactic to dictate the outcome of the court's decision and hence as an interference into Hong Kong's judicial independence.[65] The Standing Committee's power to issue Interpretations and make Decisions concerning the Basic Law notwithstanding, from the early days of the resumption of Chinese sovereignty in the right of abode saga to the oath-taking cases, the exercise of this power came to be regarded as an alarming dismantling of the boundary between Hong Kong and mainland China because it interfered with the judicial and political processes supposedly safeguarded by Hong Kong's distinctive legal framework.

One way in which Hong Kong responded to such intrusions into its autonomy and selfhood is through protest. As lawyer and writer Antony Dapiran surmises, protests in Hong Kong are not only a manifestation of societal concerns or sentiments of discontent but an expression of identity: the very possibility of demonstrating on the streets arises from the freedom of assembly and of expression guaranteed by the Basic Law and the Bill of Rights, and similar actions by people in other parts of China would almost certainly have been suppressed.[66] The government's decision to introduce laws relating to national security under Article 23 of the Basic Law in 2003 sparked fears that the new legislation, if passed, could have a significant chilling effect on speech and access to information; according to a public opinion poll conducted by the University of Hong Kong, only 16.4 percent of the respondents supported the legislation.[67] Yet the government seemed determined to pass the legislation,

---

[61] *Interpretation of Article 104 of the Basic Law of the Hong Kong Special Administrative Region of the People's Republic of China by the Standing Committee of the National People's Congress (November 7th, 2016).*

[62] *Chief Executive of the HKSAR v. President of the Legislative Council* [2016] HKEC 2487 (CFI).

[63] *Chief Executive of the HKSAR v. President of the Legislative Council* [2017] HKLRD 460 (CA).

[64] *Chief Executive of the HKSAR v. President of the Legislative Council* [2017] 4 HKLRD 115.

[65] Johannes Chan, "A Storm of Unprecedented Ferocity: The Shrinking Space of the Right to Political Participation, Peaceful Demonstration, and Judicial Independence in Hong Kong," 16 (2) *International Journal of Constitutional Law* (2018), 373–388 (379).

[66] Antony Dapiran, *City of Protest: a Recent History of Dissent in Hong Kong* (Hawthorn: Penguin, 2017).

[67] Klaudia Kee, "Most People Office Security Bill, Poll Shows," *South China Morning Post*, June 28th, 2003.

and in the face of the administration's obstinacy Hong Kongers took to the streets to express their opposition. Perturbed by the mass turnout, the government finally relented and withdrew the bill. The success of the 2003 protest marked it as a moment of triumphant solidarity and resistance, and inaugurated a tradition of peaceful protests. Occupy Central, a seventy-nine-day civil disobedience movement demanding democratic elections which was triggered by the Standing Committee's 2014 Decision, can be said to constitute another landmark in this tradition.

In 2019, people in Hong Kong marched once again, this time in protest against proposed amendments to an ordinance that were meant to enable the extradition to mainland China of fugitives who had escaped to Hong Kong from across the border.[68] The Fugitive Offenders and Mutual Legal Assistance in Criminal Matters Legislation (Amendment) Bill 2019 sparked widespread fears that even ordinary Hong Kong residents and those who were not, strictly speaking, fugitives could potentially be surrendered to the mainland for trial: as Cora Chan notes, the legislation, if passed, would have "lift[ed] the current absolute bar against rendition to China, a bar that has been considered a firewall that segregates Hong Kong's common law system that adheres to the liberal rule of law from China's socialist legal system."[69] The peaceful protests took place on two separate days in June of 2019: according to the organizers, one million people took part on the first day, and when the government refused to formally withdraw the bill but merely suspended it, two million people marched on the second day.[70] The Chief Executive, Carrie Lam, refused to give a direct answer to a reporter's question of whether she could only formally withdraw the bill if she had Beijing's approval, further confirming the impression that Hong Kong's autonomy was shrinking.[71]

The protests over the extradition bill are still unfolding at the time of writing. In one sense, they are a continuation of the tradition of protest that began in 2003: people took to the streets out of concern over the dismantling of the "firewall" separating Hong Kong's legal system from that of the mainland, and the use of "Kongish," or a mixed code of Romanized Cantonese and English specific to Hong Kong, further attests to the consolidation of identity as a dimension of the protests.[72] Yet unlike in 2003, when the administration

---

[68] For a detailed account of the origins and development of the anti-extradition bill protests, see Albert Chen, "A Perfect Storm: Hong Kong-Mainland Rendition of Fugitive Offenders," 49(2) *Hong Kong Law Journal* (2019), 419–431.

[69] Cora Chan, "Demise of 'One Country, Two Systems'? Reflections on the Hong Kong Rendition Saga," 49(2) *Hong Kong Law Journal*, 447–459 (448).

[70] "Hong Kong: Timeline of Extradition Protests," BBC.com, September 4th, 2019. www.bbc.com/news/world-asia-china-49340717.

[71] "Hong Kong: Carrie Lam Pressed on Her Power to Withdraw Extradition Bill," BBC.com, August 13th, 2019. www.bbc.com/news/av/world-asia-china-49327098/hong-kong-carrie-lam-pressed-on-her-power-to-withdraw-extradition-bill.

[72] Lisa Lim, "Do you Speak Kongish? Hong Kong Protesters Harness Unique Language Code to Empower and Communicate," *South China Morning Post*, August 30th, 2019.

under Tung Chee Hwa, Hong Kong's first Chief Executive, backed down in the face of mass demonstrations, Lam's staunch refusal to formally withdraw the bill eventually led to violence; a *cri de coeur* by the protestors, in the form of a graffiti slogan, states that "it was you [Carrie Lam] who taught me peaceful marches are useless."[73] As the summer wore on that year, the use of teargas and rubber bullets by the police became almost a weekly occurrence, and protestors in turn responded by throwing bricks and Molotov cocktails at them. The protestors also vandalized businesses they perceived to be pro-China and caused extensive damage to the building of the Legislative Council, an institution which at the time of the protests was dominated by pro-Beijing politicians.[74] Lam eventually agreed to withdraw the bill, but by then the violence had reached a point of seemingly no return. This violence, so atypical to a city with an international reputation for being safe and orderly, can perhaps be read as a sign of desperation, or a raging against the fading away of an identity within a politics of disappearance.

The Spectacle of Law

To put my argument so far in another way, a spectre has haunted Hong Kong since the early 1980s: the possibility that despite China's promise to uphold its high degree of autonomy, Hong Kong might one day become "just another Chinese city," a phrase that periodically emerges in local political and popular discourse as the ultimate doomsday scenario and which the *Asian Wall Street Journal*'s chief editorial writer once called "the worst thing you could say" about the city.[75] Such fears shed light on Hong Kongers' affective attachment to the Basic Law and their visceral reaction to challenges to the integrity of "One Country, Two System": if the rights and freedoms which they enjoy are eroded, then so is their sense of individuality and community. *Ten Years* had such resonance because it captured the anxiety, unease, and even panic which this haunting sparked: the wearing away of liberties in the film is unsettling not only because it is legally problematic but because it throws into question longstanding beliefs about what a Hong Konger is.

As cultural, media, and film scholars have demonstrated, Hong Kong film has played an important role both in reflecting emerging ideas about identity and in shaping those ideas through their representations of self and community. An overview of Hong Kong cinema over the past few decades suffices to make this point. Between the late 1970s and the mid-1980s, a group of young directors consciously moved away from the kung fu films and light comedies which had dominated the local market, both by cultivating a new aesthetic

---

[73] Jeffie Lam, "Anger of the Young at Hong Kong Government Now Goes Beyond the Extradition Bill," *South China Morning Post*, July 3rd, 2019.

[74] Emma Graham-Harrison, Lily Kuo, and Verna Yu, "A Battle for the Soul of the City: Why Violence has Spiralled in the Hong Kong Protests," *Guardian*, October 6th, 2019.

[75] William McGurn, "China's Island of Discontent," *Asian Wall Street Journal*, July 13th, 2004.

sensibility and by focusing on Hong Kong itself as their subject. Ann Hui, Allen Fong, Mabel Cheung, Patrick Tam, and other directors who became known as the "Hong Kong New Wave" focused their attention on hotly debated political and social issues in the territory, and brought to the big screen local sites which had hitherto been considered unworthy of cinematic portrayal: for instance, Hui's *The Story of Woo Viet* (胡越的故事;1981) addresses the vexed question of the colonial administration's treatment of Vietnamese refugees and contains scenes from the detention camps, and Allen Fong's *Father and Son* (父子情; 1981) takes viewers deep into Hong Kong's working-class housing estates. The New Wave directors therefore gave Hong Kong a "starring role" in their work.[76] In the 1990s, Hong Kong cinema gave visual expression to the cultural hybridity of a people who have "lived a life without a proper nationality, being neither Chinese nor British": as Sheldon Lu argues, films such as Peter Chan's *Comrades, Almost a Love Story* (甜蜜蜜; 1996) and Wong Kar-wai's *Happy Together* (春光乍洩; 1997) portray drifting, culturally protean subjects whose "fluid, deterritorialized, transnational, and mobile mechanism of national affiliation" reflects the sensibility of a community that fully identifies with neither the cultural traditions of the departing colonial master nor the unequivocal patriotism demanded by the incoming sovereign.[77]

Post-handover Hong Kong cinema has been, to a great extent, troubled by the same transformative pressures on identity that I have discussed so far, and in this sense has mirrored the crisis of disappearance in the territory. The signing of the CEPA free trade agreement led to the rise of mainland Hong Kong cinematic co-productions, and they have had a significant influence on the film industry: in order to attract investment and gain access to the lucrative mainland market, Hong Kong films have had to "sacrifice their Hong Kong characteristics in order to gain an entry permit." This has meant the use of fewer Hong Kong actors, closer attention to the tastes and interests of mainland viewers, and conformity to Chinese government regulations and censorship norms.[78] As cultural critic Chu Yiu-wai notes, it was "an open secret that Hong Kong directors must self-censor their work in order to enter the mainland market."[79] Moreover, genres such as gangster films and erotic films are not allowed to enter the mainland, and comedies that "played a characteristic Hong Kong sense of humour also needed to be adapted to the tastes of mainland audiences, sacrificing most, if not all, of their Cantonese

---

[76] Law Kar, "Overview of Hong Kong's New Wave Cinema," in *At Full Speed: Hong King Cinema in a Borderless World*, edited by Esther C. M. Yau (Minneapolis: University of Minnesota Press, 2001), pp. 31–53 (44).

[77] Sheldon H. Lu, "Filming Diaspora and Identity: Hong Kong and 1997," in *The Cinema of Hong Kong: History, Arts, Identity* (Cambridge: Cambridge University Press, 2000), pp. 273–289 (275–276).

[78] Chu Yiu-wai, *Lost in Transition: Hong Kong Culture in the Age of China* (New York: SUNY, 2013), p. 107.

[79] Chu, *Lost in Transition*, p. 110.

wit." Chu predicts that if the boundaries between the Hong Kong and main-land film industries continue to blur then "Hong Kong cinema will lose its distinctive character."

In recent years, the pressures of co-production have led some filmmakers to turn away from the China market, and the result has been the development of a vibrant, alternative independent film scene in the city.[80] In contrast to big budget productions which are expected to generate substantial profits at main-stream cinemas, the work of independent filmmakers is cheaper to produce, more experimental in style, and usually exhibited at less commercially-oriented forums such as the Hong Kong International Film Festival. The founding of the local distributor *Ying E Chi*, which is committed to the promotion and distribu-tion of independent films and which co-organizes the Asian Film Festival with the arthouse cinema Broadway Cinematheque, also attests to the momentum of this sector.[81] Compared to the more mainstream directors, independent film-makers can explore questions of identity, community, and culture without having to keep questions of market expectations or political sensitivity as firmly in view. *Ten Years*, which was first screened at the Asian Film Festival, is an instance of an independent Hong Kong film that was produced on a shoestring budget.[82]

Given the longstanding exploration of questions of identity in Hong Kong cinema, it is instructive to approach films focusing specifically on the law as a domain where the complex connections between law and identity are given visual form. As the previous sections have shown, constitutional controversies in Hong Kong are often moments when identity comes under stress. However, questions about formations of selfhood are rarely, if ever, articulated as such in the law courts and the legislature, where broader cultural questions are virtu-ally always reframed as doctrinal ones. In those forums, the ongoing reflection on what it means to be a Hong Konger is formulated as disagreements about the existence of a legitimate aim or rational connection, the meaning of "sedition" or "subversion" in the national security bill, the role of the NPCSC, or the range of offences that could lead to rendition under the extradition bill, amongst other things. This translation of the cultural into the formalistically legal has the benefit of satisfying an institutional need for closure: while it may be unrealistic to expect a complete resolution to problems raised by the cultural politics of disappearance, it is possible to pronounce a final verdict on whether a right has been breached, or whether a bill ought to be passed, or whether the NPCSC has the power of final interpretation. However, this transformation also comes at a cost: by placing constitutional controversies within a strictly doctrinal frame, it precludes these institutions

---

[80] Chris Berry, "Hong Kong Watcher: Tammy Cheung and the Hong Kong Documentary," in *Hong Kong Culture: Word and Image*, edited by Kam Louie (2010), pp. 213–229 (218).

[81] Berry, "Hong Kong Watcher," p. 218.

[82] "Low-budget Film on Hong Kong Future Turns into Blockbuster," *ejinsight.com*, January 6th, 2016.

from addressing the controversies' far-reaching ramifications to a self-understanding so inextricably tied to the constitutional principle of "One Country, Two Systems."

In this book, I will demonstrate that film constitutes a medium that registers the impact of the constitutional controversies on identity.[83] Moving beyond the limits inherent in the language of doctrine, film's diverse generic conventions, multiple modes of cinematographic and sonic expression, varied thematic possibilities, and attunement to cultural complexity enable it to give form to the way in which a conception of selfhood becomes constructed from the guarantee of individual rights, the rule of law, a distinct legal system, and democratic development, and to chronicle how that process of construction has taken place from the 1980s to the present day. Moreover, film captures, sometimes obliquely, sometimes directly, the range of affects to which the city's constitutional transitions and transformations have given rise: through the eye of the camera, we witness, for instance, the ambivalent feelings toward the impending resumption of Chinese sovereignty following the signing of the Joint Declaration in 1984, the anger generated by the 2014 NPCSC Decision that led to Occupy Central, and the panic sparked by the extradition bill that fueled the protests and violence of 2019. Marginalized in legal debate, the language of film articulates concerns about who Hong Kongers are and who they might become at the heart of the constitutional controversies I examine. To fully understand constitutional law and its relationship to identity in modern-day Hong Kong, it is necessary to turn our gaze from the hallowed chambers of the courtrooms and the legislature to the cinema screens.

In each of the following chapters, I provide a detailed reading of a single film or a cluster of related films in the context of a particular moment of constitutional contention. I begin with the early 1980s, when the Chinese and British

[83] "Law and Film" is a vibrant area of scholarship. Steve Greenfield, Guy Osborn, and Peter Robson, *Film and the Law*, 2nd ed. (Oxford: Hart, 2010) is often regarded as the founding text. For studies with a jurisprudential focus, see Peter Goodrich, "Screening Law," 21(1) *Law & Literature* (2009), 1–23; Paul Kahn, *Finding Ourselves at the Movies: Philosophy for a New Generation* (New York: Columbia University Press, 2013); William P. MacNeil, *Lex Populi: The Jurisprudence of Popular Culture* (Palo Alto: Stanford University Press, 2007); and Richard K. Sherwin, *Visualizing Law in the Age of the Digital Baroque* (Abingdon: Routledge, 2011). For studies of documentary form, see Regina Austin, "Documentation, Documentary, and the Law: What Should be Made of Victim Impact Videos?," 31(4) *Cardozo Law Review* (2010), 979–1019; Jessica Silbey, "Filmmaking in the Precinct House and the Genre of Documentary Film," 29 *Columbia Journal of Law & the Arts* (2005), 107–180; and Marco Wan, "Gay Visibility and the Law in Hong Kong," 32(3) *International Journal for the Semiotics of Law* (2019), 699–713. For studies of law and media, see Richard K. Sherwin, *When Law Goes Pop: The Vanishing Law between Law and Popular Culture* (Chicago: University of Chicago Press, 2000) and *West of Everything: Law and New Media*, edited by Christian Delage, Peter Goodrich, and Marco Wan (Edinburgh: Edinburgh University Press, 2019). For studies of law and identity in the American context, see Carol Clover, "Law and the Order of Popular Culture" (1998), reprinted in *Trial films on Trial: Law, Justice, and Popular Culture*, edited by Austin Sarat, Jessica Silbey, and Martha Merrill Umphrey (Tuscaloosa: Alabama University Press, 2019), pp. 17–39 and Eric Smoodin, "'Compulsory' Viewing for every Citizen: 'Mr Smith' and the Rhetoric of Reception," 35(2) *Cinema Journal* (1996), 3–23.

governments signed the Sino-British Joint Declaration. This was a seismic legal event, as it marked the beginning of the change of sovereignty and put in motion the process of setting up a new constitutional order for the territory. Many people in the colony had mixed emotions about the prospect of the retrocession: the idea of an end to British colonization was a source of national pride, but at the same time the thought of being taken over by a communist state was a cause of great apprehension. In the wake of the Declaration, officials from China intensified their calls on Hong Kongers to "love the motherland." Such imperatives from the authorities are a core part of mainland Chinese political discourse, but they sounded largely unfamiliar to Hong Kong ears. What did it mean to be told to "love the motherland," especially in light of the contradictory emotions Hong Kongers had about reunification? And how can such love be represented in cinematic terms? In Chapter 1, I posit that Ng See-Yuen's *The Unwritten Law* (法外情; 1985), in which a young lawyer defends a prostitute who, unbeknownst to him, is his birth mother, gives visual form to the love between "the motherland" and Hong Kong by allegorizing it as the love between mother and son. Moreover, with the end of British governance in sight, Hong Kong society started to reflect upon the rhetoric of the rule of law upon which much of the colonial regime was built. I will further contend that Ng's film, appearing at the moment when decolonization became a certainty, takes part in this critical reflection of the extent to which justice was upheld under the colonial authorities.

In Chapter 2, I situate Johnnie To's popular comedy, *Justice, My Foot!* (審死官; 1992), which revolves around a lawyer defending a woman falsely accused of murdering her husband, in light of the drafting of the Basic Law and passage of the Bill of Rights in the early 1990s. I argue that To's film can be approached as a screening of a nightmare scenario on the minds of many viewers at the time: a Hong Kong-style lawyer trying to defend the innocent and maintain justice in a Chinese-style legal system that disregards basic human rights and that is plagued by corruption and nepotism. I will then explore the function of humor in the film to show how *Justice, My Foot!* repackages anxieties about the Sinicization of law into a marketable cultural product for mass consumption.

The implementation of the Bill of Rights ordinance galvanized Hong Kong's women's rights movement in the early 1990s, even though the colonial government did not necessarily have gender equality in mind when it introduced the bill. In Chapter 3, I explore the curious coexistence of the consolidation of women's rights on the one hand and the rising popularity of misogynistic and degrading depictions of women in film on the other, with a particular focus on Andrew Lau's *Raped by an Angel* (香港奇案之強姦; 1993). I also discuss the influence of the film censorship regime on representations of sexual violence in Hong Kong cinema in this period.

In Chapter 4, I interpret Joe Ma's *Lawyer Lawyer* (算死草; 1997), a farcical comedy of seemingly little jurisprudential value, as a response to debates about the future of the common law after 1997. In the years leading up to the handover there were discussions of whether the common law should continue to be cited in Hong Kong after China resumed sovereignty, and if so, what kind of authority English precedent should have. While some staunch common law lawyers argued for preserving English law's privileged status, more reform-minded jurists argued for cutting the territory's "constitutional umbilicus" from England by relying on local cases.[84] I will contend that the lawyer in Ma's film wins his case by relying on an English precedent case that is hinted at, but not explicitly mentioned, and further suggest that his highly unorthodox way of citing precedent provides an indication of how Hong Kong can conceive of the place of the English common law after 1997.

The mass demonstration against national security laws in 2003 constitutes the first major constitutional controversy of the postcolonial era that I examine. As many commentators observed at the time, the Article 23 protest was also a process of identity formation: since the rally against national security laws presented itself as a fight to protect the city from the intrusion of repressive Chinese legal norms, it created a bond among the protestors and their supporters and fostered a sense of what it means to be a "Hong Konger." One of the participants in the 2003 protest was Tammy Cheung, an independent filmmaker who went on to become one of Hong Kong's most renowned documentary makers. Cheung attempted to capture the event on film, and the result was *July* (七月; 2004). Her challenge was to make a cinematic record that was not only visual but affective: in other words, a record that not only presents the factual unfolding of the protest but communicates the sensation of being in the midst of its charged atmosphere and enables viewers to share the sense of community that it created. In Chapter 5, I explore what it might mean to create a record of a constitutional controversy through an analysis of the themes, structures, and cinematography of Cheung's film.

In Chapter 6, I investigate how disputes over the interpretation of the Basic Law's provisions on Chief Executive elections are refracted in Hong Kong's gangster or "triad" films. These disputes became increasingly acrimonious after 1997: pro-democracy legislators, lawyers, and activists in the territory accused the Chinese government of failing to honor guarantees for democratization enshrined in the constitutional document, while the Chinese government accused the pro-democracy camp of attempting to bring chaos and undermine Chinese sovereignty in the name of democratization. I examine a group of gangster films centered around conflicts over how a new leader in the criminal syndicate should be chosen and argue that key terms in the city's election debate are integrated into the films' dialogue and signal a conscious cinematic engagement with the constitutional impasse. I will then set Herman Yau's *The Mobfathers* (選老頂; 2016) in conversation with the writings of

---

[84] Daniel R. Fung, "Paradoxes of Hong Kong's Reversion: the Legal Dimension," in *Hong Kong and the Super Paradox: Life after Return to China*, edited by James C. Hsiung (London: Basingstoke, 2000), pp. 105–125 (109).

Robert Cover to offer an interpretation of the film as a visual expression of the jurispathic violence Beijing imposed on Hong Kong in the course of the election controversy.

Chapter 7 draws on the work of trauma theorists such as Cathy Caruth to argue that Occupy Central can be understood as a form of cultural trauma. Focusing on independent documentaries about the movement, including Chan Tze-woon's *Yellowing* (亂世備忘; 2016); Evan Chan's *Raise the Umbrellas* (撐傘; 2016), Nora Lam's *Road Not Taken* (未竟之路; 2016), and James Leong's *Umbrella Diaries: The First Umbrellas* (傘上:遍地開花; 2018), I examine how different filmmakers tried to capture in their work an event with which Hong Kong society is still, to a great extent, coming to terms. I will also address the continuities between Occupy and the anti-extradition bill protests, and discuss the role of cinema in the most recent episodes of unrest.

I bring this book to a close with a reflection on constitutional time and return to a phrase that continues to resonate in discussions of Hong Kong's legal order: "remain unchanged for fifty years." To "remain unchanged" is to engage in a suspension of time, to create a temporal hiatus whereby a system, an idea of who one is, and a way of life are preserved. I approach Wong Kar-wai's *2046* (released in 2004), in which a writer conjures up a place where nothing changes in the science-fictional stories he creates, as an exploration of the potential finality of the Basic Law and Hong Kong identity, and of what it might mean to suspend time through a constitutional document.

By investigating how films about the law represent the intertwining of law and identity, and by asking what happens to these representations when constitutional controversies arise, this book takes as its subject the interconnections of two things that make Hong Kong unique: its dynamic film industry and the constitutional experiment known as "One Country, Two Systems." More than anything, though, this is a book about a community, both rooted and diasporic: it is concerned with how ideas about rights, freedom, the common law, and the rule of law have shaped that community's continuing efforts to understand itself, and with how film gives visual expression to the always provisional outcome of those efforts. In some ways, Hong Kong is a city constantly in search of an identity: "Fragrant Harbour", a "Borrowed Place" living on "Borrowed Time," the "Pearl of the Orient," and "Asia's World City" are just a few of the identities that others have given to it or that it has adopted over time. It is perhaps inevitable that a subjectivity whose appearance, as Abbas points out, "is posited on the imminence of its disappearance" is always in search of an appropriate set of images for itself, a reflection with which it is comfortable.[85]

For Abbas, the proliferation of images of Hong Kong is something we should be on guard against: the danger of disappearance means that there is a tendency to replace and substitute Hong Kong with fetish objects, clichés,

---

[85] Abbas, *Hong Kong*, p. 7.

and other visual fixations.[86] Yet perhaps it is not necessary to be so pessimistic. A politics of disappearance can fuel creative responses to the legal conundrums and cultural transformations which a community faces; those who are operating within such difficult and volatile conditions – lawyers, judges, and jurists as much as filmmakers, scriptwriters, and film producers – cannot but be inventive and resourceful in order to thrive and perhaps even simply to survive in what, in yet another identity formulation for Hong Kong, Leo Ou-fan Lee calls "city between worlds."[87] Finally, it may be that the possibility of disappearance is part of what makes Hong Kong so adept at coming up with such fascinating, diverse, and evolving images of itself, from Stephen Chow's popular comedies to Wong Kar-wai's more idiosyncratic reworkings of genre. Perhaps it is not wrong to think of the politics of disappearance as, ultimately, the force which keeps Hong Kong truly spectacular.

[86]   Abbas, *Hong Kong*, p. 8.
[87]   Leo Ou-fan Lee, *City between Worlds: My Hong Kong* (Cambridge: Harvard University Press, 2008).

1

Love in a Time of Transition:
Ng See-yuen's *The Unwritten Law*

Ng See-Yuen's *The Unwritten Law* (法外情; 1985) occupies an important place in the cultural imagination of modern-day Hong Kong, not only as one of its most enduring courtroom dramas but as one of its most memorable films *tout court*. It tells the story of Lau Chi-pang, a promising young lawyer, newly returned to Hong Kong from his legal studies in England, who decides to take on a case defending a lowly prostitute, Lau Wai-lan. Wai-lan is accused of murdering the son of a business tycoon. She in fact killed him in self-defense – he was a psychopath and had handcuffed and attacked her in a state of sexual frenzy – but no one would believe the version of events of a poor, aging prostitute. Chi-pang is the only lawyer willing to take up her case.

The key to the story is the relationship between lawyer and defendant: unbeknownst to both of them, Wai-lan is Chi-pang's birth mother and was forced to give him up to an orphanage when he was a baby because of her poverty. She sent him presents regularly as he grew up, but never saw him face to face. One of the last presents she sent him was a pocket watch meant as a memento before he left for his studies abroad. Wai-lan discovers Chi-pang's real identity by accident in the course of their interaction as legal counsel and client: during one of their pretrial meetings, she notices that the lawyer carries a pocket watch identical to the one she gave her son. When she sees the engraving on the watch, she realizes that it is the same one. Overcome with shame at the contrast between her own wretched state and the promise and social status of the young lawyer, Wai-lan is determined to keep the truth of their relationship a secret, both from Chi-pang himself and from wider society, out of fear that it would ruin his fledgling career if it ever came to light. During the murder trial, things take a dramatic turn just when Chi-pang seems close to securing an acquittal for Wai-lan: the prosecution summons the nun who headed the orphanage in which Chi-pang grew up to testify to the kinship between the defendant and her lawyer, in an attempt to demonstrate a conflict of interest that would necessitate a retrial. However, to the audience's surprise, the nun lies and denies that Wai-lan and Chi-pang are related. Wai-lan wins her case, and Chi-pang remains unaware that she is his mother. The film ends with a shot of Wai-lan with tears rolling down her face. The tears express complex emotions: they are tears of relief at the outcome of the trial, tears of joy at seeing Chi-pang as a grown man and a defender of justice, but also tears of heavy grief at having a son who does not, and cannot, recognize her. Above all, they are the tears of love of a mother for her child. We will return to this final shot later in this chapter.

There are a number of factors contributing to the film's iconic status. The first is context: *The Unwritten Law* stood out at a time in Hong Kong film history when the city was dominated by lowbrow comedies and when film-goers were losing interest in the genre's formulaic plotlines and predictable gags. Typical of the reviews at the time was the comment that "we are surrounded by comedies, and *The Unwritten Law* is like a breath of fresh air."[1] The film is also particularly memorable because it is one of the first locally produced representations of law in Hong Kong cinema. As another reviewer noted, "how many Hong Kong films can you think of with such a lengthy trial scene? It takes courage to experiment with a plot like this one."[2] The casting also played a role in the film's success: Deanie Ip and Andy Lau played Wai-lan and Chi-pang respectively, and their delicate portrayal of the mother–son relationship was so touching that they were cast together in the award-winning *A Simple Life* (桃姐) by the Hong Kong New Wave Director Ann Hui twenty-six years later, in 2011. *A Simple Life* tells the story of another quasi mother–son relationship, this time of Chung Chun-to, an aged servant, and Roger Leung, the master of the house who had grown up under her care. A survey of the reviews of this latter film indicates that the actors' dynamic in *The Unwritten Law* left a deep impression on the city: one commentator calls them Hong Kong cinema's "classic mother-son team,"[3] while another observes that when Deanie Ip and Andy Lau are mentioned "in a single breath [. . .] memories of old Hong Kong classics" like *The Unwritten Law* come to mind.[4] The continued resonance of this pioneering courtroom drama in the territory's collective memory makes it a good starting point for an investigation of the relationship between law, film, and identity in the Hong Kong context.

In this chapter, I will show that the complex affective responses of many Hong Kongers to the seismic constitutional and political changes brought about by the Sino-British Joint Declaration are encapsulated in the film's mother–son relationship. The Joint Declaration, signed by Chinese Premier Zhao Ziyang and British Prime Minister Margaret Thatcher in 1984, stipulated that Hong Kong would return to mainland China in 1997. As we will see next, in the years after the treaty was signed Chinese officials increasingly called on Hong Kongers to "love the motherland" in preparation for the city's upcoming

---

[1] Kang Ti, "Ng See-Yuen's Innovation," *Ta Kung Pao*, September 29th, 1985.

[2] Bai Fei, "*The Unwritten Law* Is Worth Our Praise," *Ta Kung Pao*, October 10th, 1985.

[3] "Andy Lau and Deanie Ip Team Up to Play Master and Servant," *Hong Kong Top Ten Blogspot*, February 23rd, 2011. http://hktopten.blogspot.de/2011/02/20110224-andy-lau-and-deanie-ip-team-up.html.

[4] "A Simple Life," *A Nutshell Review*, March 5th, 2012. http://anutshellreview.blogspot.de/2012/03/simple-life-tao-jie.html.

reunification. However, for Hong Kongers who grew up in the British colony, such official imperatives to love the motherland were largely unfamiliar and felt foreign. They therefore struggled to articulate their responses to them. What does love for the motherland look or feel like, and for the purposes of my analysis, how might it be expressed in a cultural product such as film? Love, as the cultural critic Rey Chow reminds us, needs to be historicized; its meaning, nature, attachments, and expressions are specific to its temporal context.[5] In this chapter, I will explore the relationship between Hong Kong's multifaceted, ambivalent, and self-contradictory love toward its motherland in the early 1980s, when reunification became a looming reality, and its representation as the touching yet deeply sorrowful love between mother and son in *The Unwritten Law*.

1.1 Loving the Mother(land)

Few constitutional events are as momentous as the transfer of sovereignty over a territory from one nation to another, and it would be difficult to overstate the anxiety, unease, and apprehension that many Hong Kongers felt toward the retrocession in the early 1980s. As one concerned resident noted, "the issue of sovereignty is of paramount importance since any guarantees secured for the preservation of the status quo will be pulverized if a change of government in China results in undue or even destructive interference and meddling with the internal affairs of the territory."[6] The Joint Declaration signaled that the countdown to the end of colonial governance had begun, but many questions about the city's future remained unanswered. One commentator expressed the extent of the uncertainty about post-handover arrangements through the metaphor of horseracing, a quintessential Hong Kong pastime of the period, by asking: "Who is going to be the trainer? Who the rider? Will we be racing on sand or on grass? Will the race be cancelled because of a typhoon? No one can predict anything."[7] Hong Kongers were nervous, not only about what the rules of the game were going to be after 1997 but whether there was going to be a game left to play at all.

The impending transfer of sovereignty and its accompanying uncertainties were profoundly unsettling because Hong Kong and mainland China were very different places in the early 1980s. Hong Kong was an international financial center with a thriving stock market, while China was a socialist state that had only started the slow process of opening up to the outside world a few years before, in 1978. Would Hong Kong's capitalist framework be dismantled under Chinese rule? Despite Deng's insistence that "China will

---

[5] Rey Chow, *Ethics after Idealism: Theory – Culture – Ethnicity – Reading* (Bloomington: Indiana University Press, 1998), pp. 133–149.

[6] Peter Leung, "If Sovereignty Has to Revert to Mainland . . .," *South China Morning Post*, August 3rd, 1984.

[7] "On the Theory of Hong Kong Poison Governing Hong Kong," *Ming Pao Daily News*, January 14th, 1984.

always keep its promise" to honor Hong Kong's autonomy,[8] and despite repeated reassurances from Chinese government officials to similar effect, the idea of "One Country, Two Systems" had only limited success in reassuring the people of Hong Kong. As the legal scholar W. S. Clarke noted at the time, "the wild swings in Chinese policies since 1949 [the year the People's Republic of China was founded] are understandably worrying to the people of Hong Kong, especially now that they are being asked to have faith in the promises of the present leaders in Beijing. [. . .] Ten years ago China was in the throes of the Cultural Revolution, [. . .] who is to say what colour of political philosophy will prevail in Beijing ten years from now?"[9]

The prospect of retrocession was also troubling because, as Chow points out, for many people it felt less like a return to a familiar place of ancestral origin than a movement "between colonizers," whereby the city and its inhabitants were shuttled, without their consent, from one national sovereign to another.[10] As we saw in the Introduction, it was the postwar generation of people born in Hong Kong who, coming of age in the 1960s, first developed a separate, local identity. The historian Steve Tsang underscores that despite their ethnic affiliations with their mainland counterparts – the vast majority of Hong Kong residents are Chinese – Hong Kongers had such a hazy understanding of mainland China that by the early 1980s, "when a Hong Kong person of Chinese origins referred to 'China' he was not always clear what he had in mind."[11] Sometimes China was understood as a "geographical" locality, sometimes a "cultural" entity. It was also possible that he only had a vague notion of a "mythical China that did not have a clearly defined territorial outline" and that generated little more than a sense of otherness.

Two words appeared with great frequency in Hong Kong's political discourse in this turbulent period. The first word was, unsurprisingly, "sovereignty." The Sino-British negotiations of 1982 to 1984, which culminated in the Joint Declaration, were in essence negotiations about the nature of sovereignty over Hong Kong. The term "sovereignty" recurred in the media as Hong Kongers tried to grasp the exact nature of sovereign power they would be subjected to after the handover in the course of the meandering negotiations between the British and the Chinese governments. The Joint Declaration brought home the hard reality that Hong Kong's future ruler would be the Communist state across the border. As Harvey Stockwin, a prominent political commentator at the time, noted, with the signing of the treaty "it was no longer a question of whether China would take over, but when. This required time for

---

[8] Deng Xiaoping, "China Will Always Keep Its Promise" (December 19th, 1984), *Deng Xiaoping on the Question of Hong Kong* (Hong Kong: New Horizon Press, 1993), pp. 41–46 (43).

[9] W. S. Clarke, "Hong Kong under the Chinese Constitution," 14 (1) *Hong Kong Law Journal* (1984), 71–81 (79). See also Albert Chen's response to him in "Further Aspects of the Autonomy of Hong Kong under the PRC Constitution," 14(3) *Hong Kong Law Journal* (1984), 341–347.

[10] Chow, *Ethics after Idealism*, pp. 149–168 (149).

[11] Steve Tsang, *A Modern History of Hong Kong* (Hong Kong: Hong Kong University Press, 2007), p. 196.

digestion."[12] The certainty of a "communist sovereignty" was difficult to stomach. One political scientist at the University of Hong Kong tried to spell things out in unequivocal terms for his readers: "One country [. . .] means one *sovereign* state [. . .] That is the simple fact on which there can be no argument. Sovereignty must be taken seriously. It will belong to China."[13]

"Love" was the other word that appeared frequently in Hong Kong's political discourse in the early 1980s. This was because the transfer of sovereign power over the city to mainland China was often described through metaphors of family union and, more specifically, of a return of a child to the mother(land). The English term "motherland" is a translation of *zhu guo/zho gwok*, 祖國," which literally means ancestral land, with an emphasis on family, heritage, and lineage. As a bilingual city, both the Chinese and English terms are significant as metaphors for conceptualizing the relationship between Hong Kong and the mainland: the former places the emphasis on a more general feeling of kinship, while the latter gives more a specific, maternal form to the bond. "The people of China and Hong Kong are one family," the pro-China *Ta Kung Pao* announced.[14] It went on to say that "the motherland cares for the well-being of Hong Kong." As the new constitutional order crystallized, Chinese officials repeatedly called on their Hong Kong "compatriots" not only to love Hong Kong but to love the motherland. Deng himself noted that the future governance of the territory must rest with people who love both Hong Kong and the motherland.[15] Speaking at a banquet at the end of 1984, Xu Jiatun, the head of the Hong Kong branch of the New China News Agency, said he hoped Hong Kongers would, among other things, "further uphold the spirit of loving the motherland and Hong Kong."[16] A year later, Ji Pengfei, who oversaw Hong Kong affairs in China's State Council, said it would be desirable for them to contribute to the development of both the mainland and their own city "under the banner of loving the motherland and loving Hong Kong."[17] To mainland China, the Declaration meant that Hong Kong, cruelly snatched away by imperialist Britain over a century ago, would finally return to the embrace of its loving parents.

Conceptualized in the language of filiation, kinship, and union, the transfer of sovereignty gave rise to an imperative to love. Such edicts are an integral part of the governmental discourse in the mainland, but they sounded distinctly strange to Hong Kong ears in the 1980s. To be sure, nationalist sentiments were not completely unimaginable and mainland China was not an entirely

---

[12] Harvey Stockwin, "Must Hong Kong Stay Stuck in Wonderland?," *South China Morning Post*, October 27th, 1985.

[13] Peter Harris, 1997: "The Handover without a Whimper," *South China Morning Post*, June 2nd, 1098.

[14] Cited in "Peking Role in Economy Urged," *South China Morning Post*, September 15th, 1983.

[15] Deng Xiaoping, "One Country, Two Systems" (June 22–23, 1984), in *Deng Xiaoping on the Question of Hong Kong*, pp. 6–12 (11).

[16] "Xu Calls on All to Co-operate," *South China Morning Post*, December 31st, 1984.

[17] "Ji Calls for Co-operation," *South China Morning Post*, December 17th, 1985.

foreign entity, for the majority of Hong Kongers were Chinese and many had parents or grandparents who had settled in Hong Kong from across the border. However, the strong sense of local identity, combined with grave concerns of the political repression and economic backwardness of China at the time, meant that few Hong Kongers could fully identify with their mainland counterparts. As Tsang succinctly put it, most Hong Kongers "felt they should be proud of being Chinese and should desire the early departure of the British 'imperialists'," but "the idea of being handed over to a Communist regime, whose atrocious record some had experienced first-hand and others knew of through relatives and friends, terrified them."[18] He adds that even though there had been a surge of patriotism in Hong Kong after Richard Nixon's visit to China catapulted the country onto the world stage in 1972, especially among students in higher education, their enthusiasm "did not last" and subsided a few years later "as the vicious nature of the power struggle in the People's Republic of China was unveiled," a power struggle epitomized by the downfall of the "Gang of Four" shortly after Mao Tse-tung's death in 1976.[19] By the early 1980s, "being Chinese in Hong Kong was primarily an ethnic and cultural affiliation and generally did not mean being a Chinese citizen or national of the PRC," and while there may not have been any overt crisis of identity, the tension between the two – ethnic and cultural affiliation on the one hand, distinct political status on the other – was keenly felt.[20] Writing as a columnist in the newspaper *Ming Pao*, the novelist Eunice Lam Yin-nei puts a very different spin on the metaphor of family reunion: "if the country is the parents, then it should know the fear, doubt, mistrust and panic of its children. A relationship in which the children only feel fear towards the parents is obviously a terrible relationship, and it's a relationship neither the parents nor the children would want."[21] Lam's acknowledgment of the metaphor reflects an acceptance of the familial affinities between Hong Kong and China, but it also challenges the political discourse's presumption of happy unity.

Given most Hong Kongers' ambivalent feelings toward the outcome of the Joint Declaration and the impending retrocession, the idea of "loving the motherland" was a highly complex one. Their conflicting attitudes toward China meant that this "love" was characterized by both belonging and alienation, warmth and wariness, closeness and remoteness, familiarity and foreignness. One survey on local attitudes toward the prospect of the transfer of sovereignty demonstrated "a clear case of a conflict of emotions."[22]

This "conflict of emotions" translated into a longing for a deferral of the handover; to want unification, while simultaneously not wanting to see the prospect of its realization, became a state of mind associated with loving the

---

[18] Tsang, *A Modern History of Hong Kong*, p. 220.
[19] Tsang, *A Modern History of Hong Kong*, p. 191.
[20] Tsang, *A Modern History of Hong Kong*, p. 195.
[21] Eunice Lam Yin-nei, "Fear," *Ming Pao Daily News*, March 8th, 1984.
[22] "Loyal . . . but the Doubts Remain," *South China Morning Post*, November 24th, 1984.

motherland in the early 1980s. An open letter by a concerned Hong Kong resident provides a glimpse of this state of mind: the writer notes that while she is a "patriot" and takes pride in the country's successes, she also believes that the time is not right for reunification, for "people appear to be happier the way things are in Hong Kong, to what it presently is in China."[23] She contends that it is "better to wait until things become more settled and peaceful" because "the world today is in a state of confusion." In other words, there was not only a wish to return to the motherland but also a yearning to postpone this return to some point in the indefinite future. A columnist observes in a similar vein that while people did feel "a sense of belonging to their 'motherland'," they simultaneously felt that there was as yet "nothing in common" between themselves and their counterparts across the border.[24] The sense of affinity was real, but the thought of integration was difficult to many.

To conclude, official calls to "love the motherland" in the 1980s sounded patently mainland Chinese and therefore emphatically un-Hong Kong. To put it bluntly, they sounded like Communist calque and failed to capture most Hong Kongers' feelings toward the incoming sovereign. The strangeness of the formulation to local ears did not mean that there was no love for China in Hong Kong; it was simply that this love was not the straightforward joy of reunion or national pride at reunification that marked the use of the phrase in mainland Chinese political discourse. The love of Hong Kongers for the motherland was a much more complex one marked by contradictory feelings, conflicting emotions, incompatible moods, and incongruous states of mind. This affective response gave rise to a longing for deferred unification. In the following sections, I will show that *The Unwritten Law* captures the city's unique cultural moods and emotive structures. Through its representation of the dual feelings of affinity and estrangement in the mother–son relationship between Wai-lan and Chi-pang, the film provides a point of entry for probing this multifaceted and highly textured form of love.[25]

1.2 The Personal Is the National

"Wherever there are Chinese, there is Chinese culture – and wherever there is Chinese culture, there are strong national sentiments."[26] For mainland Chinese officials such as Xu, love for the motherland is linked to patriotism and national loyalty. However, given the relative lack of familiarity with such public mandates of affective attachment toward the nation in colonial

---

[23] Chow Mi-to, "Time Not Right for Unification," *South China Morning Post*, June 6th, 1983.

[24] Leung, *South China Morning Post*, August 3rd, 1984.

[25] For a study of Hong Kong cinematic representations of other family relations between the territory and China, such as the female "mainland cousin," see Shu-mei Shih, *Visuality and Identity: Sinophone Articulations across the Pacific* (Berkeley: University of California Press, 2007), pp. 103–114.

[26] Chris Yeung, "Xu Urges Teachers to Widen Links," *South China Morning Post*, November 21st, 1985.

Hong Kong, as well as the difference between what was expected in the governmental discourse and what was felt in the city, the love could only be articulated in a form more readily comprehensible to Hong Kongers: personal love. In *The Unwritten Law*, national love between motherland and filial territory finds expression in the personal love between mother and child. The personal here is the national, both in the allegorical sense that the film can be read as a representation of Hong Kong's reunification with China and in the affective sense that the sentiment of Hong Kong's national love for the motherland is given form or "a local habitation and a name" in the personal love between Wai-lan, the prostitute accused of murder, and Chi-pang, her son.[27] Theirs is not a story of a happy family reunion. Instead, the film evokes a complex, delicate love whereby the reunion between mother and son, much like the transfer of Hong Kong's sovereignty to China, is neither completely desired nor completely unwanted by the audience of the time.

The interpretation of non-Western literature and film in an allegorical mode has been contentious since Fredric Jameson asserted in the 1980s that, in the parlance of the time, all "third-world texts" are "necessarily [...] national allegories."[28] This dogmatic claim that there is only one way of approaching non-Western texts – that these texts are *necessarily* allegorical in nature – is indeed problematic. However, the response to Jameson's position cannot be that scholars of non-Western material can *never* read them as allegories. Rather, Jameson notwithstanding, we should continue to be attuned to their potential as national allegories, without reducing their richness and complexity to one mandated interpretative frame. In the case of *The Unwritten Law*, the fact that a film about the law appeared in the midst of critical constitutional change suggests that an allegorical reading could, in this context, be a sensible one. The starting point for approaching the film's connection to its legal environment is to make explicit the markers of national identity in its portrayal of the two main characters. Throughout Ng's film, Chi-pang is cinematographically aligned with colonial Hong Kong, while Wai-lan is associated with mainland China.

Newly returned to Hong Kong from his studies in Britain, Chi-pang hastens to visit the orphanage in which he grew up. As he enters the gates, the camera focuses on the name of the institution: Saint Mary Orphanage. As the name indicates, the orphanage is a European institution, presumably set up by the Jesuits. Its head, Sister Maria, is a Cantonese-speaking Caucasian nun. Chi-pang is puzzled by the stillness of the place. He comes across the gardener, who tells him that the orphanage seemed empty because it had closed down: "The landowner says he will take back the place for further development," the gardener says wistfully. He also tells Chi-pang that Sister Maria has returned

---

[27] William Shakespeare, *A Midsummer Night's Dream*, Act V Scene 1.

[28] Fredric Jameson, "Third-World Literature in the Era of Multinational Capitalism," 15 *Social Text* (1986), 65–88(69). See also Aijaz Ahmed's powerful critique of Jameson's position in "Jameson's Rhetoric of Otherness and the 'National Allegory'," 17 *Social Text* (1987), 3–25.

to Europe. In light of the film's immediate context of the transfer of sovereignty, the allegorical significance of the orphanage seems clear: like Hong Kong, it is a colonial institution whose time is coming to an end, and the "landowner" is taking back the place. The change is shockingly sudden to Chi-pang, just as the idea of retrocession was to most Hong Kongers. Like mainland China, the "landowner" has original title but is unfamiliar to the audience. The colonial overseer has already departed, and the place as it exists now will soon be demolished. As Chi-pang wanders around the grounds of the orphanage, we are given flashbacks of his happy days there: games with the other children in the playground, the presents he received from his mysterious benefactor (whom we know is his mother), the kind words and attention of Sister Maria. A song about childhood memories, sung by the actor who plays Chi-pang, is played in the background. Chi-pang's wanderings at the orphanage capture a sense of loss and nostalgia for safer, more blissful times that echo comparable local sentiments associated with the fear of the upcoming handover. Though his memories are specific to his time at the orphanage, the feelings that they evoke tap into the immediate affective environment in which the film was produced.

Chi-pang's return to the orphanage suggests the possibility of reading him as a figure for the people of colonial Hong Kong in the early 1980s: like them, he grew up in a European space which is now on the verge of disappearing; like them, he feels powerless to prevent the change from happening; like them, he experiences wistfulness and a sense of longing for the past. His status as a colonial figure is further underscored by his legal education abroad. The film opens with a sequence of Chi-pang's graduation from law school. Chi-pang's professor congratulates him on obtaining a first-class honors degree, and the sequence ends with Chi-pang proudly holding both his degree certificate and the scepter for the top student in his cohort. The graduation ceremony takes place in London, the center of empire, and the sequence is the only one in the entire film in which the dialogue is in English. Western orchestral ceremonial music plays in the background. The film therefore opens by introducing Chi-pang not only as a talented lawyer but as a product of British colonial education. The first shot in the sequence is of Chi-pang walking down the steps of an impressive baroque building; the grandeur of the edifice evokes the hallowed English common law into which Chi-pang is being inducted. In colonial society, a British education is regarded with awe: as Kwan, the paralegal who is assigned to assist Chi-pang, says enviously at their first meeting: "Mr. Lau was properly trained at a British law school, what can he not accomplish?" The head partner of the firm instructs Kwan to put in extra effort when working with Chi-pang, because Chi-pang had newly returned from Britain. Chi-pang constitutes what was commonly regarded as the best of Hong Kong society at the time: young, intelligent, handsome, ambitious, and, importantly, British-educated.

The portrayal of Wai-lan, by contrast, evokes a strong sense of Chineseness. As Mary Farquhar and Chris Berry have observed, the nineteenth-century Opium War by which China lost Hong Kong to Britain has long been narrated as a form of "humiliation" and "as the paradigm experience of a wound to the Chinese national body" in Chinese film.[29] The depiction of China as a lowly, downtrodden prostitute whose body is repeatedly taken advantage of by her clients can be thought of as a continuation of this mode of representation. The film also takes pains to depict the social world of the prostitutes in which Wai-lan is embedded as a Chinese arena. The only sustained vision of this world is given in a sequence in which Chi-pang visits Wai-lan's former brothel in an attempt to gather more information favorable to her case. As we enter the brothel, we hear traditional Chinese opera music playing on the radio. A Chinese altar for paying homage to household deities hangs prominently on the wall facing the camera, and pieces of red paper in Chinese writing (which are supposed to bring luck) make up the reminder of the décor. The prostitutes are mostly dressed in traditional attire and drink Chinese tea rather than Western wine. As Chi-pang walks in, the prostitutes are gathered around a table playing a Chinese gambling game, and one of them is cooling herself with a Chinese straw fan. The vast differences in economic circumstances between the brothel and the lawyers' world echo the divergent economic situations between Hong Kong and China at the time. While the brothel is of course part of colonial Hong Kong in the narrative, the presentation of Wai-lan's *milieu* with such traditional markers of Chineseness visually delineates it as a space that seems cut off from the colonial spaces of the rest of Hong Kong in the film. These markers set it apart visually not only from the French champagne, Western music, foreign dances, and English dinner jackets of the social domain of the lawyers and judges but also from the European architecture of the orphanage in which Chi-pang grew up.

The circumstances in which Chi-pang was placed at the orphanage, revealed through a flashback to the day Wai-lan brought him there as a baby, bolster this allegorical reading. Curiously, the audience does not at first see Wai-lan's face in the flashback. In the first shot, the camera is positioned behind her, so that we only see a woman wearing a traditional Chinese cheongsam walking up to the gate. The emphasis of the shot is therefore not on Wai-lan herself but on the traditional Chinese attire. The second shot makes the evocation of Chineseness even more apparent: it is a shot of her shoes, again of a traditional Chinese style – they are black velvet shoes, with a floral pattern, of a kind not often found on the streets of modern-day Hong Kong. It is only in the third shot that we see Wai-lan walking slowly and reluctantly, with a sorrowful expression on her face, up to the main building of the orphanage. She begs Sister Maria to take the child, as she could not care for him herself. While there is of course no exact factual parallel

---

[29] Mary Farquhar and Chris Berry, "Speaking Bitterness: History, Media and Nation in Twentieth Century China," 2(1) *Historiography East and West* (2004), 116–144 (123).

with the way Hong Kong was taken from the motherland – far from begging a colonial power to take Hong Kong, China lost Hong Kong to Britain after its defeat in the Opium War – what is important here are Wai-lan's more fundamental sentiments of grief, reluctance, and powerlessness in the scene. Just as the motherland had to relinquish Hong Kong to a foreign power due to the force of circumstances, so Wai-lan had to hand over her child due to her helpless situation. The pain of a mother giving up her baby parallels the pain of the motherland giving up her people.

Finally, Wai-lan's constant but distant presence in Lau's life as he grew up also echoes China's relationship with Hong Kong. Wai-lan asks Sister Maria not to tell Chi-pang about his origins, yet she watches over him secretly throughout his life. In the flashback, we see Chi-pang as a primary school student reading a book in the playground of the orphanage while Wai-lan and Sister Maria watch him from the corridors of a building nearby. In another flashback, we see Chi-pang leaving for his studies in Britain. It was Wai-lan who scraped together the money for his tuition and his ticket abroad; her abusive husband disfigured her with a hot iron in an attempt to wrest the cash from her. Despite her sacrifices, she does not want her son to see her. From another building nearby, she sobs while bidding Chi-pang a silent farewell. The motherland is here imagined to watch over her child from afar while the colonial institution takes all the credit for raising him. She is far away, across the border, but always close by, watching over him with tenderness, care, and love.

The Unwritten Law's story of a mother's reunion with the child that she once had to give up to foreign care resonates with the historical narrative of the motherland's reunion with the territory it once had to relinquish to foreign administration, a historical narrative that circulated ubiquitously in Hong Kong in an era dominated by the Sino-British negotiations, the Joint Declaration, and all the uncertainties and soul searching that they generated. The film's two layers of meaning start to become discernable when we foreground the implicit markers of national identity in the presentation of the two main characters: Chi-pang is associated with colonial Hong Kong through his background in the orphanage and his education, and Wai-lan is associated with a sense of Chineseness through the film's depiction of the world of the prostitutes, as well as the sentiments and circumstances surrounding the loss of her child. The mother recognizes her child, but the son, estranged after all these years under foreign tutelage, no longer recognizes her.

1.3 The Sentimentality of Love

If, as I have been arguing, Chi-pang and Wai-lan can be read as representations of 1980s Hong Kong and China respectively, then it follows that the question of whether the mother would be reunited with her son in *The Unwritten Law* can be read as a cinematic engagement with the issue of the reunification of the motherland and her lost territory. The family reunion cannot happen if Chi-pang does not know the truth about his client's identity, and the uncertainty of whether he will find out who she really is constitutes one of the main dramatic tensions in the film. How does *The Unwritten Law* manage audience reactions to family reunification through its plot and cinematography, and what does this question in turn tell us about the question of how the film relates to its legal and historical contexts?

One way of approaching these issues is through the film's sentimentalism. By all accounts, *The Unwritten Law* is a sentimental film, in the sense that it seems designed to elicit an overflow of emotion and often tears from the viewers. Reviewers repeatedly used adjectives such as "moving" (動人), "touching" (感人), and "stirring" (感動) to describe its impact on the audience when it was first screened at the local cinemas.[30] The more critical reviewers accused the director of being "emotionally manipulative" (煽情), but they also acknowledged the film's affective charge, for at the core of their accusation of manipulation is precisely the recognition of the film's ability to pull at the viewers' heartstrings.[31] The film's sentimentalism arises from the fundamental dilemma that a mother's love cannot be acknowledged by her own son: Wai-lan yearns to be united with Chi-pang at last, but she also does not want Chi-pang to know her true identity because his career would be ruined if anyone ever found out that he was the illegitimate child of a lowly prostitute: "For his future, I cannot let anyone know that his mother is a whore! I cannot let anyone know that his mother is a murderer!" The intensity of the mother's love is matched by the overarching importance of the son's misapprehension.

The film's cinematography also contributes to its sentimentalism, as epitomized in a sequence in which Wai-lan reflects upon her situation in a prison cell at night. She has just discovered that Chi-pang is her son. As the truth sinks in, her thoughts are interrupted by memories of various tragic incidents from her life, and the narrative cuts between the past and the present through a series of flashbacks. In the first flashback, she tells Sister Maria: "I will do my very best to support him financially. For the sake of his future, please hide the truth of his origins from him [. . .] Just tell him that the person supporting him is a benefactor called Mr. Nobody . . .." The name "Nobody" is poignant: even though she will sacrifice her own body again and again through sex work in order to support him financially in the years to come, she resigns herself to remaining nothing to him in his life. In the next flashback, we see her abusive husband attempting to wrest the money for Chi-pang's studies from her. As she tries to run away, he hits her full in the face with a hot iron and disfigures her. The camera zooms in on her face: she sits there sobbing in pain, as blood oozes from a long, deep scar on her left cheek. We know that the disfigurement

[30] Ma Chi, "Goodness and Love That Touch Us – *The Unwritten Law*", *New Evening Post*, September 30th, 1985.

[31] Lu Feng, "*The Unwritten Law* Excels At Manipulating Our Emotions," *Sing Tao Daily*, September 25th, 1985.

will ruin the livelihood for a woman who makes a living by her beauty, and it is presumably this episode that reduced Wai-lan to soliciting in the least salubrious parts of Hong Kong. The camera then cuts back to the prison cell to show the present-day Wai-lan touching the old scar as she thinks back to her husband's attack, and this shot is followed by a close up of a thick bundle of cash which Wai-lan hands over to Sister Maria.

The juxtaposition of these temporally distinct moments in Wai-lan's life amplifies her suffering by piling them one after the other and also underscores that she endured the suffering to secure a better future for Chi-pang. Years of hardship have made this maternal body scarred, gaunt, and cowed. Wai-lan deserves to finally embrace her son and be rewarded for her years of self-sacrifice, but the narrative has made clear that in a society where social standing and reputation are such prized assets that an innocent woman without any of those assets is left without legal representation, any association with her would ruin Chi-pang's future. The film manages the audience's emotive reactions by cuing, shaping, and directing their responses to the idea of reunion: it elicits strong sympathy for reunion, but it also cultivates a firm appreciation of the need to remain apart. The film's sentimental charge arises from situating viewers at the intersection of two reactions which pull in different directions and which are ultimately at odds with each other.

How could we theorize the film's sentimentalism? One film review describes *The Unwritten Law* as a *wenqinpian* (溫情片): this is a common Chinese term for sentimental film, but a transliteration of the term would be something along the lines of "warm sentiment film," in the sense of a film that generates warm, loving, and tender feelings on the part of the viewers.[32] This characterization of the film is worth probing, if only because it stands out among a sea of reviews that, whether positively or negatively, chose to highlight the emotional intensity or excess of the narrative. It may be productive to think about *The Unwritten Law* as a form of *wenqinpian* in light of Rey Chow's work on sentimentalism.[33] Chow extends the definition of sentimentalism beyond its conventional, Euro-centric associations with pathos, pity, and distress.[34] She notes that the common understanding of sentimentalism as a form of "emotional excess" is "only a clue to a much broader range of issues" in Chinese cinema.[35] She observes that the sentimental in Chinese film is often associated with domesticity or the home, a point reflected in *The Unwritten Law*'s focus on maternal life and family relations. More importantly, Chow also points out

---

[32] Deng Xin, "How to Gauge Current Film Trends: Viewers Nowadays Seem to Warm to Sentimental Films," *New Evening Post*, October 14th, 1985.

[33] Rey Chow, *Sentimental Fabulations: Contemporary Chinese Cinema* (New York: Columbia University Press, 2007). Chow deliberately defines the term "Chinese cinema" broadly to encompass films from the People's Republic of China, Hong Kong, Taiwan, as well as those by directors who are ethnically Chinese and based in the United States.

[34] The clearest exposition of sentimental literature remains Janet Todd, *Sensibility: An Introduction* (London: Methuen, 1986).

[35] Chow, *Sentimental Fabulations*, p. 15.

that one possible Chinese translation of the term "sentiment" is *wenqin* (溫情), literally, "warmth." She glosses the importance of warmth to sentimentalism in this way: "being warm, to be exact, is being in the middle between the extremes of hot and cold"; as such, warmth signifies a fascinating middle ground between polar opposites.[36] This idea of sentimentalism as a form of in-between-ness is critical to Chow's understanding of the term. As an intermediate state between extremes, the sentimental in the context of Chinese-language cinema is better understood as "an inclination or a disposition toward making compromises and toward making-do with even – and especially – that which is oppressive and unbearable". Occupying such a middle ground is emotionally demanding, as it takes energy and effort to be "making-do" or maintaining a "compromise" when one is placed between two problematic or undesirable extremes.

In light of Chow's argument, I would suggest that the sentimentality of love in *The Unwritten Law* is premised on the viewers' position of in-between-ness, making-do, and compromise. By placing them in a position marked by divergent reactions and emotional vacillation regarding the family reunion between Wai-lan and Chi Pang, the film cues viewers to perform the complex emotional work necessary to accommodate opposing reactions, and it is this emotional work which forms the core of the film's stirring or moving quality. The film is touching, even heartrending, precisely because it situates the audience in the difficult middle space of the two poles of desiring and not desiring the reunion. To return to the overlap between the personal and the national, I would further suggest that the *viewing* position characterized by conflicting reactions to Chi-pang and Wai-lan's reunion parallels the *political* position characterized by conflicting emotions about the unification of Hong Kong to China. The contradictory feelings of wholehearted embrace and outright rejection toward the motherland that constituted the affect of Hong Kongers' political position resonate with the irreconcilable emotions toward family reunion that constituted the affect of the audience's viewing position. The love in the mother–son relationship in the film overlaps with, echoes, and evokes the love in the relationship between Hong Kong and mainland China that formed the *zeitgeist* of the territory in the aftermath of the Sino-British Joint Declaration.

Sister Maria's speech in the courtroom takes on new significance in light of this understanding of the film's sentimentalism. The nun is summoned back from her retirement in Europe by the prosecution to testify to the real relationship between Wai-lan and Chi-pang. Both the defendant and her lawyer are shocked to see her. The prosecutor cross-examines her and asks her directly whether Wai-lan is Chi-pang's mother. Crucially, Sister Maria hesitates as she ponders over how to answer. At long last, she takes a deep breath, looks the prosecutor directly in the eye and lies: "I'm sorry . . . NO!!!"

---

[36] Chow, *Sentimental Fabulations*, p. 18 (original italics).

Having denied the kinship, she exits the witness stand and leaves the prosecutor standing dumbfounded in the middle of the courtroom.

The testimony constitutes the climax of the film. Sister Maria's hesitation is deliberately highlighted in the sequence: it is over one minute long, and in this time viewers are kept in suspense over her response along with the prosecutor and the jury in the courtroom. What gives rise to the dramatic tension of this moment? In terms of the plot, the tension in the sequence comes from the fact that neither answer is desirable for the reasons already stated: saying "no" means Wai-lan cannot be reunited with Chi-pang, but saying "yes" means ruining Chi-pang's future. The flashbacks during this sequence make the dilemma clear: the camera cuts first to Sister Maria's memories of Wai-lan and then to her memories of Chi-pang, thereby indicating that she has in mind the well-being and happiness of them both.

However, in allegorical terms, I would suggest that the power of this sequence comes not simply from the withholding of the nun's answer but from the way it taps into the overlap between two interrelated affects, the love between the mother and her son on the one hand and the love between Hong Kongers and the motherland on the other. The long sequence defers the answer, and in doing so maintains that delicate balance between conflicting attitudes toward family reunion/political reunification that I have been tracing. The suspense is powerful because it "keeps and preserves," however temporarily, the delicate "compromise" between togetherness and separation, a compromise which reflects the simultaneous longing for intimacy and yearning for detachment which Hong Kongers experienced in relation to China at this historical juncture.[37]

It is also worth pausing over the final shot of the film in this light. After the verdict in Wai-lan's favor is handed down, Chi-pang walks over to congratulate her. The trial has now come to an end, and it is the time for good-byes. He smiles at her, says "take care," and walks away with his colleagues, leaving her in the company of her fellow prostitutes in the courtroom. Chi-pang's words have a ring of finality to them; "take care" (保重) implies that he does not expect to see her again. As the lawyer departs, the camera slowly zooms in on Wai-lan. The final shot of the film is a close up of Chi-pang's mother, with tears rolling down her face. The audience is crying with her: as one commentator noted, Ng's film powerfully brought "a flood of tears" to their eyes. It is possible to interpret the ending as a screening of the fantasy of deferral: the son who does not become reunited with his mother and walks away, presumably into a bright future, can be viewed as a representation of a Hong Kong that remains free from the motherland. Yet to the extent that it is a fantasy of an infinitely deferred return, the emotions that it generates are contradictory and incongruous: our tears are tears of joy at the idea of a son and a territory that remain unburdened, but they are also tears of sadness arising from the thought of

---

[37] Chow, *Sentimental Fabulations*, p. 18.

a happy family reunion that does not happen. The tears express both gladness and sorrow, relief and regret, freedom and heartache.[38] Such is the complexity of love in *The Unwritten Law*, a film that captures the sentiments of a city in a period of unprecedented constitutional change.

1.4 Love beyond the Law

So far, I have been considering the film's sentimentalism in the context of the relationship between Wai-lan and Chi-pang. The issue of sentimentalism is also related to the film's representation of law. One way of approaching the relationship between law and sentimentalism is by way of the film's Chinese title, which literally means "love outside of the law" or "love beyond the law." As one reviewer observed, "Even though *The Unwritten Law* is a courtroom drama, it is really about love [. . .] from beginning to end, love is the film's main concern." What does love have to do with law? In this section, I will focus on the trial scene to contend that love in the film forms the basis of an interrogation of the rule of law in colonial Hong Kong.

In the final thirteen years of the British rule, between 1984 and 1997, there gradually came into view a more critical reflection on the colonial discourse on the rule of law as Hong Kong society collectively examined the legacy of the departing sovereign. As it looked back at its own history, there emerged a remembrance that while the major elements of the rule of law did exist in the 1980s and the 1990s, the "gift" of the rule of law was not as longstanding as the British administration made it out to be: as Ming K. Chan argues in a seminal article, there were "significant lapses and gaps" in the colonial justice system, even if we acknowledge that "the rule of law is definitely a foremost British legacy for Hong Kong."[39] I have discussed some of these "lapses and gaps" in the Introduction. *The Unwritten Law* can be regarded as part of this reflection on colonial justice. Through Wai-lan's treatment by the justice system, Ng's film provides visual indications of how the guarantee of the rule of law might have been more of a structuring myth than a lived reality for much of the time Hong Kong was a colony.

Early in the film, Chi-pang is introduced to all the major figures in the legal profession, including judges, senior barristers, and police commissioners, at a fancy cocktail party thrown by his girlfriend's father, a seasoned barrister. The fact that the introductions arise from Chi-pang's own personal relations, as well as these figures' readiness to welcome him into their circle because he is the likely son-in-law of a prominent barrister, suggests that the colonial lawyering world is more of a cozy coterie than a world of impartial advocates and judges. When his girlfriend's father later urges Chi-pang to drop the case,

---

[38] "Loyal . . . but the Doubts Remain," *South China Morning Post*, November 24th, 1984.
[39] Ming K. Chan, "The Legacy of the British Administration of Hong Kong: A View from Hong Kong," 151 *China Quarterly* (1997), 567–582 (570).

he tells him point blank that he will be ostracized in the profession should he dare act against the famous businessman whose son attacked Wai-lan. Wai-lan herself understands the inequalities ingrained in the system. As she observes, "no one will believe" her testimony because her attacker "came from high society" while she is "nothing but a whore, the cheapest kind of whore". In the course of the trial, the attacker's psychiatrist who is summoned to give evidence denies that the attacker was ever a client at his clinic, and he dares to lie in open court because he knows that no one will believe the words of a prostitute rather than the assertions of a respected member of the medical profession. By exposing how the law sided with the rich and powerful and overlooked the people most in need of its protection, the film suggests that the premise of the rule of law, that everyone is equal before the law and no one is above the law, was more rhetorical than real in colonial Hong Kong.

In contrast to the self-interest and the inequalities that characterize the domain of law, the film offers the domain of love as the place where justice can be found. A number of critics have underscored the incompatibility between law and love. Writing in the mode of a critical legal studies scholar, Peter Goodrich argues that the jurisdictions of love form part of the "minor jurisprudences" which have been repressed by the law. The "science of law" as we know it does not leave much room for love.[40] Joshua Neoh similarly contends that "law and love are alternative relational paradigms."[41] The film accentuates the divergence between the two in its depiction of the way the lawyers constantly misinterpret expressions of love. Just before the trial begins, Wai-lan says to Chi-pang: "I am so sorry." What Chi-pang hears is an apology for an earlier decision to terminate him as her defense counsel, a decision which she reconsiders. However, beyond the surface meaning of her words is a much more profound apology: she is saying sorry for having given birth to him despite her economic circumstances, for abandoning him at an orphanage, for not giving him the best in life. Within the courtroom, a mother's heartfelt apology to her son for not being by his side is heard as the apology of a client to her lawyer for an issue of legal representation. This exchange takes place across the two sides of the dock, with metal bars separating the two characters. The physical barrier between them visually underscores the miscommunication between speaker and listener.

Another moment of misinterpretation occurs during Wai-lan's own testimony to the court. Chi-pang tells her to speak freely in front of the judge and the jury. Untrained in legal language, Wai-lan hesitates and looks around the room. When she finally speaks, she confesses to staying up all night agonizing over how to defend herself. She concludes her speech by saying: "I have to thank god . . . for He has given me what I desire the most." As she says her final

[40] Peter Goodrich, *Law in the Courts of Love: Literature and Other Minor Jurisprudences* (Abingdon: Routledge, 1996), p. 2.

[41] Joshua Neoh, "Law and Love in Abraham's Binding of Issac," 9 *Law and Humanities* (2015), 237–261(261).

line, she looks directly into Chi-pang's eyes. Chi-pang looks back at her with a blank smile. The audience of course knows that she is grateful for seeing her son again, and for knowing that he has grown up to be a compassionate and upstanding person. Yet what Lau and the rest of the court hear is that she is simply grateful for the representation of a dedicated lawyer and the support of her friends. A final instance emblematic of the divergence is the prosecutor's reaction to Sister Maria's characterization of maternal love. When asked whether the defendant is Chi-pang's mother, she says:

> From my perspective as the Head of an orphanage, what matters most is not whether the woman physically gave birth to the child. What matters most is whether the woman cared for the child, whether she loved the child, whether she was willing to even sacrifice herself for the child. Only a woman who is capable of all of those things can be called a mother.

Her response about what constitutes maternal love exasperates the prosecutor: "Sister Maria, I did not invite you to come all the way here to hear your philosophizing [about motherhood]." His reaction suggests that the lawyer has no patience for, and fails to understand the articulation of the meaning of love: all he hears is empty "philosophizing."

The film aligns love with justice by suggesting that at the core of love is the spirit of self-sacrifice. It makes clear that justice must be fought for, and it is only when we are willing to sacrifice ourselves that a just verdict can be achieved. *The Unwritten Law* is full of self-sacrificing women, and their acts of selflessness constitute an important aspect of the film's sentimentalism: the narrative is so moving because we see these women give up the little that they have for other people. Moreover, the fact that the lawyers are all men whereas those who make sacrifices are all women underscores the divergence between law and love. There is of course Wai-lan, who sacrifices herself for her son. The spirit of self-sacrifice is also reflected in the acts of the other prostitutes, who address each other as "sisters" as an expression of their love and devotion to one another. They pool together their hard-earned money for Wai-lan so that she can afford a lawyer, and in fact it is one of Wai-lan's "sisters" who first approaches Chi-pang and begs him to take the case. Then there is Chu Niu, yet another prostitute, who was also assaulted and injured by Wai-lan's attacker. Chu was initially reluctant to step forward as a witness because she was too traumatized by her experience, but she finally agrees to do so. She breaks down in tears as she retells the incident in court, but she endures re-traumatization to help ensure that Wai-lan does not receive an unjust sentence. There is also the nurse at the psychiatrist's clinic, who happens to have grown up at the same orphanage as Chi-pang and who runs into him by chance at a café. It is because of her love for a fellow orphan and her trust in him that she agrees to sacrifice her career at the psychiatrist's office and testify against her employer. Had she not presented the attacker's medical record as evidence in court, the psychiatrist's testimony would not have been exposed as a lie and Wai-lan would have been found guilty.

Finally, there is Sister Maria. In strictly legal terms, Sister Maria commits perjury by lying about the relationship between Chi-pang and Wai-lan. Yet one of the key points of interest in *The Unwritten Law* is that while it is Sister Maria who is the law breaker in the film, it is also Sister Maria who ensures that justice is done. We can understand her answer to the prosecutor – the emphatic "No!!!" – in terms of the divergence between law and love, between ideology and self-sacrifice, and between the demands of the court and the demands of justice. The film makes clear that it is an act of ultimate self-sacrifice, even damnation, for a nun to lie in open court in this manner: when Sister Maria takes the stand, the camera zooms in on her placing her hand on the Bible, as she swears "*in the name of God*, to speak absolutely no falsehood." The point is re-emphasized when she is pressed for a final answer a few minutes later. The camera zooms in on her hand again, this time to show it tightly clutching the crucifix she wears around her neck. These moments indicate that Sister Maria risks her own salvation if she lies. Yet that is ultimately what she decides to do, and it is her answer, that perjurious but virtuous speech act, that ensures that Wai-lan is not unjustly found guilty of murder. Her refusal to give in to the law's demand for the answer that would have disqualified Chi-pang as Wai-lan's lawyer and necessitated a retrial in which the defendant would have been left with no legal defense exposes colonial law as more of a limit to, rather than a vehicle for, justice. By showing that love can, against all odds, clear the name of even a helpless, downtrodden woman such as Wai-lan in a legal system which privileges power and status, and by exposing the inequalities in that system, the film interrogates the ideology of law in colonial Hong Kong and remains hopeful of the existence of something else, a utopian "beyond" or "outside" of that ideology, where justice can be done.

Conclusion

In this chapter, I have explored the complex emotions and conflicted attachments that arose in Hong Kong in the aftermath of the Joint Declaration. These emotions and attachments, so critical to our understanding of Hong Kong's relationship to China, are often elided in the more legalistic analysis of the constitutional provisions or documents governing that relationship. Through its capacity for allegorical representation, a film such as *The Unwritten Law* gives us a window into the affective landscape to which the international treaty between Britain and China gave rise in the early 1980s. Toward the end of the decade, another incident relating to China would spark a strong, emotive reaction in Hong Kong. In the next chapter, I will examine the city's legal responses to the Tiananmen Square crackdown in Beijing and explore how anxieties about law and identity to which it gave rise are refracted in a film that appeared in its wake.

The imperative to "love the motherland" is one which will recur in Hong Kong. It will eventually filter through from Chinese officials' edicts into the city's popular discourse, though perhaps not in the form which the authorities anticipated: speaking in 2017, a Hong Kong student said that "China is like the biological mother you recently reunited with [...] There's no love at all."[42] While both mainland and local governmental officials express bafflement and even outrage at the alienation which many of today's young Hong Kongers feel toward the motherland, the cinematic images from the 1980s suggest that that sense of alienation was already there, in a more incipient form, from the first stages of decolonization. From at least the time of the Joint Declaration, the love which Hong Kongers felt toward the motherland was more ambivalent and internally incoherent than that expected by the authorities; against that backdrop, it is perhaps unsurprising that the increasingly insistent nature of the calls to love the motherland made by the authorities after 1997 also ran the risk of becoming increasingly estranging.

[42] Ben Bland, "China Tensions Give Hong Kong an Identity Crisis," *Financial Times*, June 29th, 2019.

2

Laughing at the Law:
Johnnie To's *Justice, My Foot!*[*]

In Johnnie To's *Justice, My Foot!*(審死官; 1992), a woman in Qing Dynasty China named Yeung Sau-chun finds herself framed for the murder of her husband. The real culprits are Yeung's brother-in-law and his wife, the Yiu-Tin couple, whose motive for the murder is to monopolize the family fortune. In order to save herself and her unborn child, Yeung flees from her native province, only to find herself abandoned and penniless in the countryside. By a stroke of good fortune, however, she meets the kindhearted wife of the famous litigation master Sung Sai-kit. Taking pity on the helpless, pregnant woman, Madam Sung takes Yeung back to the Sung residence. Sung is initially reluctant to help Yeung, but Madam Sung eventually persuades him to defend the innocent woman against the true murderers in court so that she can clear her name.

The problem for Sung is that the trial is to take place in a Chinese courtroom which is plagued by corruption, bribery, and nepotism; marred by the abuse of judicial power; run by incompetent judges and vengeful law enforcement officers; and premised on the rule of man rather than the rule of law. The Commissioner of Shanxi province is the brother of Madam Yiu, the wife of Yeung's brother-in-law, and he attempts to use his position to secure a favorable verdict for the murderers. Moreover, Sung had antagonized the Magistrate of Guangzhou city through his flippant attitude and his lack of respect on previous occasions, and the magistrate is determined not to allow Sung to win this case. Finally, the Inspector General is unhappy with Sung because of what he regards as his insolent attitude. The court officials therefore seek to protect the guilty and use the trial as an occasion for personal vengeance. The stakes are high not only for Yeung but also for Sung himself: should he fail, he will face severe punishment, including torture, for daring to challenge the position of these officials.[1]

---

[*] A version of this article was originally published in the *Cardozo Law Review*, 31 *Cardozo Law Review* 1313 (2010). The author has made modifications to the article for this version. These changes were not reviewed or approved by the *Cardozo Law Review*.
[1] *Justice, My Foot!* is the remake of an earlier film (with the same Chinese name) by Yeung Kung-lcong entitled *The Judge Goes To Pieces* (1948). To's film differs significantly from the original

The film therefore contains all the elements of a legal tragedy involving a gross miscarriage of justice. However, the most striking aspect of *Justice, My Foot!* is that it is extremely funny. Sung is played by the comedian Stephen Chow, who is famous in Hong Kong for a unique brand of humor known as "Moleitau" – a phrase which is difficult to translate but which loosely refers to a combination of slapstick, toilet humor, situational comedy, and word play. *Justice, My Foot!* was the most successful film in the Hong Kong Box Office when it appeared in 1992.[2] One film critic gave it what is arguably the greatest praise one can give in Cantonese to a comedy: he said that some parts of *Justice, My Foot!* are so funny that they make you "spit out your rice in laughter."[3]

In this chapter, I examine the seemingly paradoxical relationship between humor and injustice. While the film does have a happy ending, many of the funniest scenes center on the flawed legal process, and this dimension of the narrative is worth probing. Why did this specific cinematic representation of Chinese law appear in early 1990s Hong Kong, and how is it related to questions of Hong Kong identity?[4] Law and humor are more closely connected to each other than may first appear: as Peter Goodrich has observed, generations of burgeoning lawyers have been "induced and lured" into the law "through jocular cases, absurd scenarios, strange disputes, and perverse outcomes," so much so that humor can be regarded as a conduit of "juristic knowing."[5] Taking this insight from Goodrich's argument as a point of entry into the film, I will investigate what comedy can tell us about law's role in the construction of selfhood and also reflect upon the nature of the laughter arising from the visualization of law in a comic mode.

In Section 2.1, I will situate *Justice, My Foot!* in light of the political and constitutional developments in Hong Kong in the aftermath of the Tiananmen Square Incident in Beijing on June 4th, 1989. I will underscore the

---

and pays comic homage to it by including two pictures of Ma Si-tsang, the actor who played the original Sung Sai-kit, on the family altar in the Sung residence. Ma is in effect cast as the parents of the current Sung. In one picture, Ma appears as himself (Sung's father), while his image is altered to look like that of a woman in the other picture (Sung's mother). The presence of Ma in the film is of course a sign of respect to the makers and actors of the 1948 film, yet his position on the family altar suggests that the older film is already dead and has limited influence on To's own version. The original may have responded to the legal changes of its own time in ways which are beyond the scope of my analysis here.

[2] The film grossed HK$49,884,734 (approximately US$6,395,479). See *Hong Kong Films 1992* (Hong Kong: Motion Picture Industry Association, 1993), p. 151.

[3] Law Lai, "Review: *Justice, My Foot!*," *Next Magazine*, July 10th, 1992, p. 109.

[4] For discussions of the representation of law in Mainland Chinese film, see *Cinema, Law and the State in Asia*, edited by Corey K. Creekmur and Mark Sidel (Basingstoke: Palgrave Macmillan, 2007), pp. 161–231; Alison Conner, "Courtroom Drama, Chinese Style," 12 *Journal of Comparative Law* (2017), 437–461 and "Images of Justice (and Injustice): Trials in the Movies of Xie Jin, " 35 *Hawaii Law Review* 805 (2013), 805–882; and Stephen McIntyre, "Courtroom Drama with Chinese Characteristics: A Comparative Approach to Legal Process in Chinese Cinema," 8 *University of Pennsylvania East Asia Law Review* (2013), 1–21.

[5] Peter Goodrich, "Proboscations: Excavations in Comedy and Law," 43 (2) *Critical Inquiry* (2017), 361–389 (363).

apprehension and dread many Hong Kongers felt toward China at this historical juncture, and toward the Chinese justice system in particular, and explain
the significance of these sentiments for our understanding of the film. In
Section 2.2, I will offer a reading of three scenarios from *Justice, My Foot!* as
the dramatization of three options available to the Hong Kong lawyer con-
fronted with the reality of the upcoming handover in 1997. In Section 2.3, I will
draw on philosophical writings on laughter and the comic to analyze the
function of humor in the film as both a means of coming to terms with political
and legal uncertainties and a commercial tactic to ensure the film's popularity.

2.1 Representing Law in Anxious Times

To begin with the obvious: the events of *Justice, My Foot!* are set in China
during the Qing Dynasty. The Chineseness of the film is evident from the
beginning; the opening sequence consists of a long shot of a scroll depicting
traditional Chinese buildings, and the words of the opening credits appear on
the screen as if they were the products of Chinese calligraphy or traditional
Chinese ink stamps. Moreover, the costumes, the decor, and details such as the
period-specific hairstyle together create the image of a courtroom with distinctly Chinese characteristics. The visual Chineseness underscores that the
film is dealing not simply with injustice or judicial corruption in a general
sense but with forms of injustice and judicial corruption specific to the Chinese
context.

However, despite the overt references to mainland China, *Justice, My Foot!*
has a distinctly Hong Kong flavor. Both Stephen Chow, the actor who plays
Sung, and the late Anita Mui, who plays his wife, are iconic Hong Kong
celebrities. Chow made an indelible mark on Hong Kong's cinematic landscape in the 1990s with a series of comedies of which this film forms a part, and
moviegoers have dubbed him Hong Kong's "King of Comedy."[6] In fact, his
influence on Hong Kong culture is so widespread that one critic asked whether
the 1990s should be called "the 'Stephen Chow' era."[7] Chow's character, Sung,
also conforms to a certain stereotypical Hong Kong self-image, in that he is not
only clever, resourceful, entrepreneurial (Sung owns and runs an inn) but also
materialistic and amoral.[8] Anita Mui, the "Canto-pop queen" who was also
known as the "Madonna of Asia" in her time, rose to fame in a period when

---

[6] Laramie Mok, "Five Stephen Chow Movies that Made Him Hong Kong's King of Comedy,"
South China Morning Post, June 22nd, 2019. For an analysis of *Hail the Judge* (1994), another
Stephen Chow comedy set in a Chinese courtroom, see my forthcoming "Hail the Spectator:
Embodiment, Film, and Justice".

[7] Wai Lo-see, "Is there a 'Stephen Chow' Era?," 351 *City Entertainment* (September 1992), 18–21.

[8] To notes that his original choice for Sung Sai-kit was not Stephen Chow but Chow Yun-Fat, but
the latter was unavailable due to a prior agreement with another film company. To praises
Stephen Chow's style of acting as "excellent, full of energy and life." See the interview with To in
Miles Wood, *Cine East: Hong Kong Cinema through the Looking Glass* (Guildford: FAB Press,
1998), pp. 116–130(p. 123).

stardom was created and bolstered through an entertainer's appearance across multiple platforms, including television, film, product advertising, and music.[9] Primarily a singer, Mui's crossover from the concert stage to the movie screen in this instance can be regarded as part of this "cross-media synergy" in the entertainment industry.[10] Mui's image was ubiquitous in Hong Kong popular culture until her death in 2003. It would not be a stretch to say that Chow and Mui together connote a certain Hong Kongness: what the audience sees is two iconic Hong Kong figures caught in a mainland Chinese legal dilemma.

The language of the film further marks it as a Hong Kong production: even though the setting is characterized by a distinctive mainland Chineseness, the dialogue is entirely in Cantonese, the dialect spoken in Hong Kong. More precisely, much of the dialogue is in colloquial Cantonese, whose vocabulary, structures, and expressions have no equivalent in Mandarin. This hurdle to translation suggests that what is at stake in the language of the film is more than a suspension of disbelief, in which the audience is implicitly asked to ignore the discrepancy between Mandarin and Cantonese. The film's dialogue can be understood as part of a process of viewer identification; as the film critic Linda Chiu-han Lai notes:

> The slang … specifically interpellates Cantonese speakers who live in Hong Kong today. The intense use of Cantonese slang privileges a distinct viewing community compris[ing] not just any Chinese person, nor even any Hong Kong citizen, but only those active residents who have partaken of everyday life and popular culture in the colony in recent years.[11]

The disjuncture between the visual and the verbal, between what we see and what we hear, thus consolidates a sense of Hong Kong identity among the viewers who are able to comprehend Chow's Cantonese humor. In other words, the distinctiveness of the film's language literally speaks to a community of spectators brought together by their common linguistic background.

The combination of the mainland Chinese setting and the distinctly Hong Kong elements within the film suggests that what *Justice, My Foot!* screens is an encounter between a Hong Kong lawyer and the problematic legal system of the mainland. Chow's figure, in particular, constitutes a blatant historical inaccuracy, in that by officially representing one party in the courtroom he behaves more like a common law lawyer familiar to a Hong Kong audience than a *songshi* or Chinese litigation master.[12] The cinema becomes an

---

[9] Lisa Cam, "Canto-pop Queen Anita Mui: Remembering the 'Madonna of Asia'," *South China Morning Post*, October 10th, 2019.

[10] Chu Yiu-wai, *Hong Kong Cantopop: A Concise History* (Hong Kong: Hong Kong University Press, 2017), p. 82.

[11] Linda Chiu-han Lai, "Nostalgia and Nonsense: Two Instances of Commemorative Practices in Hong Kong Cinema in the Early 1990s," in *Fifty Years of Electric Shadows*, edited by Law Kar and Stephen Teo (Hong Kong: Urban Council Publications, 1997), pp. 95–100 (p. 95).

[12] Michael Ng, "Fiftieth Anniversary of Chan Mon-kut's Trickery," 109 *Cup Magazine* (2011), 118–119. For a detailed study of the litigation master, especially of his role in enabling a counter-hegemonic social contestation within the legal arena, see Melissa Macauley, *Social*

imaginary space in which the people of Hong Kong saw themselves encountering problems they regarded as endemic to Chinese law and from which they believed they were normally shielded because of their home city's legal system. The significance of this encounter comes into sharper focus if we place the film in context, because the problem of China dominated the moment in Hong Kong's constitutional history in which the film appeared. China loomed large in Hong Kong's collective imagination between the signing of the Sino-British Joint Declaration in 1984 and the retrocession in 1997, but anxieties about the city's postcolonial future under Chinese rule peaked in 1989, just three years before *Justice, My Foot!* appeared, as a result of the Chinese government crackdown on students in Tiananmen Square that year. People in Hong Kong closely followed reports of the crackdown on their television screens and were gripped by fear and panic: as Johannes Chan observes, the events in Beijing "not only broke the hearts of many Chinese people, it also seemed to sound the death knell for Hong Kong."[13]

The human rights violations associated with the military crackdown are documented elsewhere, and my focus is on how they affected the way Hong Kong people thought about China, about themselves, and about the continued viability of their city's legal framework after the handover. I would like to highlight two reactions in particular.[14] The first is the widespread concern that Hong Kongers could face the same fate as the student dissidents in the mainland after 1997. There was fear that, ironically, the end of the colonial era would also signal the end of human rights and freedoms. The barrister-turned-politician Martin Lee notes that "[t]he Tiananmen Square Massacre had woken up a lot of people in Hong Kong to the fact that what happened in Beijing could happen to Hong Kong after 1997."[15] In a similar vein, another barrister-turned-politician, Margaret Ng, asks, "what would it have been like had Hong Kong been under Chinese sovereignty during these recent events?"[16] Johnnie To himself takes part in this exercise of prophesying when he observes, "where there are Chinese people, there is corruption, and I think this is the way Hong Kong officials will also behave after 1997."[17] According to an index which tracked public confidence in the city's future, after the events of 1989 "more than half of the middle and upper middle class respondents said they did

---

Power and Legal Culture: Litigation Masters in Late Imperial China (Palo Alto: Stanford University Press, 1998).

[13] Johannes Chan, *Human Rights in Hong Kong* (Hong Kong: Wide Angle Press, 1990), p. viii.

[14] For further discussions about the impact of the Tiananmen Square Incident on Hong Kong, see William P. MacNeil, "Righting and Difference," in *Human Rights in Hong Kong*, edited by Raymond Wacks (Oxford: Oxford University Press, 1992), pp. 86–120 and Steve Tsang, *A Modern History of Hong Kong* (Hong Kong: Hong Kong University Press, 2004), pp. 247–254.

[15] John Tang, "Lee Calls for Hong Kong-Mainland Confederation," *South China Morning Post*, June 8th, 1989.

[16] Margaret Ng, "Every Tuesday Viewpoint," *South China Morning Post*, June 6th, 1989.

[17] Review of *Justice, My Foot!*, *City Entertainment* (1992).

not believe China would abide by the terms of the Sino-British Joint Declaration or could refrain from meddling in the affairs of Hong Kong."[18]

The second significant aspect of Hong Kong's reaction is that the Tiananmen Square Incident was locally understood as a failure of law. People feared that the legal protections that they enjoyed would vanish under a Chinese regime. Skepticism arose as to whether the Basic Law, which was still being drafted at the time of the crackdown, could effectively safeguard Hong Kong's freedoms. The Chairman of the local Bar Association found the draft provisions on the post-handover political structure to be "unacceptable", and predicted that "many people will pack up and go [i.e. immigrate], because they will want the certainty of freedom elsewhere".[19] The constitutional document was eventually enacted in 1990, but with the events of Tiananmen Square fresh in their minds, many Hong Kongers were still gravely worried about the future. Writing in the 1990 issue of the *Hong Kong Law Journal*, Albert Chen notes in his editorial that the final version of the Basic Law was "probably disappointing to most Hong Kong people."[20] The language used to critique the law further reflects the ambient fears of the time. The *South China Morning Post* reports that the day after the massacre, a local protestor publicly set fire to a draft of the Basic Law and broke down in tears. "The Basic Law is rubbish," he says. "I don't trust the Basic Law. It's unfair and evil."[21] A politician compares the document to the bandage used in the Chinese custom of female foot-binding: he said that parts of the Basic Law were a "long, stinking foot-binding bandage that stunts the growth of democracy in Hong Kong."[22] This metaphor captures the anger and fear toward China immediately after the massacre: the law is represented as a tool with which the People's Republic – here portrayed as a patriarchal figure – violently deforms the body of a democracy which is implicitly gendered as female. As the 1980s came to a close and Hong Kong entered the 1990s, the success of "One Country, Two Systems" seemed more important but also more uncertain than ever.

In a desperate attempt to stop the exodus from Hong Kong in the aftermath of the Beijing crackdown, the colonial government intensified its efforts to introduce a Bill of Rights as an additional means of protecting freedoms in the territory after the handover. A draft of the bill was published for public consultation in March 1990, and the Bill of Rights Ordinance was enacted in June 1991. Comments on the bill that were made during its consultation and

---

[18] Bernard Fong, "Slow Growth in Public Confidence since June," *South China Morning Post*, December 12th, 1989.

[19] Jennifer Cooke, "Tang Urges All-Out Bar Fight on Basic Law," *South China Morning Post*, January 19th, 1990

[20] Albert H. Y. Chen, "Editorial," 20(2) *Hong Kong Law Journal* (1990), 145–150 (145).

[21] S. Y. Wai, "Protestors Ask NCNA Chief to Explain Violent Events," *South China Morning Post*, June 5th, 1989.

[22] Denise Wong, Joe Wu, and Laura Chan, "'Stinking Bandage' in the Basic Law," *Hong Kong Standard*, October 23rd, 1992.

development further pointed to widespread unease. Henry Litton, a Queen's Counsel who also later became a Court of Final Appeal judge, observes that the Bill of Rights Ordinance is "a very odd document" and that "it gets more odd with closer acquaintance."[23] Another commentator argues that it is "nothing but a Macbethian Witches broth" and that "some diabolical mind has been stirring in the pot."[24] The presence of references to Western texts such as William Shakespeare's *Macbeth* and the Bible in the assessment of the bill again reflects unease towards China; the language can be regarded as constitutive of a fantasy to use texts from the Western canon to counter a Chinese reality. The Human Rights Commission called the bill "hypocritical" and warned that it constituted a "broken promise which sells out the interests of Hong Kong people" and "leaves the protection of human rights in Hong Kong without any improvement."[25]

In addition to concerns about the adequacy of the Basic Law and the Bill of Rights as legal means of safeguarding rights and freedoms, Hong Kong was also rattled by disagreements over the composition of the Court of Final Appeal that was to be established to replace the Privy Council as the final arbiter of legal disputes after the retrocession. Both the Joint Declaration and the Basic Law stipulate that Hong Kong's highest court, when established, may invite judges from other common law jurisdictions to sit on the bench when the facts and circumstances of a case so required.[26] The appointment of overseas judges was meant to ensure that legal cases in the territory would continue to be decided through common law reasoning and in accordance with international human rights standards. The exact number of overseas judges that could sit on the court became a legal and political flashpoint. China insisted that the maximum number of overseas judges on the court be restricted to one, but the Bar Association argued that it was up to the Court of Final Appeal itself to decide the exact number.[27] Even though a ratio of four local judges to one foreign judge on the five-member court had already been agreed upon by the Sino-British Joint Liaison Group, a consultative organ set up by both the British and Chinese governments to implement the Joint Declaration and ensure a smooth transition, China's vocal stance compounded fears about future interventions in the city's judicial independence.[28]

The production of *Justice, My Foot!* largely coincided with the public debate about the Bill of Rights and the promulgation of the Basic Law, and its

---

[23] Henry Litton, "Much Wrong with the Bill of Rights," *South China Morning Post*, April 3rd, 1990.

[24] Neville de Silva, "Bill of Rights Little More than Paper Tiger," *Hong Kong Standard*, March 26th, 1990.

[25] "Group Plans Protest over Bill of Rights," *Hong Kong Standard*, March 6th, 1990.

[26] Sino-British Joint Declaration Annex I, Section III and Basic Law, Article 82.

[27] Lindy Course, "Bar Chairman Takes Parting Shot at Plan for Final Court," *South China Morning Post*, January 14th, 1992.

[28] Chris Yeung and Doreen Cheung, "China Warns Over Final Appeal Court," *South China Morning Post*, October 25th, 1991.

appearance overlapped with the heated discussion about the composition of the Court of Final Appeal. Between 1989 and 1992, the public in Hong Kong became increasingly apprehensive about whether the territory's legal structure could be maintained after the 1997 handover. Given the role of law in the construction of identity, these apprehensions were about nothing less than the possibility of maintaining Hong Kongers' selfhood after that date. In this light, the film's depiction of problems like the abuse of judicial power, corruption, bribery, and judicial incompetence in the Chinese legal system can be interpreted not only as a visualization of local concerns about the future of Hong Kong's judicial system but as part of what Ackbar Abbas calls the politics of disappearance whereby the contours of the "Hong Konger" as a cultural category came under considerable pressure.[29] Through the on-screen encounter between Sung and the mainland legal system, the local audience saw its worst fears about their home's legal future realized: the Hong Kong lawyer trapped in a courtroom in which the rule of law is replaced by the rule of man.

2.2 The Hong Kong Lawyer's Choice

Faced with the imminent return of the city to the mainland and the possibility of the entrenchment of an unreliable and corrupt judicial framework, what could lawyers in Hong Kong do? What options were available to them as they looked into the not-too-distant future? The film indicates three options and also implicitly points toward the option that they should choose. They could (i) turn to corruption, (ii) retire from the world of law and pursue another career, or (iii) confront the problems of the Chinese legal system with courage and integrity. The remainder of this section discusses three scenes that dramatize these options.

In the first scenario, the Hong Kong lawyer chooses to become corrupt, accepting bribes from the guilty parties and thereby obtaining financial benefits through the sacrifice of those who are innocent but poor. Sung is presented with this option early in the film when he is asked to defend the son of a bank owner. The son, Chan Tai-man, has seriously injured another man in a brawl, and the victim later dies from his injuries. The bank owner, knowing that the family of the deceased will sue his son, hopes to employ Sung as his defense lawyer. Sung is offered a box of silver as a deposit. He initially refuses to help but eventually agrees after the bank owner orders his servants to bring in two additional carts of gold. "If you win, all this will be yours," the bank owner tells Sung. Sung rises from his seat and emphatically responds, "No." For a brief moment, the audience believes that he has the integrity to refuse the offer, but this expectation is defeated when Sung continues his sentence: "No, I want half

---

[29] Ackbar Abbas, *Hong Kong: Culture and the Politics of Disappearance* (Hong Kong: Hong Kong University Press, 1997).

even if I lose." By choosing to forgo justice for financial gain, the Hong Kong lawyer chooses the path of the other corrupt Chinese officials.

However, the film suggests that this is not the path that the Hong Kong lawyer should take. After he wins the court case for Chan, Sung is handsomely rewarded and returns home in high spirits. He brings a new toy for his newborn son in celebration, only to be told that his son had fallen into a well and drowned prior to his return. The audience is told that this is not the first time Sung has lost a child. In fact, none of his previous children had been able to live beyond the age of one because of Sung's corrupt and immoral behavior; his willingness to defend the guilty for personal gain has led to divine retribution in the form of the premature death of his children. "Retribution ... This is retribution," Sung laments to his wife. The film suggests that regardless of a lawyer's resourcefulness and intelligence, the deliberate failure to uphold the ideals of justice will lead to unhappiness outside of the courtroom.

In the second scenario, the Hong Kong lawyer chooses to retire from the law and pursues an entirely different career path. This second option is reflected in Sung's decision to open Yuet Loi Inn. Following the latest death of his son, Sung swears to abandon his life in the law and decides to run an inn, a career which he presumably believes will involve fewer morally contentious choices. When Madam Sung brings Yeung to their residence and urges Sung to help her clear her name, Sung resolutely refuses, insisting that his legal career is over and that he is now exclusively in the hotel and restaurant business.

However, the film seems to mock the idea that the Hong Kong lawyer could ever avoid the law entirely. Sung is repeatedly depicted as emasculated following the loss of his identity as a legal personage. Since he is untrained in the hotel and restaurant business, there is little he can do at the Inn. Bored, idle, and listless, he begins to take an interest in his wife's toilette. Madam Sung is irritated by his behavior: "You're a man, why are you taking an interest in my toilette? Do you have too much time on your hands?" Sung regards his own ennui as an erosion of masculine identity: "At my age, I can't be seen walking around with nothing to do, because people would laugh at me. It's a pity I've quit my job [in the law]." Madam Sung chastises him for "not being enough of a man" when he refuses to come to the rescue of the defenseless Yeung. The crisis of Sung's masculinity forms the basis of a comical exchange between husband and wife:

Madam Sung:	You see that she's in despair and you refuse to help. What kind of a man are you?
Sung:	Don't say that again, or I'll beat you.
Madam Sung:	You're not a man!
Sung (raising his fist):	Don't think I won't do it just because you're pregnant ...

Madam Sung:	You're not a man! You're not a man! You're not a man!
Sung [relenting]:	Okay fine . . . I'm a woman then. Harrumph!

The sexual politics of this scene are conservative, in part because they are structured by the gender hierarchy of Qing-Dynasty China and also because ideas of gender equality were still only emerging in early 1990s Hong Kong, a point I will return to in the next chapter. Sung's emasculation is made more explicit when he is attacked inside his own inn: he is unable to fight off the intruders and has to be rescued by his wife. At the end of the fight, Sung says, "It's a good thing not too many people saw that I had to be rescued by a woman." But when he raises his head he realizes that the fight was witnessed by the entire village, and the villagers are all laughing at him. The sequence of the fight ends with the image of Sung humiliated, his head buried in the bosom of Madam Sung in a gesture of shame, sobbing while the rest of the village looks on in derision.

It is possible to go further and argue that losing one's identity as a litigation master or lawyer constitutes not only a form of emasculation but also a form of castration in the film. The Cantonese expression for retiring from the law is "sealing one's pen" (in that a pen was needed in order to file a complaint to the court, and litigation masters constituted a relatively small class of literate people in Chinese society at the time). Significantly, the pen is represented as a phallic object in the story, whereby the phallus connotes knowledge and power. As a way of ensuring that Sung will never return to the law, his wife forces him to take an oath before the entire village, and he swears: "If I ever pick up my pen again . . . then my next child will be born without a penis." The equivalence between "pen" and "penis" is made explicit in the oath. This oath is one reason why Sung initially refused to come to the aid of Yeung: "I've sealed my pen . . . If I pick it up again and my child is born without a penis, can you give the penis back to me?" Within a rigid gender hierarchy in which masculinity is privileged, and femininity devalorized, the loss of one's identity as a litigation master or lawyer (the loss of a pen) amounts to the loss of one's identity as a man (the loss of a penis), which in turn translates into a loss of positive qualities such as courage, determination, and strength.

In the third scenario, the Hong Kong lawyer faces the problems of the legal system with integrity and courage, and fight for justice despite seemingly insurmountable obstacles. In the final trial scene, Sung finds himself before court officials who are hostile to him. This seems to be a lost battle from the beginning. Moreover, the Yiu-Tin couple bribes Sung's key witness, Yeung's maid Xiao Mei, who was present at the scene of the crime. However, despite these difficulties Sung manages to win the case, because he possesses incontrovertible evidence – in the form of a letter written by the Commissioner of Shanxi to the Magistrate of Guangzhou – that a bribe of 5000 catties of silver had changed hands between the sender and the receiver. Moreover, through his gags and antics Sung induces the Magistrate of Guangzhou to bicker with his wife in open court, in the course of which they unwittingly reveal where the silver they had illicitly accepted is stored and therefore lead Sung directly to the evidence he needed. The film seems to suggest that when the Hong Kong lawyer complements their intelligence and resourcefulness with a commitment to justice, they will be able to surmount the obstacles brought about by the return to a Chinese legal system. Out of the three options available to them, this final option of squarely confronting the problems of the system is thereby presented as the desirable one.

2.3 The Function of Humor

To return to the question of humor, one would think that a film capturing the anxieties of a population so terrified by the events of 1989 and so nervous about the future of law would align itself more with tragedy than with comedy. Between 1989 and 1992, the number of Hong Kong residents who immigrated to other countries more than doubled, and newspapers of this period contained regular articles about people who queued overnight at various consulates and embassies in an attempt to obtain an application for a foreign passport.[30] To be forced to flee one's homeland due to worries about the impending collapse of its judicial edifice and the disappearance of one's very identity is no laughing matter. So how can we think about the humoristic depiction of law in the film?

One possibility is to return to the three scenarios examined earlier. The audience's interest in each of these situations is sustained by various filmic techniques that create comical effects. In the first situation, the trial of Chan for murder leads to a tragically unjust verdict: the family of the deceased is left without a remedy due to Sung's willingness to defend the guilty party in exchange for gold. Far from eliciting anger or pity, however, the trial scene provokes laughter through Sung's witty cross-examination. First of all, he subverts the legal requirement of causation through exaggeration and distortion. The victim was beaten by Chan the day before the trial and died on the day of the trial; hence, there is a time gap between the brawl and the death. Sung then asks, "If I hit someone, and he dies eight or ten years afterwards, can I be accused of murder?" Much of the comical effect is created by the establishment of such an absurd analogy; Sung retains a lawyerly analogical reasoning but twists its content to sidestep the issue of causation. He further argues that since death is inevitable, the question of whether his client caused the victim's death is irrelevant. When the father of the deceased counter-argues that the victim was obviously in the prime of his life and was therefore not

---

[30] The number of people who emigrated from Hong Kong rose from 30,000 in 1987 to 66,000 in 1992. See *Hong Kong 1994*, edited by Renu Daryanani (Hong Kong: Hong Kong Government Printer, 1994), p. 412. See also Fanny Wong, "More Hong Kong People Plan to Emigrate," *South China Morning Post*, June 6th, 1989.

someone who would die so suddenly, Sung reprimands him for his poor grasp of evidence: "Can you tell when I'm going to die? . . . If you can't tell when I'm going to die, how can you be sure that your son wasn't the kind of person who would drop dead all of a sudden?"

Once again, the logic of Sung's riposte – since you cannot tell when I will die, you cannot tell when your son will die, and therefore your counter-argument is fallacious – maintains the form of a conventional legal argument, but its absurd content undermines its own formal structure. Sung's cross-examination creates a topsy-turvy legal world, in which the plaintiff becomes the defendant and the defendant becomes the plaintiff. In addition to the dialogue, the figure of the magistrate as a befuddled old man who is in constant need of guidance from Sung in order to reach a verdict creates a comical distance between the conventional image of a magistrate or judge and the person overseeing the proceedings here.

In the second situation, in which Sung is presented as an emasculated figure due to his self-imposed exile from the law, the humor is heightened by the gender bending that results from the de-masculinization. When Sung wakes up the morning following his refusal to represent Yeung in court, he finds that his wife has dressed him in women's clothing, put makeup on his face, and given him a woman's haircut. His servant, Ah Fok, mockingly tells him through his giggles that Sung is even more beautiful than his wife in this ridiculous costume. Sung rushes off to court, only to be stopped by his servant who needs to retrieve the papayas that Madam Sung had stuffed into Sung's garment to give him female breasts; Ah Fok was in the middle of preparing dinner and the papayas were the ingredients for that evening's dessert.

The humor of the third situation, in which Sung confronts the corrupt court officials at the trial, is brought about in multiple ways. When Sung enters the courtroom at the beginning of the sequence, he receives bouquets of flowers from his fans, one of whom asks for his autograph, and the superimposition of Stephen Chow's image as a movie star in real life onto his image as a litigation master in the narrative compounds the sense of absurdity. The bickering between the Magistrate of Guangzhou and his wife constitutes another instance of this meshing together of disparate situational elements; the intrusion of a domestic dispute into the courtroom undermines the gravity of the trial and pulls it back from the brink of tragedy. At the level of linguistic play, the insertion of Cantonese colloquialisms or street language into the sequence creates a contrast between the solemnity of the courtroom proceedings and the casualness and at times rudeness of Sung's expressions. The narrative is further punctuated by a self-reflexive mockery of the conventions of Cantonese drama, and the excessive crying and the exaggerated hand gestures of the victim can be read as a tongue-in-cheek critique of the ridiculously contrived movements which characterize the genre.[31] Finally, there is Chow's signature slapstick

---

[31] Wai Lo-see, "Is there a 'Stephen Chow' Era?," 20.

comedy and toilet humor, and the inclusion of farting magistrates and
a pooping baby in the case can be read as strategic interventions designed to
disrupt the potentially tragic register of the proceedings.

Chow's "Moleitau" humor clearly contributes to the popularity of *Justice,
My Foot!*, but its role deserves further examination in light of the constitutional
and political developments that form part of the film's context. Goodrich has
argued that humor can be "proleptic": laughter in the courtroom can rupture
the reasoning process and interpretative premises upon which judgments are
rendered, thereby enabling us to perceive, however momentarily, how legal
logic might be structured otherwise: "the future is glimpsed, and the shape of
change previewed in the iteration occasioned by [. . .] the clash and corres-
ponding fissures generated by the intercession of humor in the humorless, of
the ludic in the legal."[32] In Hong Kong, this glimpse of the future, of how legal
decisions might be made differently beyond 1997, is precisely what was
troubling. There is therefore a darker side to the comedy, and a latent disquiet
in the laughter. Henri Bergson's argument that laughter is often sustained by
negative impulses is apposite here: he posits that if we examine laughter
intently, we can probably discern "something less spontaneous and more
bitter, the beginnings of a curious pessimism which becomes the more pronounced as the laugher more closely analyses his laughter."[33] In a similar vein
to Bergson, Simon Critchley notes that "[w]e often laugh because we are
troubled by what we laugh at, because it somehow frightens us."[34] Thinking
about the film in light of these observations, it is possible to surmise that the
laughter which the comic register induces masks something viewers may not
have wished to confront directly, something they could only look at in medi-
ated form.

Critchley goes on to point out that what troubles or frightens us may be
related to our notion of place or nationhood: humor can "put one back in one's
place with anxiety, difficulty and indeed shame of where one is from."[35]
I would argue that it is precisely feelings of anxiety or difficulty about *place*
that the humor of *Justice, My Foot!* both expresses and conceals. Through its
narrative of a Hong Kong lawyer's confrontation with a corrupt Chinese legal
system, the film captures fears that elements of law such as the right to a fair
trial, judicial independence, and due process which many people regarded,
consciously or unconsciously, as boundary markers between Hong Kong and

---

[32] Goodrich, "Proboscations," 373.
[33] Henri Bergson, *Laughter: An Essay on the Meaning of the Comic*, trans. by Cloudesley Brereton
      and Fred Rothwell (London: Macmillan, 1911), p. 199. For further foundational theorizations
      of humor, see Herbert Spencer, "The Physiology of Laughter," in *Essays: Scientific, Political,
      and Speculative* (London: Williams and Norgate, 1891), Volume II, pp. 452–467 and
      Sigmund Freud, "Jokes and their Relation of the Unconscious" (1905) in *The Standard Edition
      of the Complete Psychological Works of Sigmund Freud*, edited and trans. by James Strachey
      (London: Vintage, 1960), Volume 8.
[34] Simon Critchley, *On Humour* (Abingdon: Routledge, 2002), pp. 56–57.
[35] Critchley, *On Humour*, p. 74.

the mainland could be dismantled. The visualization of such negative affects is not pleasant to watch. Yet through the mediation of humor, the film not only allows local viewers to come face to face with those fears but also enables those viewers to be entertained by them.

Humor in the film therefore performs quite complex work. On one level, it enables the audience to face up to their anxieties at a particular point in Hong Kong's constitutional history. But it does more than that. It actively draws on issues close to the heart of the viewers at the time and then transforms them into a form of entertainment by provoking laughter. By watching, and laughing at, the legal dilemma in which iconic Hong Kongers such as Chow and Mui are caught, the audience is confronting and amused by their nightmarish scenario. The film's commercial success is in large part due to a strategy that simultaneously taps into a source of deep-seated cultural anxiety and repackages it into consumable comic material.

The fact that the legal proceedings take place in a Chinese court of the past – the Qing Dynasty – bolsters this understanding of the cinematic repackaging and re-presentation at work here. The placing of the narrative in a different historical context not only reinforces the perception of mainland Chinese courts as backward and unenlightened but creates a comforting historical distance between the injustice on the screen and the viewers themselves. In other words, the depiction of a historical Chinese courtroom rather than a contemporary one makes possible the screening of a legal system that resonated with the viewers without that system being entirely recognizable to them.

Far from being a lightweight comedy with no jurisprudential value, it is paradoxically the fact that *Justice, My Foot!* is "only" a Stephen Chow comedy that allows it to function as the medium through which the audience of the time could confront its anxieties about law and identity. With a nod to Karl Marx, one newspaper editorial noted that the constitutional disagreements of the period were characterized by both "farce" and "tragedy," and this characterization arguably also serves as a useful way of theorizing humor in *Justice, My Foot!*: the audience laughs, but what underpins the more silly or farcical elements of the film is the collective fear of an impending tragedy as Hong Kong moved steadily toward the moment of retrocession.[36]

2.4 Conclusion

The Tiananmen Square crackdown raised questions about both whether a distinct legal system could really be maintained in Hong Kong after the resumption of Chinese sovereignty and whether Hong Kong cultural identity could fade away under Chinese rule. In her article on language and identity in Stephen Chow's comedies, Linda Lai also notes that film can contribute to our understanding of the past by commemorating it: in contradistinction to

---

[36] "End Farce over Bill of Rights," *Hong Kong Standard*, March 5th, 1990.

"monumental history," which focuses more on "dominant political events," cinematic history "attends to the micro-levels and more everyday domain of human life, such as habits of mind, (structures of) feelings, conventions of speech, customary practices and other material forms left out of the framework of monumental history."[37] While the provisions of the Basic Law or the Bill of Rights Ordinance tell us little about just how loudly the questions raised by the Beijing crackdown resonated in early 1990s Hong Kong, filmic material such as *Justice, My Foot!* can give us a sense of the anxieties surrounding rights, identity, and "One Country, Two Systems" in that period, and of how cultural products constituted a forum for coming to terms with such anxieties. Five years after *Justice, My Foot!*, as the era of Chinese sovereignty dawned in 1997, another Stephen Chow comedy appeared on the movie screens. Before turning to the year of the handover, however, I will address one more interaction between law and film in colonial Hong Kong: the simultaneous rise of women's rights and the Category III "case file" film.

[37] Linda Chiu-han Lai, p. 95.

3

Women's Rights and Censorship:
Andrew Lau's *Raped by an Angel*

In its 1991 report on gender equality, the Hong Kong Council of Women issued a damning condemnation of the state of affairs in the territory: not only did it find "pervasive and severe discrimination against the women of Hong Kong," but it found that the colonial regime had deliberately "chosen to ignore" the problem as the time of British sovereignty gradually came to a close.[1] The report underscored the local courts' reliance on outdated evidentiary rules on rape and identified inequalities in areas ranging from employment to inheritance. As we will see, the Bill of Rights Ordinance, enacted in the same year, provided a newfound legal basis for challenging such unequal practices, and equality norms emerged and gradually consolidated in its wake.

The early 1990s also witnessed the proliferation of a distinctly Hong Kong film genre: the Category III film. Named after the "restricted" category in the three-tier film classification system enacted in the late 1980s, Category III films were shown at mainstream local cinemas but restricted to viewers over eighteen years of age. Dubbed "the other Hong Kong cinema," they are usually low-budget local productions characterized by two elements: sex and violence.[2] The epitome of Category III movies is what film scholars Darrell W. Davis and Yeh Yueh-yu call the "case file" film (奇案片): these are films based on sensational criminal cases, whether real or fictitious, that supposedly happened in Hong Kong history. Adopting a term by Tom Wolfe, Davis and Yeh designate such films as exercises in "pornoviolence," in which women are shown raped and murdered by psychopathic sex killers, before having their bodies buried, dismembered, or dissolved in acid.

Category III films were immensely popular in Hong Kong in the early 1990s, but had virtually vanished as a distinct genre by the time of the handover. Surprising, then, that the time of Category III films should also be the time of women's rights: the debate surrounding both arrived with the onset of the 1990s, intensified in the first half of the decade, and died down just before the retrocession. The rise and fall of this markedly local genre coincided almost

---

[1] *Report by the Hong Kong Council of Women on the Third Periodic Report by Hong Kong Under Article 40 of the International Covenant on Civil and Political Rights* (1991), 1.

[2] Darrell W. Davis and Yeh Yueh-yu, "Warning! Category III," 54 *Film Quarterly* (2001), 12–27 (14).

completely with the trend toward eliminating gender-biased policies and implementing sex discrimination laws. Even though much has been written on Category III films, there has been curiously little examination of these parallel developments in relation to each other. As film critic Paul Fonoroff observed, "there's a PhD thesis waiting to be written on the subject of what these films say about Hong Kong society, particularly the status of women and the popular perception of our legal system."[3]

In this chapter, I will contend that representations of women in case file films are characterized by deep contradictions, and that these contradictory representations can be read as responses to transformations in the legal infrastructure relating to gender equality in early 1990s Hong Kong. On the one hand, case file films virtually always create visual pleasure by sexualizing and objectifying women, and by depicting them as victims of gruesome and even sadistic violence. On the other hand, they often interrogate their own representations of femininity by problematizing the status not only of the men in the narrative but also of the spectators in the cinema, who derive visual pleasure from such representations. While the Category III label gave film-makers great liberty in showing sex and violence, the evolving norms of gender equality meant that such sex and violence were screened in a way that was increasingly influenced by changing ideas about women's rights and female agency.[4]

In the first section, I will explore the legal developments concerning gender equality in the early 1990s, and also highlight how rape became a problem of particular concern for both local women's rights activists and the Hong Kong community at large. In the second section, I will examine the ways in which the representation of women in Category III films in general, and in case file films in particular, arose as a direct result of the implementation of a new system of censorship in the late 1980s. In the final section, I will present a close reading of one case file film, Andrew Lau's *Raped by an Angel* (1993; 香港奇案之強姦), to illustrate how the genre responded to changes in the laws relating to women. I will further demonstrate that Lau's film constitutes a prime example of how "the other Hong Kong cinema" can be understood as what William MacNeil calls *lex populi*, or the distinctly *visual* interrogation of the law in the form of popular, even trashy, entertainment.

I have chosen *Raped by an Angel* for detailed analysis for three reasons. First, it is the only Category III film that has spawned four sequels in its wake (*Raped by an Angel 2–5*), and this long afterlife attests to its iconic status within the

---

[3]   "*Love to Kill*," in *Paul Fonoroff at the Hong Kong Movies* (Hong Kong: Film Biweekly Publishing House, 1998), pp. 349–350 (350).

[4]   For a pioneering study of women in law and film, see Orit Kamir, *Framed: Women in Law and Film* (Durham: Duke University Press, 2006). Kamir explicitly focuses on the reception of an international selection of films by Western viewers. My study focuses on Hong Kong cinema, and in doing so takes up Kamir's invitation in the introduction of her book to consider more culturally and jurisdictionally specific processes of censorship and reception.

genre. Second, this film constitutes the most sustained rumination on the law among the age-restricted films: through its depiction of the confrontation between a female law student and a villain who is both a scheming lawyer and a sexual psychopath, it presents a probing exploration of the dilemmas of women seeking justice in an arena not only dominated by men but characterized by masculinist standards of proof. Indeed, one of its original titles, *Legal Rape*, though rightly rejected by the censors for suggesting that rape could ever be legal, nonetheless signals the film's explicit engagement with the law. Finally, the film is written and produced by Wong Jing, a figure who is locally synonymous with 1990s Hong Kong popular culture but who remains one of the most under-analyzed filmmakers in international film scholarship.[5] This scholarly neglect can be attributed to the lowbrow and low-budget nature of his work, yet as we will see below, Wong's script provides the basis for a specifically Hong Kong cinematic response to sex crime and the problem of gender inequality.

3.1 Women's Rights and the Problem of Rape in Early 1990s Hong Kong

Women's rights developed to a great extent because of the upcoming retrocession: Hong Kongers were worried about losing the city's "liberal traditions after the 1997 handover," and their "allegiance to gender equality and human rights" was part of efforts to ensure that "things in Hong Kong were not going to change" under Chinese rule.[6] The growth of women's rights could be attributed more directly to the enactment of the Bill of Rights Ordinance in 1991. As we have seen, the colonial government introduced the Bill in the aftermath of the atrocities in Beijing's Tiananmen Square on June 4, 1989, in an attempt to reassure Hong Kong residents that similar crackdowns would not occur in their home city, and that their rights would still be protected even after China resumed sovereignty. While the legislation was not specifically enacted with gender inequality in mind, its incorporation of international law provisions targeting gender inequality brought the problem to the forefront of public consciousness. The ordinance is modeled on the International Covenant on Civil and Political Rights (ICCPR) and replicates, in their entirety, the covenant's three articles prohibiting discrimination: Article 2, which imposes a requirement for states to ensure that citizens enjoy their rights "without distinction of any kind, such as [. . .] sex"; Article 3, which imposes an obligation on states to guarantee the "equal right of men and women" to enjoy their rights; and Article 26, which states that "all persons are equal before

---

[5] For a rare but insightful discussion of Wong Jing's corpus, see David Bordwell, *Planet Hong Kong: Popular Cinema and the Art of Entertainment*, 2nd ed. (Madison: Irvington Way Institute Press, 2011), pp. 109–114.

[6] Sally Engle Merry and Rachel E. Stern, "The Female Inheritance Movement in Hong Kong: Theorizing the Local/Global Interface," 46(3) *Current Anthropology*, 387–409 (402).

the law and are entitled without any discrimination to the equal protection of the law." When the government announced plans to introduce the bill, women's organizations recognized that it "could be used as a weapon against discrimination."[7] They responded robustly during the bill's consultation period, and a number of them made submissions on how its substantive content might be improved.[8] The Beijing crackdown made human rights and the rule of law even more integral to Hong Kongers' conception of themselves, and in the early 1990s local women's groups turned to the law almost by instinct in their fight against political, social, and economic equalities.

The Bill of Rights Ordinance led to two important developments in gender equality in Hong Kong. The first was the abolition of a longstanding rule against female inheritance of land in the area known as the New Territories. The rule derives from customary Chinese law and was preserved into the twentieth century as part of the colonial administration's strategy of maintaining stability in the colony.[9] It was intended to ensure that land was kept within a clan as it was passed on from generation to generation: the Council of Women identified the thinking at the root of the unequal treatment when it observed that "since all women were potentially other men's wives, no woman, married or unmarried, could be permitted to inherit clan land."[10] A concomitant issue was the inheritance of so-called "small houses": each indigenous male resident of the New Territories had the right to inherit 700 square feet of land on which to build a small house in his village, but women did not enjoy this right. The equality provisions of the Bill of Rights provided the necessary legal groundwork for challenging these customary rules: as the Ombudsman remarked, "with the enactment of the Bill of Rights Ordinance [...] it is arguable whether customs and practices of discriminating against women, insofar as they relate to land in the New Territories, should continue to be enforced by the courts."[11] In their analysis of rights discourse in Hong Kong, Sally Engle Merry and Rachel E. Stern have argued that cultural "translators" such as expatriate female legal scholars and Hong Kong-born female common law lawyers helped to garner the public support required for social change by showing the indigenous women how to frame their concerns in the language of international human rights.[12] The rules against female inheritance of land and "small houses" were eventually repealed in 1994.

The second development was the introduction of new legal measures to protect women, including the passage of the local Sex Discrimination

---

[7] Carole J. Petersen, "Equality as a Human Right: The Development of Anti-Discrimination Law in Hong Kong," 34 *Columbia Journal of Transnational Law* (1996), 335–389 (353).

[8] Vicky Wong, "Positive Action is Necessary to Ensure Women's Rights," *South China Morning Post*, March 4th, 1990.

[9] *Report*, 14.   [10] *Report*, 13.

[11] Simon Beck, "Women's Land Rights Laws under Attack," *South China Morning Post*, July 19th, 1992.

[12] Merry and Stern, "The Female Inheritance Movement in Hong Kong," 399–400.

Ordinance and the adoption of the Convention on the Elimination of All Forms of Discrimination Against Women (CEDAW). As the Council of Women's Report documented, sex discrimination was rife in early 1990s Hong Kong: advertisement for most professional and managerial positions stipulated that only men should apply, while most secretarial and clerical positions were reserved for women.[13] Moreover, women constantly received a lower salary than men: the Report underscored that "virtually *every* industry that provided data for male and female employees showed a tendency to pay women less money than men for the same work."[14] The legislator Anna Wu put the issue of discrimination on the table through a number of private member's bills.[15] The debate was protracted, and the government eventually proposed its own bill in an attempt to narrow down the scope of the law, but the Sex Discrimination Ordinance was eventually passed in 1995. The Council of Women's Report also urged the colonial administration to support local calls for Britain to extend CEDAW to Hong Kong; Britain had ratified it in 1986, but the protections were limited to the imperial center and did not reach the outskirts of empire. As the Council noted, "how can the British government justify its refusal to give women in the territory of Hong Kong the same protection from discrimination that has been enjoyed by women in the United Kingdom for the last decade?"[16] The protections in CEDAW were finally extended to Hong Kong in 1996.

Writing as a local academic in 1993, Harriet Samuels summarized the state of affairs relating to women's rights in early 1990s Hong Kong when she observed that debates about CEDAW, antidiscrimination, and equal pay legislation "have had the effect of raising people's awareness of the issues and of bringing the issues into the public domain."[17] The work of feminist constitutional scholars such as Petersen and Samuels has provided both a valuable analytical frame for and an important historical record of developments in the period. However, their exclusive focus on constitutional and human rights law has elided a more domestic criminal and social issue that plagued women in the territory at this historical juncture: rape.

Rape has of course been the focus of much Anglo-American feminist legal scholarship, but manifestations of the problem in Hong Kong had a specifically local dimension.[18] The surge in the number of female rape victims was of great societal concern in the early 1990s, and incidents of rape ran alongside a deepening problem of violent crimes and indecent assault against women. The *Hong Kong Standard* gravely noted in an editorial that "Hong Kong must

---

[13] *Report*, 3.   [14] *Report*, 4 (original emphasis).
[15] Petersen traces the process of legislative enactment in detail, 372–386.   [16] *Report*, 7.
[17] Harriet Samuels, "Women and the Law in Hong Kong: A Feminist Analysis," in *Hong Kong, China, and 1997: Essays in Legal Theory*, edited by Raymond Wacks (Hong Kong: Hong Kong University Press, 1993), pp. 61–86 (86).
[18] For pioneering studies, see Catharine A. MacKinnon, *Toward a Feminist Theory of the State* (Cambridge: Harvard University Press, 1989), pp. 171–184 and Carol Smart, *Feminism and the Power of Law* (London: Routledge, 1989), pp. 4–26.

face up to the fact that sexual offences are on the rise," and that in particular "rape, the third most serious crime in the canon (after treason and murder), is on the increase here."[19] In the second quarter of 1991, the number of rape cases jumped to forty-two, from twenty-six in the previous three months.[20] Worrying as these figures were, the actual number was likely even higher due to underreporting; as one District Board member asked, "these are the known cases, but what about the unreported ones"?[21] The problem was particularly serious in some of the public housing estates in the so-called "New Towns," or government planned residential developments located in the more rural areas that were designed to alleviate the problem of overpopulation in the city center. The New Town of Tuen Mun was the epicenter of the problem, and the number of women who were raped and murdered there seemed to be spiraling out of control in the early 1990s; one legislator noted with alarm that

> recent cases of rape, indecent assault and other offences have frequently happened in Tuen Mun, causing fear in many residents and disturbing the peace of life. [. . .] In April last year, a woman was raped on the staircase of Yau Oi Estate. Since then seven rape cases have occurred in Tuen Mun, and two of the victims were murdered by the rapist.[22]

Some women in the area formed concern groups and organized anti-rape seminars, and other residents took the problem to the Legislative Council and even petitioned the Governor for a solution.[23]

A news report on the female residents of Tuen Mun's Yau Oi Estate gives a sense of the state of fear the women lived in.[24] They were aware that a thirty-year-old woman had been raped a few months before at an adjacent estate, and that another victim was murdered the day before the report appeared. Most of the women agreed that they were "most at risk late at night, but they stressed that at no time was it safe to be out alone." A young female teacher who lived in Yau Oi Estate thought going out alone after dark meant "taking a very great risk"; her mother would wait up for her whenever she went out at night, "and could not sleep until she was home." She refused to take the elevators, as "strangers always seem to be lurking around." Yet the stairs were no safer, and the police noted that in every instance of rape there "the victim had been attacked in a lift or dragged along a staircase."

The crime was abetted by the poor architectural design of public housing estates. Many of the buildings were poorly lit, had open designs with no

---

[19] "Compassion, Action Needed to Curb Rape," *Hong Kong Standard*, March 2th, 1993.

[20] Jennifer Cooke, "Fourteen Percent Increase in Violent Crimes," *South China Morning Post*, July 24th, 1991.

[21] Jimmy Leung and Virginia Maher, "Women of Tuen Mun Live in Fear," *South China Morning Post*, February 25th, 1993.

[22] Speech by Michael Ho, *Hong Kong Hansard*, June 2nd, 1993.

[23] Speech by Wong Wai-Yin, *Hong Kong Hansard*, June 2nd, 1993.

[24] Leung and Maher, "Women of Tuen Mun Live in Fear."

lockable main gates or security cameras, and included numerous built-in alcoves and dark corners in which attackers could hide. One police officer warned that "toilets hidden around corners" facilitated the perpetration of sexual and other crimes, that "external drainage pipes running next to windows" provided a kind of "natural ladder" for robbers and rapists to access private residences, and that "badly-lit subways" constituted convenient but highly dangerous routes to the housing estates.[25] The Housing Authority was severely chastised by lawmakers for the appalling building design and poor security. As legislator James To pointed out, not only did the open design provide "easy access and exit points" for criminals but the labyrinthine structure of individual buildings meant that they were "an excellent hiding place" for robbers and rapists because "once you get in, it is extremely difficult to track you down."[26] He further underscored the "persistent problem" of poor lighting and expressed concerns about how the premises were becoming de facto "hangout" points for "nomadic youth gangs." This correlation of architectural design and crime is registered in a number of case file films from the period. For instance, Billy Tang's *Red to Kill* (弱殺; 1994), which tells the story of a rapist whose murderous and sexual impulses are triggered by the victims' red garments, foregrounds the setting of the crimes through numerous shots of dark corners, elongated corridors, and dimly lit staircases. It is also echoed in *Raped by an Angel*, in a scene in which a woman tries to escape from her building by running down a long flight of stairs, only to be grabbed by the hair and dragged back inside by her pursuer.

The "Tuen Mun Rapist" became an icon of fear, certainly among women but also among the territory's population at large. In the midst of the crimes, one psychiatrist gave her assessment of the as-yet unidentified criminal: first and foremost, he was likely to be "a very disturbed, pathological character."[27] He probably had a "hatred of women" that "stemmed from his childhood," even though he was "attracted to them sexually." Given how well planned the crimes were and how adept he was at escaping prosecution, he was "likely to be anything but mad" and was "likely not psychotic." He was strong, as evidenced by the way he grabbed his victims by the throat "with his bare hands" when he attacked them. Most significantly, there were "great gaps in his psychological profile": he could be married or single, social or solitary. The fact that he was strong enough to throttle his victims suggested that he was likely to be a manual worker, but then he could also be a white-collar worker who frequented the gym. Such gaps intensified anxieties as they meant that it was almost impossible for potential targets to identify him until it was too late. He was finally apprehended in August 1993. His name was Lam Kwok-wai, he was twenty-three years old, and he admitted to eight counts of rape, three counts of

---

[25] Flora Wong, "Crime-prone Buildings Worry Police," *Hong Kong Standard*, January 4th, 1993.
[26] Speech by James To, *Hong Kong Hansard*, June 2nd, 1993.
[27] "Inside the Mind of the Tuen Mun Rapist," *South China Morning Post*, May 9th, 1993.

murder, and seven counts of robbery within a sixteen-month period.[28] In three of the attacks he choked his victims to death. He was sentenced to life imprisonment, but his presence continued to be felt in Hong Kong despite his sentence as he provided the direct inspiration for the murderous, psychopathic rapists in many films of the period. Cha Chuen-yee's *The Rapist* (屯門色魔; 1994) and Wong Gam-din's *Portrait of a Serial Rapist* (香港奇案之屯門色魔; 1994) are explicitly based on events in Tuen Mun, but echoes of the "Tuen Mun Rapist" can be heard in many case file films of the time. In *Raped by an Angel*, the echoes take the form of the villain's inclination toward violence, his deliberate and meticulous planning of sexual crimes, and his strength and muscular physique. The Category III or "restricted" films under the new film classification system unexpectedly provided the perfect forum for exploring representations of the sex, violence, and terror associated with rape in the Hong Kong imagination.

3.2 Sex, Violence, and Censorship

To understand the impact of censorship on cinematic representations of sex and violence in the early 1990s, and of the ways in which the case file film responded to developments in women's rights and problems about rape in this period, we need to return briefly to origins of the film classification system in the late 1980s. In 1987, the *Asian Wall Street Journal* reported that the colonial government had been censoring films even though its own legal department had explicitly advised it that the censorship system had no basis in law.[29] In other words, the government was aware that it had no legitimate power to censor, but did it anyway. The revelation angered the public as it was discovered that the authorities were censoring for political reasons, in that they prevented films that were overtly anti-colonial or risked damaging relations with China from being shown in the territory.[30] After the scandal, the government needed to give the censorship mechanism a firm grounding, and the Film Censorship Ordinance was passed in 1988. The ordinance aimed to formalize the grounds on which a film could be censored and to clarify the vetting procedure.[31] Under the new system, the authorities would assign a censor to a film, unless they determined that it was a kind of film that could obviously be exempted from the censorship process.[32] The censor determined whether the

---

[28] Emma Batha, "Tuen Mun Rapist Loses Plea," *South China Morning Post*, August 17th, 1995.

[29] See Albert H. Y. Chen, "Some Reflections on the Film Censorship Affair," 17 *Hong Kong Law Journal* (1987), 352–359.

[30] For a discussion of pre-1988 incident of censorship in Hong Kong, see Tan See-kam, "Ban(g)! Ban(g)! *Dangerous Encounter – 1st Kind*: Writing with Censorship," 8(1) *Asian Cinema* (1996), 83–109.

[31] For a fuller explication of the censorship mechanism, see Saw Tiong-guan, *Film Censorship in the Asia-Pacific Region: Malaysia, Hong Kong and Australia Compared* (Abingdon: Routledge, 2013), pp. 41–48.

[32] Section 9, Film Censorship Ordinance.

film could be shown at the local cinemas. Before a film could be released, it would receive a categorization: a Category I film was suitable for all ages, a Category II film was not suitable for children, and – most importantly for my purposes here – a Category III film was restricted to viewers aged eighteen or above.[33]

One of the censor's main considerations when deciding whether a film would be banned or allowed to reach the cinemas with a Category III label was whether it portrayed, depicted, or treated "cruelty, torture, violence, crime, horror, disability, sexuality, or indecent or offensive language or behaviour."[34] Yet this attempt at instituting a principled approach to censorship brought problems of its own. As one local film critic pointed out, "the limits set up by the authorities are confusing and ambiguous": exactly how much of the undesirable elements such as sexuality, cruelty, or crime listed in the ordinance could one fit into a film before it would be completely banned?[35] How much sex and violence could one cram into the Category III label? These uncertainties led to a period of intense exploration and experimentation in the industry, as filmmakers and producers continuously tested the boundaries of the new classification system. While Hong Kong's experience with film regulation confirms Nora Gilbert's observation in her study of censorship in the Anglo-American context that film production can be "stirred and stimulated,"[36] rather than restrained, by censorship, it also demonstrates that the exact impact of censorship can vary greatly in different legal and cultural contexts: whereas Anglo-American censorship led to more nuanced ways of conveying meaning by instilling the need "for subtext,"[37] "for diverse and ever-shifting modes of communication," and for "silences that speak louder than words," censorship in Hong Kong actually led to ever more extreme depictions as Category III films became a de facto "safety zone" for investigating the very representability of sex and violence.[38] As Bordwell observed, "now that an over-eighteen audience had been defined" by the film classification system, "peripheral companies began cranking out low-budget pornography and gorefests."[39] The Category III label on a film's advertising material, prominently displayed as a triangle with "III" in the middle of the image, functioned as a warning but also "as a temptation, and perhaps as a dare" to the audience to see how far the film would go in its visualization of taboo subjects.[40] The classification itself thus paradoxically "became a marketing device" by enticing viewers with the promise of "such representations up to the limits of the

---

[33] Section 12(1), Film Censorship Ordinance. Category II was further subdivided into IIA (not suitable for children) and IIB (not suitable for young persons and children) in 1994.

[34] Section 10(2)(a), Film Censorship Ordinance.

[35] Law Miu-lan, "The Storm of Case File Films is Coming for Us," 369 *City Entertainment* (June 3rd – June 16th, 1993), 35–41(40).

[36] Nora Gilbert, *Better Left Unsaid: Victorian Novels, Hays Code, and the Benefits of Censorship* (Palo Alto: Stanford University Press, 2013), p. 2.

[37] Gilbert, *Better Left Unsaid*, p. 35.   [38] Bordwell, *Planet Hong Kong*, p. 96.

[39] Bordwell, *Planet Hong Kong*, p. 79.   [40] Davis and Yeh, "Warning! Category III," 24.

permissible."[41] One of the most striking aspects of Category III films is that they were not shown underground: since they were deemed suitable for screening at local cinemas, they competed with other mainstream local productions for the attention of adult viewers. By 1992, a mere four years after the Film Censorship Ordinance came into effect, about half of the local productions were Category III films.[42] *Raped by an Angel* was one of the top thirty local titles in the year it was released.[43]

The case file film is "the exemplar" of Category III films, for it is within this domain that the experimentation and boundary testing reached their greatest intensity.[44] *Raped by an Angel*, like many case file films, has a Chinese title that foregrounds Hong Kong as the scene of the crime: it is known in Chinese as "A Hong Kong case file – Rape." Productions based on sensational local court cases were not entirely new: the 1970 murder of a couple at Lung Fu Shan forms the basis of Ann Hui's *The Secret* (瘋劫; 1979), and the *Three Wolves Murders* in the 1960s, in which the son of a tycoon was kidnapped and murdered by three men wearing wolf masks, has been the subject of a television program and also of Taylor Wong's *Sentenced to Hang* (三狼奇案; 1989). In fact, *Sentenced to Hang* was the first film in Hong Kong history to receive a Category III rating. Yet the films of the early 1990s are marked by a degree of sex and violence unseen in the productions that came before, in part because they are based on cases of clinical sexual depravity: in addition to stories about the Tuen Mun Rapist, there was Danny Lee and Billy Tang's *Dr Lamb* (羔羊醫生; 1992), based on the rape and murder of female passengers by the taxi driver Lam Kor-wan in the 1980s; Herman Yau's *The Untold Story* (八仙飯店之人肉叉燒包; 1993), based on the story of a man in the nearby Portuguese colony of Macau who killed his employer and his family and then stuffed their remains in pork buns; Norman Chan's *The Final Judgment* (紙盒藏屍之公審; 1993), based on the murder of a woman whose body was found in an abandoned paper box; and Cha Chuen-yee's *Legal Innocence* (溶屍奇案; 1993), based on the murder of a woman whose body was dissolved in a bathtub filled with acid. The films mix fact and fiction and are rarely faithful to actual events; some of them, such as *Raped by an Angel,* are labelled as case file films even though they are invented stories.

Given the sadistic and even murderous sexual violation of women that constitutes the mainstay of case file films, it is unsurprising that this strand of Hong Kong cinema sparked vigorous debate within the community. They were often condemned as an unequivocally "bad influence" on viewers, and their nature as low-budget productions led to accusations of rampant commercialism.[45] The films' defenders, however, underscored their stylistic innovations: one critic attributed their popularity to their unique

---

[41] Davis and Yeh, "Warning! Category III," 21.   [42] Bordwell, *Planet Hong Kong,* p. 79.
[43] Bordwell, *Planet Hong Kong,* p. 97.
[44] Law Miu-lan, "The Storm of Case File Films is Coming for Us," 36.
[45] Sek Kei, "The Case File Film Controversy," *Ming Pao Daily News,* June 2nd, 1993.

cinematography,[46] and a leading film critic of the time, Sek Kei, commended producers for moving beyond the hackneyed formulas of comedies, period dramas, and martial arts films.[47] Furthermore, filmmakers mixed and matched elements from established American genres such as slasher films, erotic thrillers, exploitation films, horror, softcore pornography, and rape-revenge films, taking what they thought were the most thrilling or transgressive elements of each in the process of probing and pushing the new classificatory boundaries. The gore of slasher films, the mystery of erotic thrillers, the psychological investment of rape-revenge films, and the titillation of softcore porn all went into the creation of the case file film, such that its "III classification by itself does not give away what kind of film one may encounter" in the cinema.[48]

What went unnoticed in these debates about case file films, much of which focused on their gore and horror, was the ways in which they dramatize women's encounter with the law. While of course not all case file films deal explicitly with legal rules or processes, a number of them do engage with law, and in those films the justice system is often portrayed as woefully inadequate to bringing justice to women. Moreover, they reflect a changing conception of female agency through their depiction of female leads not simply as passive or terrified victims but as women who are strong enough to fight back against their aggressors or an unjust judicial process, even if these women may not be entirely successful in the end. In Clarence Fok's *Remains of a Woman* (郎心如鐵; 1993), another film based on the case of the body dissolved in acid, the murderer is acquitted by the court. However, the ending of the film strongly hints that he gets his comeuppance when the ghost of the victim comes back to haunt him; she tells him: "I will be with you forever and ever and ever," and as the film closes we hear his cry of terror as well as the sound of her laughter. *Remains of a Woman* suggests that even though the law fails women, they are the ones who ultimately triumph. In *The Final Judgment*, a man is wrongly accused of murder on the basis of the prosecution's dubious "scientific evidence," and the film depicts a colonial justice system more invested in shoring up its own authority through such "evidence" than in finding the real culprit. The narrative portrays the suffering which the wrongful conviction inflicts not only on the man but on his wife: she gets conned of all her savings by a crook posing as a lawyer; she is forced to sell her body in order to earn money to raise their daughter; she is despised by the neighbors for being the spouse of a convicted murder; and she bears the burden of the long and fruitless process of appealing the case all the way to the Privy Council in England. The film underscores her willpower as she fights to clear her husband's name, but it also makes clear that her admirable energy and determination only make the

---

[46] Law Miu-lan, "The Storm of Case File Films is Coming for Us," 36.
[47] Seki Kei, "Case File Films Are More Realistic," *Ming Pao Daily News*, June 12th, 1993.
[48] Davis and Yeh, "Warning! Category III," 24.

tragedy greater as no single person can be a match for the colonial legal machinery. At the end, her husband purposefully makes her doubt his own innocence in the hope that she will let go of him and start a new life with their daughter. *The Final Judgment* is based on the wrongful conviction of a man, but it is as much a tale about its consequences on a woman as it is about its consequences on him. As we shall see, *Raped by an Angel* portrays a judicial system that not only fails to help the female victims but actively inflicts harm on them, such that the protagonist decides to take matters of justice into her own hands. Time and time again, the case file film provided a forum for exposing, probing, and re-examining the gendered basis of the law.

The space opened up by the new censorship regime enabled a process of experimentation with film style and subject in the early 1990s which, combined with the growing influence of the women's rights movement as well as the resonances of societal discussions about rape, gave form to a distinctly Hong Kong cinema. The new genre that emerged from the 1988 film classification system took the physical violation of women's bodies, the psychological trauma of ill-treatment, and the law's disavowal of female victimization as its main premise, and provided a forum for reconsidering the position of women in society and the supposedly gender-neutral foundations of the legal edifice. In the remainder of this chapter, I will provide a close reading of *Raped by an Angel* to show how the case file film can challenge the ways in which viewers *see* the legal process.

3.3 Interrogating Law in a Case File Film

3.3.1 The Law Student as Heroine

The film centers on three characters: Yau, Chu, and Mark. Yau is a spirited, intelligent female law student and also works as a part-time model. Chu is her best friend and is also a part-time model. Mark is a lawyer. He is charming and courteous on the surface but is actually a psychopath with a penchant for violent sex. He sets his sights on Yau and Chu after seeing them in a commercial on television. Yau is unimpressed by his fake charms, but Chu proves an easier target. Mark's psychopathic character is manifested in the way he meticulously sets a trap for Chu in order to possess her: he moves into the apartment next door to her and proceeds to convince onlookers in their building that he and Chu are an intimate couple. He then steals the key to Chu's apartment and makes a show of entering and leaving her residence at his leisure. Chu of course has no idea that he is entering the apartment, but onlookers become convinced that Mark is entering as Chu's boyfriend and are unlikely to question future break-ins. When Yau goes away for a weekend, Mark walks into Chu's home, overpowers her, chains her to a chair, and brutally rapes and torments her. He also films the violations in an act of sadistic humiliation. When Yau returns and finds out what has happened, she convinces Chu to press charges against Mark.

Mark is brought to trial, but his years of practice as a lawyer have taught him how to manipulate legal evidence to his advantage. The jury believes Mark's version of events, and Chu loses her case.

With his innocence secured by the acquittal, Mark re-enters Chu's apartment to seek vengeance on her for daring to initiate legal proceedings against him and kills her in the process. Mark then comes after Yau. Yau, however, is prepared for him. Knowing that the law will not protect her, she sets a trap of her own for him. Instead of waiting for Mark to attack, she actively lures him into the trap. I will discuss their confrontation in some detail later, but for now, it suffices to note that she defeats Mark, and the psychopathic rapist and murderer is finally arrested by the police.

Yau's identity as a law student is integral to the critique of the legal process in *Raped by an Angel*. Early in the film, her criminal law professor explains how rape is dealt with within the justice system: "I have seen many instances in which the lawyers raise questions about the victim's sex life, in order to portray her as a promiscuous person or as someone of loose morals." The pivotal issue in the legal treatment of rape is one of perception: as Yau's professor explains, the key to discrediting the victim's testimony is by painting an "image" ("形像") of licentiousness, for a jury is more likely to infer that there is consent to sex if the victim has had multiple sexual partners or given consent to the same person in the past. In other words, how a victim is *seen* by the jury has a significant impact on the outcome. The professor's explanation echoes a key point made by pioneering scholars of both feminist film theory and feminist legal theory. The film scholar Laura Mulvey has posited that the conventional feminine role, even in late twentieth-century liberal societies, is one in which women are "simultaneously looked at and displayed" within a masculinist scopic regime, so much so that they "can be said to connote *to-be-looked-at-ness*."[49] The legal scholar Catharine MacKinnon has made a comparable point about women as the object of male vision in her analysis of rape law. MacKinnon shows that the law is profoundly and problematically gendered because the "socially reasonable" and "objective" point of view which the legal system adopts to determine whether a woman has given consent to sex is in fact the male point of view.[50] As such, "to measure the genuineness of consent from the individual assailant's point of view is to adopt as law the point of view which creates the problem." Yau's law professor, like Mulvey and MacKinnon, underscores the importance of the field of vision, and the centrality of the act of looking in rape cases makes film a particularly powerful medium for interrogating the premises of the law.

Raped by an Angel underscores that within both a patriarchal legal system and patriarchal society, the ability to structure the field of vision is a masculine

---

[49] Laura Mulvey, *Visual and Other Pleasures*, 2nd ed. (Basingstoke: Palgrave MacMillan, 2009), p. 19.

[50] MacKinnon, *Toward a Feminist Theory of the State*, p. 181.

prerogative. In its opening sequence, a woman is shown returning home, stripping off her work clothes, and turning on the television. The camera then cuts to a masked figure outside her window. The masked figure watches her every move. This is followed up a close up of the woman, as we continue to watch her walk around in her underwear. The eye of the camera overlaps with the eye of the masked figure: it is he who controls the field of vision, placing her within this field while she is unaware of being watched. More importantly, the camera places the viewer in the spectatorial position of this figure: we experience what it is like to be in a position of power within a patriarchal system, of controlling the field of vision and of having this woman as the object of our gaze. The viewer is therefore co-opted into Mark's point of view.

A similar dynamic occurs in a later segment. Here, Yau and her friends are having a party when they get a prank call. Chu is worried by the call, but Yau takes over the phone and addresses the caller defiantly: "Who are you?" At the end of the call, however, Yau gets a shock: the caller addresses her by her name, and it is at this point that she realizes that the caller can see her. She looks outside the window and realizes that he must have called from a phone booth beneath her apartment, but by then the phone booth is already empty. This scene visually underscores the imbalance of power between them; Mark controls the field of vision and places Yau within his gaze. By the time she tries to look back, he is already gone. The camera again places the viewer in the same spectatorial position as the caller: we watch Yau take over the phone and then watch her respond to the call, just as the caller would have watched her from the phone booth. The relationship between seeing and power is further underscored in a scene in which Mark holds Chu prisoner in her own apartment. Mark first gags her and ties her to a chair. He then proceeds to film her: he holds up a giant recorder, turns it on with a sadistic smile, and slowly walks around her as she trembles in fear. At the end of the process, Mark looks up from the camera and says "Cut! [That was a] good take" as if he was a film director. The woman is here captured, both literally and physically, in the eye of the camera.

Given the problems with the law's response to rape which Yau's professor highlights, it is perhaps surprising that Yau would still urge Chu to place her faith in the legal system after Mark imprisoned, raped, and tortured her. One might ask how a bright law student learning about the imperfections of the criminal justice system would not have at least given thought to the trauma which a trial could potentially inflict on Chu. However, at this point in the film Yau does not seem to have fully absorbed the lessons about the gendered nature of law. In the sequence of the class on rape law, Yau arrives late and enters the classroom only after her teacher has discussed the problems of perception. The professor chides her in front of the whole class not only for missing a crucial part of the lecture but also for failing her mid-term paper. Yau's education is not yet complete, and she urges Chu to trust the law. Chu's decision to prosecute Mark will lead to public humiliation, and finally to her death.

3.3.2 The Rape Victim in Court

The film's trial scene calls attention to the ways in which the law can cast a female rape victim as the guilty party when its procedures and rules of evidence are manipulated by someone who is well-versed in them. After Chu presses charges against him, Mark is taken to the police station and then brought to the dock. The camera cuts between Mark and Chu as they give their accounts of what happened to the police and to the jury. Chu denies being in a relationship with Mark, and insists that they had been no more than passing acquaintances before the attacks happened. The camera then cuts to Mark, who insists that Chu is his long-term girlfriend. The shot/counter-shot technique underscores the importance of perception in the film's portrayal of the legal process: as the focus moves between them, Chu's version of events is continuously undermined by Mark's narrative which portrays her as a cold-hearted gold digger who falsely accuses him of rape to punish him for refusing to lend her money. The series of testimonies by Chu, followed by their dismantling by Mark, confirms that control over the field of vision in the law is a masculine prerogative.

Mark ensures that the image he paints of Chu is bolstered by witnesses through a series of elaborate ruses. For instance, he deliberately smears lipstick onto the side of his mouth after meeting Chu at the office so that his secretary, who saw Mark with Chu earlier in the day, would interpret the lipstick as evidence of passionate kisses given by Chu. On another occasion, he steals into Chu's apartment in the middle of the night while she is asleep and walks out of her front door when he hears the cleaning lady take out the trash in order to give the cleaning lady the impression that he has spent the night with Chu. There are multiple shots of the cleaning lady gossiping about Mark and Chu with the doorman, which suggest that the doorman also falls victim to the illusion, meticulously constructed by Mark, that he and Chu are in a serious, loving relationship. When these three people – the secretary, the cleaning lady, the doorman – are summoned to the witness stand, their testimonies only serve to substantiate Mark's version of events. Chu's strongest evidence against Mark would have been testimony by Mark's ex-girlfriend, whom he had abused on multiple occasions. However, Mark pre-empts her testimony by threatening to make public a sex tape they once made together. Terrified by the prospect of the tape being released, the ex-girlfriend backs down from testifying against him.

The victim's silence becomes a source of weakness within the adversarial space of the courtroom and allows Mark to reinforce his image of her by filling in the gaps in her narrative. His lawyer begins by asking Chu about her sexual history: "do you enjoy an active sex life?" Surprised by the question, Chu is already visibly nervous. The helplessness of the victim as she is subjected to relentless cross-examination is accentuated through the cinematography: Chu is filmed with a camera placed slightly above her so that her image looks smaller on the screen, whereas the lawyer is filmed with a camera placed slightly below him so that his image is enlarged. When asked how it could be that Mark did not leave any seminal fluids on her body if he really raped her, Chu confesses that she is not entirely sure. This confession of uncertainty provides the lawyer with an opportunity to strengthen the perception of events that Mark carefully created: when Chu breaks down and says "I don't know! I really don't know!," the lawyer aggressively provides a narrative for her: "Of course you don't know! [...] You actually enjoyed the process, but when you went to the bank and found that the amount he deposited was smaller than what you expected, you decided to frame him to punish him, did you not?" Her hysterical response contrasts with Mark's own polished performance in the courtroom. When cross-examined on the bruises on Chu's wrists and ankles, Mark confesses to tying her up but claims that the sexual bondage was her idea: "She told me she liked it [...] Yes, I did tie her up [...] she told me to do it, and I am willing to do anything for her!" The criminal here appropriates the victim's torment, turning it into his own act of self-sacrifice to elicit the sympathy of the jury and furthering his depiction of her as a liar and schemer. After she loses her case, Chu says in despair: "how will people *see* me now?," but her awareness that the judicial process can be manipulated by her attacker to affirm a damaging public image of her has come too late.

As a police inspector tells Yau in the aftermath of the trial, "Hey lady, everything depends on the evidence," and he patronizingly reiterates that the police cannot put a man behind bars without proof of wrongdoing. Yet the film's representation of the legal process underscores the problem with reliance on such evidence, which is that it often sidelines the woman's point of view and allows the male point of view to structure reality. By carefully laying the groundwork, the male lawyer-villain succeeds in controlling the jury's under-standing of events, showing them only what he wants them to see and using the victim's silence as opportunities for bolstering his narrative. Unknown to him, however, the trial has provided a valuable lesson to Yau. It has completed the legal education of this law student by giving her insight into the importance of structuring perception within the existing legal and societal framework. It is ultimately this insight that will enable her to triumph over the villain.

3.3.3 My Criminal, Myself

Yau knows that Mark is coming for her and decides to set the terms of the show down. She moves into Chu's apartment, next door to where Mark lives. When Mark asks her why she is there, she looks him straight in the eye and says "Oh, I just needed a quiet place to study for my law exams. You should come over sometime." Her defiance only makes him even more determined to possess her. The confrontation between Yau and Mark takes place on a dark and stormy night, in a building left empty except for the two of them. At the beginning of this sequence, we see Yau making dinner and running a bath for herself. When Mark appears, she tries to escape. The film draws on the conventions of horror for its climax: the isolated victim, the empty building, the thunder and lighting, the disconnected phone line, the malfunctioning lights, and the music combine to create a fast-paced game of cat and mouse between the rapist and his target.

The confrontation is staged as a battle for control over the field of vision. As part of his obsessive planning to possess Yau, Mark offers her a gift in the aftermath of Chu's trial, seemingly as a gesture of reconciliation. The gift is a life-sized figure of a clown, which Yau places in her living room. When Mark finally puts his plan in motion, he dresses himself up as the gift and poses in its place. Yau does not realize that the figure has been swapped, and that Mark is now in the apartment with her. The camera zooms in on Mark as he slowly opens his eyes, a focus that underscores his scopic power. Mark watches Yau's every move in his disguise, and he grabs her while her back is turned. The crux of Mark's strategy to overpower Yau in the apartment is identical to his plan to overpower Chu in the courtroom: by structuring the field of vision so that other people only see what he shows them, and by ensuring that he is in a position of sight while they are in a position of blindness in relation to the truth.

Yau's counter-strategy, however, is exactly the same: take control of the field of vision. The trial has taught Yau two things about rape: first, that perception matters and, second, that perception is often manipulated to the advantage of men. Her response can therefore be understood as an appropriation of the law's scopic dynamic, this time to the advantage of women. Knowing that Mark is spying on her through a hole he had drilled in the wall, one night prior to the actual confrontation she performs a seductive dance in her living room to induce him to walk into the trap she has set for him. While she does not immediately succeed – he does not take the bait until a few days later – the encounter destabilizes the power relations between the two: the rapist still holds the woman in his gaze, but she is in control not only of the performance but, judging from Mark's widened eyes and quickening breath, also of its effects. Yau's performance of her own femininity becomes part of her arsenal against him.

As Mark watches Yau's strip tease, so do the viewers; the eroticism ostensibly directed at the villain is also directed at the film's audience. The tantalizing nature of the dance is underscored by Chingmy Yau, the actress who plays Yau, when she jokingly said at a press conference that her performance was inspired by a show that she had once seen at a strip club.[51] Such explicit eroticism is part of what earned the film a Category III rating; the dance is simultaneously staged as a trap for one man (in the narrative) and for the entertainment of a larger audience (on the movie screen). In cinematographic terms, the camera in the final segments of *Raped by an Angel* aligns the eye of

---

[51] "Chingmy Yau Says Experience At Strip Club Proves Useful," *Ming Pao Daily News*, May 26th, 1993.

the audience with the eye of the villain, and thus places viewers in the same spectatorial position as Mark. In other words, one of the stylistic innovations of this particular case file film is that it makes the audience see through the eyes of rapist. This alignment works on two levels: it is at times deliberate, for instance when the audience watches the striptease, or in another scene where we see the hands of the criminal cutting Yau's phone lines from the height and angle of his head; at other times, it is less a literal merging than an overlap in cognitive range, such that the audience only knows as little or as much as Mark knows at that stage in the narrative.

The overlapping visions of the viewers and the rapist enabled by the film's camerawork create a number of effects. First, they draw the audience into the scene of the crime by co-opting them into the place of the criminal: in the striptease scene as well as at multiple other moments in the plot, the camera enacts an identification of the viewers (in the darkened cinema) with the rapist (in his darkened living room, watching through the hole in the wall), and the merging of the fields of vision constitutes the basis of a merging of identities. This overlap places the audience in a complex and unsettling position: they understand that they should condemn the rapist as they watch his plan unfold, but at the same time they are titillated, entertained, and quite possibly aroused by the eroticism that the film deliberately aims at them. This double reaction of condemnation and involvement becomes even more problematic in the actual rape scenes. When Mark rapes Chu, he walks into her apartment and catches her by surprise. In the midst of the struggle, the white t-shirt on Chu's body gets wet, and the garment clings to her figure and half reveals her breasts and nipples. As Mark backs her against a wall, he rips open her shirt to reveal her voluptuous upper body, and the scene is again shot from the man's point of view.

These scenes constitute what the criminologist Alison Young calls "crime-images," in which viewers are "implicated" in the enactment of a crime through the cinematographic merging of scopic fields.[52] This implication between the viewers and the rapist is complex because it is characterized by both distance (we are only watching someone else commit a crime) and proximity (we identify with the person committing the crime as we are within the same scopic regime). Young notes that these moments give rise to two opposing kinds of cinematic pleasures: first, there is pleasure in the "judgment" or condemnation of the act; this reaction arises from the distance between the viewers and the wrongdoer. Second, there is pleasure in the "perpetuation" or continuation of the act; this reaction arises from the viewers' identification with the wrongdoer.[53] To put Young's point slightly differently, within a patriarchal framework there is always a kind of pleasure in seeing the sexual violation of a woman's body; the very alignment in the fields of vision means

---

[52] Alison Young, *The Scene of Violence: Cinema, Crime, Affect* (Abingdon: Routledge, 2010), p. 72.
[53] Young, *The Scene of Violence*, p. 41.

that every cognitive act of condemnation or every moment of revulsion is accompanied by a counter current of fascination, identification, and desire. Much as the film invites us to disapprove of Mark's actions toward Chu and Yau, the cinematography also places us in a spectatorial position to acknowledge their appeal. Like their Category III labels, case file films express disapproval of sexual violence but simultaneously promise the visual pleasures that they generate. The question is not so much whether the film should have been banned or whether certain scenes should have been excised, but how the cinematography enables the film to trouble its own morally problematic viewing pleasures.

The answer to this question is related to the second effect of the cinematic alignment between the criminal and the audience: the limitation of the audience's field of vision. The viewers only see what Yau is willing to show Mark through the hole in the wall. What Mark does not see, the audience does not see, which means that the audience does not see what Yau is not willing to show. The commonalities between the eye of the criminal and the eye of the audience means that the trap which Yau sets for Mark is also a trap she sets for the spectators, insofar as we are as much in the dark as to her plans as he is. As Mark pursues her through the building, we see several close up shots of her looking frightened. Like Mark, the viewers truly believe that she is trying to escape from the building in a state of panic, when in fact her plan is to stay within the apartment. As Mark runs after her, he steps into a strategically placed steel jaw trap hidden beneath clothing that only appears to be randomly scattered on the floor. The jaw trap, a kind of *vagina dentata* signaling Yau's status as a castrating woman fighting back against the patriarchal system, catches the audience as much as Mark by surprise.[54] As Mark screams in pain, Yau pushes him sideways into the bath tub, which turns out to be filled not with water but with corrosive acid. Again, the audience sees the trap only when Mark does. The most critical part of the trap, however, is yet to come: in the midst of the struggle inside the darkened apartment, Yau swaps places with a childhood friend who happens to be dying of AIDS. When Mark grabs the woman he is pursuing and penetrates her, he believes that he has finally triumphed over Yau. At that point, Yau emerges from the backroom and turns the light on, to reveal that Mark has had unprotected sexual intercourse with someone who is HIV positive. The camera zooms in on Yau's face, and the triumphant look in her eyes indicates that this moment signifies the closing of the trap: Mark's punishment is that he is going to die from AIDS (This *denouement* indicates that, despite its progressive engagement with the law's problematic approach to rape, the film is not free of the prejudices of the time when it comes to other issues). The friend is willing to be part of the trap

---

[54] For a psychoanalytically-informed discussion of the figure of the castrating woman, see Barbara Creed, *The Monstrous-Feminine: Film, Feminism, Psychoanalysis* (London: Routledge, 1993).

because she is angry at what Mark did to Chu; the narrative makes clear that she is already dying from her illness and sacrifices herself as one last moral act to avenge her friend. Since Mark only sees women as helpless objects of his lust and domination, he cannot have imagined the bonds of sisterhood which would make a woman sacrifice herself for an injustice done to another woman, nor can he have foreseen the intelligence, the agency, and the meticulous organization of these childhood friends.

Ultimately, Mark falls into the trap because he underestimates Yau, and because Yau defines, manages, and restricts his field of vision: he sees her as helpless when in fact she is in a position of power; he misidentifies the objects in the apartment; he mistakes the woman who offers herself as bait to him for the woman he is seeking to violate. In the trial, Chu's dilemma was that the law placed its faith on the maxim that evidence is that which is *evident*. By skillfully manipulating the facts before the jury, the lawyer-villain sidelines the woman's version of events and buries her trauma under a set of seemingly self-explanatory circumstances. Yau's strategy here capitalizes on both the reliance on perception and the possibility of actively creating misperception that is characteristic of the law, and turns the law's logic against the rapist. The criminal's greatest strength becomes the final weapon ensuring his comeuppance.

The film therefore does not simply invite the viewers to observe the defeat of the criminal, but makes them undergo the process of his entrapment cinematographically. Rather than simply showing us a situation whereby the criminal is tricked by Yau's carefully arranged facts and staged evidence, it implicates us through a cinematographic determination of viewing positions. It makes us understand what it feels like to be a subject in that position, and enables us to *experience* the sting of being brought down by someone who manipulates our field of vision. At the end of the film, the film's cinematography prompts two reflections on the relationship between film, women, and the law. First, it brings about an awareness on the part of the viewers that the visual pleasure which they derive from watching the representation of sexual violence as a form of entertainment is entangled with, and ultimately inseparable from, the pleasure which the criminal derives from committing such sexual violence in the film. The merging of scopic positions draws the audience into the crime-image, bringing them closer to the wrongdoing, and to the victim's suffering, than the average viewers of a low-budget movie would expect to be brought, thereby encouraging a critical consideration of the impact the film could have upon them. Second, the film heightens our awareness of the complex ways in which perceptions can be maneuvered in the context of rape by placing us in two different positions in the scopic field: the position of someone who watches Chu fall victim to Mark's control of the field of vision in the courtroom, and the position of becoming victim ourselves to Yau's control of Mark's – and our – field of vision in the final sequence. It thereby encourages us to rethink the maxim that evidence is simply that which is evident, and cultivates a mindfulness that circumstances and testimonies pointing to a seemingly clear verdict may not be as reliable as they seem to be at first glance. *Raped by an Angel* therefore encourages us to think hard about how evidence structures perceptions of femininity, about how we may unwittingly perpetuate the gender bias of a justice system through our own, unexamined, perceptions of women who step forward as rape victims, and about the potential we all have, as members of a society, to create a new, fairer, and more accurate set of images for them.

3.4 Conclusion

In this chapter, I have provided a reading of case file films, and of *Raped by an Angel* in particular, as a forum for engaging with problems of gendered justice in a time of changing ideas and norms about women's rights and sex equality in colonial Hong Kong. I have demonstrated the ways in which *Raped by an Angel* portrays sexual violence against women as an element of popular entertainment, while simultaneously raising questions about viewer complicity and the law's treatment of rape victims. The heyday of the case file film was short-lived: the novelty of the genre wore off within a few years of its emergence, and it seemed to have exhausted its energies by the handover in 1997.

I will close this chapter with a discussion of the relationship between case file films and feminism. The origins of these films in the context of the experimentation and exploration of styles and subjects following the establishment of the new censorship regime mean that it is difficult to label them as unequivocally pro- or anti-feminist: as producers and directors felt their way around the contours of the classification system, they produced representations of sex that uneasily negotiated the emerging norms of sex and gender in the period. While some of the films furthered the feminist cause by exposing the justice system's masculinist interpretative logic, it can be argued that they also undermined it through, among other things, their portrayal of the rapist-villain. In all of the case file films of the early 1990s, rape and other forms of sexual violence are committed by sexual psychopaths. The villains are all unequivocally evil, deranged, and merciless, and they all confirm, and perpetuate, the stereotype of the rapist as a violent stranger who hides in dark corners to prey on unsuspecting women. The most extreme example is the villain of *Red to Kill*, depicted as an inarticulate, simian monster with superhuman strength that emerges at night. Even though some of the actual cases that formed the inspiration for the films did indeed involve criminals with clinically proven psychopathic traits, such cinematic portrayals mask the reality that perpetrators of rape are often men who not only are known to the victim but are close to them and are trusted by them. It is not uncommon for perpetrators to be boyfriends or family members, figures who bear no resemblance to the sexual psychopaths of case file films. Without undermining the interrogation of law which the "other Hong Kong cinema" enacts, it is important to remember that this interrogation takes place in a context in which the industry was still exploring its own boundaries and subjects, and in which it was responding unevenly to the changing legal environment of the time.

4

The Common Law after 1997:
Joe Ma's *Lawyer Lawyer*

Joe Ma's *Lawyer Lawyer* (算死草; 1997) revolves around a court case in late nineteenth-century Hong Kong. A man is framed for murder and is sentenced to death by the colonial court. At the eleventh hour, his lawyer saves him by arguing that, on the true interpretation of the provision on the death penalty in the Qing Penal Code, the man should be freed. The film appeared at a pivotal point in Hong Kong's constitutional history: 1997, the year of the city's retrocession from Britain to China. One of the major controversies about "One Country, Two Systems" around this time concerned the place of English precedent in the Hong Kong courts after the handover: what status or authority should English cases have, and how should they be cited? In this chapter, I suggest that *Lawyer Lawyer* can be understood as providing an answer to these questions.

Local viewers seemed aware that *Lawyer Lawyer* could be read as an intervention into debates about the continuation of Hong Kong's legal system when it first appeared. As film critic Paul Fonoroff wrote in the *South China Morning Post*, the film came out "as the new judicial process" was coming "under critical scrutiny," and can be regarded as "an attack on pre-July 1 [1997] notions of justice."[1] Fonoroff's comment underscores the link between Ma's film and the legal debates of the time, and the fact that the territory's leading English-language newspaper made the editorial decision to publish an opinion piece on a Chinese-language film – a rare occurrence – further suggests that *Lawyer, Lawyer* is an important cultural text for understanding the interconnections between film, law, and identity in this moment of constitutional transition.

I will give the basic narrative arc of Ma's film in Section 4.1. In Section 4.2, I will examine the disagreements about the place of English precedent in post-handover Hong Kong which forms the film's immediate legal context. In particular, I will highlight the different views on the desirability of continued reliance on English cases after 1997, and underscore the anxiety and uncertainty about the impact of the transfer of sovereignty on the legal system. In Section 4.3, I will demonstrate that the lawyer's interpretative move in the film

---

[1] Paul Fonoroff, "Nothing Funny about Lawyers," *South China Morning Post*, August 15th, 1997.

trial is premised on another fictional case, the one brought by Shylock against Antonio in William Shakespeare's *The Merchant of Venice*, and that the outcome of Foon's murder trial is in fact determined by a clever and unexpected use of an English precedent case in a Hong Kong court. In Section 4.4, I will show how the use of Shylock's case can be read as both a comment on the place of English precedent in the courts of post-handover Hong Kong, and a part of the process of forming a postcolonial identity.

4.1 The Narrative Arc of Joe Ma's Film

The film opens in the southern Chinese province of Guangdong, where viewers are introduced to Chan Mong-kut, a man both revered and feared by the local inhabitants for his intelligence, and his servant Foon. Chan is played by the comedian Stephen Chow, whose appearance in this film is further testimony to his centrality to 1990s-Hong Kong cinema which I discussed in Chapter 2. After a comical quarrel between master and servant, Foon abandons Chan and leaves China for the British colony of Hong Kong. Things take an unfortunate turn in Hong Kong, and Foon is framed for murder. When Chan's wife reads about the upcoming murder trial in the newspaper, she and her husband rush to Hong Kong to rescue Foon, and Chan is employed as his defence counsel.

The colonial court in *Lawyer Lawyer* is portrayed in a negative light: its rules are arcane and convoluted, the (Caucasian) judge is arrogant and unsympathetic, and the witnesses are corrupt. Worst of all, the court privileges procedure over justice; the judge instructs the jury to disregard Chan's defence because he had spoken at the wrong time during the trial and had not followed the rules and protocols of the courtroom. According to the judge, the rules of procedure must be followed to the letter. Moreover, it transpires in the course of the proceedings that the barrister on the opposing side is in fact the real murderer, yet the judge instructs the jury to disregard the relevant evidence, again because it was not presented according to proper procedure. Despite overwhelming evidence of Foon's innocence, the court refuses to deviate from its strict adherence to procedural rules; it finds him guilty of murder and sentences him to death by hanging. Chan can hardly bring himself to believe that English justice could allow such an outcome: "Your Honour, surely we don't need to follow the rules so closely?" he exclaims.

The camera then cuts from the courtroom to the scene of the execution. A guard leads Foon up to the execution stand and puts the rope around his neck. All seems lost for Foon, but Chan saves the day at the last moment. He does so through an act of interpretation, arguing that on a proper construction of the provision on the death penalty in the Penal Code, Foon's death did not in fact constitute the necessary outcome of the sentence. His argument is as follows: the Chinese term for death by hanging is "huan shou zhi xing/wuan sao ji ying" (環首之刑), which literally means "a sentence whereby a hoop is placed around one's neck" (huan/wuan (環) = hoop or circle, shou/sao (首) =

neck, zhi/ji (之) = of, xing/ying (刑) = punishment or penalty). Chan argues that since the rope had already been placed around Foon's neck, the sentence had already been carried out to the full according to the strict letter of the sentence; nothing in the expression "wuan sao ji ying/ wuan sao ji ying" (環首 之刑) stipulates that the hoop needs to be tightened. Chan's legal interpretation is perversely literal, but the judge cannot deny Chan the force of his argument given that he himself had insisted that the rules of procedure in the courtroom be followed to the letter in a similarly literal fashion. Foon is therefore released. The final sequence takes place one year after the trial: Chan and his wife pose for a second wedding photo to celebrate the overcoming of differences between them which had formed the subplot, and the audience is told that Foon has also married the woman he loves.

4.2 Anxieties and Uncertainties about English Precedent in Hong Kong, Circa 1997

How did Hong Kongers react to the prospect of the retrocession in the final years of the 1990s, the historical juncture in which the film appeared? In many ways, their complex affective responses were a continuation of the conflicting emotions that emerged in light of the Sino-British negotiations and the signing of the Joint Declaration in the early 1980s, which I discussed in Chapter 1. Many people in Hong Kong continued to show ambivalence towards China, even if the outright panic of the early 1990s sparked by the June 4 crackdown had gradually subsided in the course of the decade. For instance, the *SCMP* reports that while many students graduating from high school in 1997 felt "joy and pride" that the territory will no longer be under foreign rule, their positive sentiments were "tinged with worry" because "they could not forget what happened in Tiananmen Square."[2] Daniel Fung, the city's first Solicitor General, summed up the mood when he acknowledged that "whilst Hong Kong enjoyed a robust and liberal legal and independent judicial system," there were fears that "all that would disappear down some juridical black hole after China resumed her sovereignty."[3] Furthermore, a glance at the news headlines of the period reveals ongoing concerns associated with China's resumption of sovereignty, such as the potential rise of corruption and bribery in the courts, the replacement of the English language by Chinese as the medium of judicial proceedings, and possible attempts to politicize the selection of judges after the handover.[4]

[2] Stella Lee, "Squaring Up to Face the Future," *South China Morning Post*, July 1st, 1997.
[3] Daniel R. Fung, "Paradoxes of Hong Kong's Reversion: The Legal Dimension," in *Hong Kong and the Super Paradox: Life after Return to China*, edited by James C. Hsiung (Basingstoke: Macmillan, 2000), pp. 105–125 (107).
[4] See, for example, Niall Fraser, "Graft-busters Gird for New Battle," *South China Morning Post*, July 1st, 1997; Linda Choy, "Court Decision Sparks Fury on Short Notice," *South China Morning Post*, July 24th, 1997; Greg Manuel, "Translation of Attempted Rape Annoys Lawyers," *South China Morning Post,* June 3rd, 1997.

Running alongside the ambivalence towards the incoming sovereign was an ambivalence towards the departing one, as Hong Kong society continued to reflect upon the legacy of colonial rule. A coalition chose the occasion of the handover to protest not only against the imprisonment of the June 4 dissidents in the mainland, but also "Britain's failure to set up a democratic political system in Hong Kong" prior to 1997, and it further objected to the mere "lip service" which the colonial administration paid to "the plight of the working class people" in the city.[5] Moreover, a commentator writing about her worries about Hong Kong's future could not help bringing up how her father held a lifelong grudge against the colonial administration because he experienced at firsthand how it "discriminated against locals while protecting and favoring the English-speaking population."[6] The constitutional transformation from British colony to Chinese Special Administrative Region brought to the surface the complicated feelings towards Britain and China that co-existed, in different combinations and with varying degrees of intensity, in the years leading up to the handover.

Disagreements about the place and authority of English case law after the handover can be understood in light of the ambivalence not only towards the Chinese resumption of sovereignty, but also towards the legacy of colonial rule. On the one hand, it was obvious that continued reliance on English case law was crucial in maintaining the credibility of the legal system, and the desire to hold onto the common law was part of the city's affective attachment to a longstanding legal cornerstone. On the other hand, the handover meant that there was now a strong argument for Hong Kong to develop its own, indigenous, case law and to move away from a reliance on cases that were decided based on socio-cultural conditions vastly different from its own. This countervailing tendency was an important dimension of the city's desire to distance itself from its colonial past.

Prior to the handover, local judges in the Hong Kong courts were bound by the decisions of the Privy Council and traditionally regarded themselves bound by decisions of the House of Lords; the former was the colony's court of final appeal, and the latter was "the supreme tribunal for the identification of English law."[7] Hong Kong's judges were not formally bound to the English Court of Appeal or to the other English courts, but they generally followed their decisions, on the basis that it was desirable for the common law not to diverge amongst countries in which it operated, that the English courts provided a greater range of decisions for the guidance of the local lawyers, and that adherence to English law would promote certainty.[8] The transfer of

---

[5] Linda Choy, "Serious Side to Alternative Celebration," *South China Morning Post*, July 1st, 1997.

[6] Fong Wai-hung, "Three Sides to My Family's Fortune," *South China Morning Post*, July 1st, 1997.

[7] Peter Wesley-Smith, *An Introduction to the Hong Kong Legal System*, (3rd edn, Hong Kong: Oxford University Press, 1998), p. 84.

[8] Wesley-Smith, *Introduction*, p. 85 (my italics).

sovereignty introduced complications to this relatively straightforward schema. The status of English law in post-handover Hong Kong is governed by Article 8 of the Basic Law, which states that "laws previously in force [i.e., during the colonial period] in Hong Kong" including "the common law, rules of equity, ordinances, subordinate legislation and customary law shall be maintained" unless they contravene the Basic Law itself or are subsequently amended by Hong Kong's legislature. However, even though Article 8 deals with the common law and equity as they existed at the time of the handover, it is silent on their place after the transition. This silence created much uncertainty and debate, and different views were posited on the desirability of maintaining Hong Kong's fidelity to English case law.

Peter Wesley-Smith, a former Dean of the Faculty of Law at the University of Hong Kong, has pointed out that while institutional factors such as the vast holdings of common law reports in local universities and the scarcity of textbooks on local law likely meant that English law would still continue to be cited, it would be "unnecessary, anachronistic and undesirable" for the Hong Kong courts to remain strictly bound by English precedent cases.[9] In a similar vein, the Solicitor General described abandoning the notion of binding English law as a move which would enable Hong Kong to cut its "constitutional umbilicus from the United Kingdom" and which would free it "from an earlier culture of relying for judicial inspiration on predominantly English case law."[10]

While Wesley-Smith and Fung regarded a move away from a strict reliance on English cases as binding precedent as a positive one, there were many who did not share their views and were concerned that such a move would represent a significant erosion of the common law system. In his introduction to one of the most cited works on legal precedent, the Hong Kong-based editor of the volume noted that while "democracy (of a sort) exists here, and the English system of common law prevails," concurrently "a body of opinion says that neither of these institutions is desirable."[11] The volume was published in 1987, just three years after the Joint Declaration, and the fact that one of the seminal works on legal precedent begins with a note about the uncertain survival of the common law in Hong Kong after the retrocession shows that anxieties about colonial precedent were born almost at the same time as the treaty stipulating that Hong Kong would once again become part of China. Such anxieties intensified as the years passed, and reached a climax around the time of the actual transfer of sovereignty. In an article published on the day of the handover, the *SCMP*'s legal correspondent notes that "when lawyers discuss

---

[9] Peter Wesley-Smith, "The Common Law of England in the Special Administrative Region," in *Hong Kong, China and 1997: Essays in Legal Theory*, edited by Raymond Wacks (Hong Kong: Hong Kong University Press, 1993), pp. 5–41 (39).

[10] Fung, "Paradoxes of Hong Kong's Reversion: The Legal Dimension," p. 109.

[11] Lawrence Goldstein, "Introduction" in *Precedent in Law*, edited by Lawrence Goldstein (Oxford: Clarendon Press, 1987), p. 1.

the future of Hong Kong's criminal law they often sound like environmentalists concerned with preserving an endangered species."[12] He goes on to predict that, in legal terms, the success of "One Country, Two Systems" will "depend not so much on what is changed as on what is left alone." In a similar vein, a law lecturer expresses his hope that a legal profession "steeped in common law tradition would provide protection" against Chinese-style corruption. Another lecturer notes that in the area of commercial law there would likely be "a strong move towards local precedent" and predicts that "the courts and advocates will distance themselves from British jurisprudence."[13] However, in the same article the Chairman of the American Chamber of Commerce warned that the business community would be wary of too much change in the law: "The assumption is that the legal system will stay the same. If there is significant tinkering it could affect business confidence." There were also concerns about the possible updating of Hong Kong's Companies Ordinance from an English model to one which would incorporate American, Canadian, New Zealand, and Australian traditions. One lawyer suggested that the move away from the English model could be "politically driven by a desire to sever ties with Hong Kong's colonial past" rather than by any genuine desire to improve the city's company law.[14] While the debate over the Companies Ordinance is more concerned with the place of English legislation rather than case law, it points more generally towards anxieties about moving away from the English common law after 1997; such moves were often regarded as a lamentable wearing away of the common law. Article 8 of the Basic Law did little to clarify the status and use of English precedent in post-handover Hong Kong, and the disagreements continued.

Lawyer Lawyer thus appeared at a time of uncertainty about the future of English authorities in the Hong Kong Courts. There were fears that deviations from such English precedent would undermine Hong Kong's legal edifice, yet there were also strong voices for freeing the Hong Kong courts from the shackles of colonial cases and for developing local case law. In light of such hopes, fears and unease, how could Hong Kong proceed so as to maintain a balance between preserving the common law system that has served Hong Kong well and escaping from the ideological shackles of colonial law? In the next two sections, I will argue that Chan's interpretative move in the film could be read as a response to this issue.

4.3 Citing Shakespeare

To return to the scene of legal interpretation with this chapter began, Chan's argument is premised on a strictly literal interpretation of the law: he posits

---

[12] Cliff Buddle, "Common Law Will Defend Itself," *South China Morning Post*, July 1st, 1997.
[13] Patricia Young, "Companies Put Confidence in Judicial System," *South China Morning Post*, June 27th, 1997.
[14] Sheel Kohli, "Doubts Increase Over Rule of Law," *South China Morning Post*, June 2nd, 1997.

that on a true reading of the wording of the sentence, "huan shou zhi xing/ wuan sao ji ying" (a sentence whereby a hoop is placed around one's neck) only stipulates that a hoop is to be placed around the defendant's neck, and that there is no requirement that the hoop be tightened. Foon's sentence had therefore been carried out to the full the moment the hoop was placed around his neck. This argument seems strange in part because of its strict literality, and in part because it is so unanticipated by the audience. It makes one wonder about its genesis: how did Chan come up with this interpretative strategy at the last moment? There are multiple answers to this question. One view is that it is derived from observation: Chan's first encounter with English law through his interaction with the judge and the barrister in Foon's trial taught him that English lawyers stick closely to the letter of the law, and with his intelligence he quickly learned from his opponents and turned their way of reading to his own advantage.

However, there is another possible view, which is that Chan learned this mode of literal interpretation not from Foon's case, but from another, less obvious, source. I would suggest that there is in fact another court case which Chan is relying on here, one which is not named explicitly in the film but presence of which can be detected by the careful viewer. This is a fictional case, which is appropriate given that we are concerned with a film trial. The case which Chan relies on here is the case of *Shylock v. Antonio* in Shakespeare's *The Merchant of Venice*, in which Portia traps Shylock through a perversely literal reading of his bond. In that case, as is well known, Shylock the Jew lends money to Antonio the merchant, and it is stipulated in the bond that should Antonio fail to repay his debt, Shylock will be entitled to a pound of his flesh: "Three thousand ducats for three months, and Antonio bound."[15] Antonio agrees to the bond in order to give his friend financial backing to woo Portia. In the trial scene in Act IV Scene 1 of the play, Shylock insists on the pound of flesh to which he is entitled. Portia intervenes in the case disguised as Balthazar, a learned doctor from Rome. Much to Shylock's delight, she initially agrees that he is entitled to a pound of flesh from Antonio, but her agreement is in fact a trap: she notes that the bond entitled Shylock to nothing more and nothing less than a pound of flesh, which means that (i) he cannot draw any blood while cutting the flesh (as blood is not explicitly stipulated in the bond), and (ii) he must perform the impossible task of cutting exactly one pound of flesh. Her perversely literal reading of the term of "a pound of flesh" in the bond uses the very law which Shylock relies upon to deny what he seeks; sticking strictly to the term means that it becomes impossible for him to obtain the pound of flesh he is entitled to.[16]

---

[15] William Shakespeare, *The Merchant of Venice* (first published 1598, Signet Classic 2004), I.3.9–10.

[16] For discussions of *The Merchant of Venice* in the frame of "Law and Literature," see Peter Julian Millett, *Villainy in Venice* (Hong Kong: University of Hong Kong Occasional Publication, 2005); Paul Raffield and Gary Watt (eds.), *Shakespeare and the Law* (Oxford: Hart,

The interpretative strategy at work in Shakespeare's play and in Ma's film creates a set of intertextual relations between them; at the core of both texts is a mode of legal interpretation which many people would regard as perversely literal. When we consider the multiple parallels between Portia's argument in Shylock's case and Chan's argument in Foon's case, it becomes possible to argue that the former informs and directs the latter.

First of all, there is a parallel in the way Shylock and the judge initially insist on an absolute fidelity to the wording of the law because they believe their own understanding of the wording to be the only possible one. In the trial scene of *The Merchant of Venice*, Shylock insists on a pound of Antonio's flesh according to the strict letter of his entitlement because he does not believe that it can be denied according to the wording of the bond. Similarly, in *Lawyer Lawyer* the judge insists upon an unswerving adherence to the strict letter of the rules of procedure because he sees them as the means to establish order in an otherwise unruly colony. "I crave the law" says Shylock, and this craving arguably also reflects the judge's desire for absolute obedience to the rules of colonial law.[17] Neither of them understood that literality is a sword that cuts both ways.

Second, the very perversity of the reading allows the interpretative act to form the narrative climax in both texts. Fidelity to the rules of procedure or interpretation is sacrificed in favor of a dramatic or cinematic denouement. In Shakespeare's play, Shylock is trapped by a singularly unconvincing reading of the terms of his bond; in a real court of law such an interpretative argument would not have carried weight. As Terry Eagleton points out, Portia's reading of the bond is "'true to the text' but therefore lamentably false to its meaning [...] Her interpretation is *too* true, too crassly literal, and so ironically a flagrant distortion."[18] Yet it is precisely this perversity which lends the reading its dramatic force; the fact that Shylock is punished by the very law he relies on constitutes the irony and hence the tragedy of the scene. Similarly, the judge in *Lawyer Lawyer* is trapped by an overly literal interpretation of the sentence: he had previously insisted on a literal reading of the law, so he must now agree to Chan's literal interpretation of the sentence. Parodying the judge's own logic, Chan insists that "the law is the law, and not a single word or punctuation can be changed"; it is the perversely literal quality of the interpretation which constitutes its cinematic force because the judge is now trapped in his own interpretative framework and has no choice but to allow Foon to walk free. Like Portia's argument, Chan's interpretation is "aberrant because too faithful" and as such would not have been accepted in a real-life

---

2008), pp. 235–299; Gary Watt, *Equity Stirring* (Oxford: Hart, 2009), pp. 214–218; Richard Weisberg, *Poethics and Other Strategies of Law and Literature* (New York: Columbia University Press, 1992), pp. 94–104; and Kenji Yoshino, *A Thousand Times More Fair* (New York: HarperCollins, 2011), pp. 29–59.

[17] *The Merchant of Venice*, IV.1. 205.

[18] Terry Eagleton, *William Shakespeare* (Oxford: Blackwell, 1986), p. 37.

court room, but it is precisely for this reason that it provides an appropriately comic denouement to an otherwise tense execution scene.[19]

Thirdly, there are parallels in the way Chan and Portia capitalize on the consequences of their literal interpretation. In Shakespeare's play, Portia does not merely deny Shylock the terms of the bond, but actively takes away what he already owns independent of the bond. It is a ruthless interpretation, and critics have argued that such ruthlessness can be understood as premised on anti-Semitic sentiments.[20] In *The Merchant of Venice*, the law is clear that dire consequences await a Jew who dares to shed Christian blood. Portia tells Shylock that if he takes the flesh and draws blood from Antonio, he will lose all his possessions:

> Take then thy bond, take thou thy pound of flesh,
> But in the cutting it, if thou dost shed
> One drop of Christian blood, thy lands and goods
> Are (by the laws of Venice) confiscate
> Unto the state of Venice.[21]

She also tells him that even if he refrains from taking Antonio's flesh, the fact that he, as a Jew and hence a non-citizen, attempted to do so would mean that he would still lose his possessions, and possibly his life:

> It is enacted in the laws of Venice,
> If it proved against an alien,
> That by direct, or indirect attempts
> He seek the life of any citizen,
> The party 'gainst the which he doth contrive,
> Shall seize one half his goods, the other half
> Comes to the privy coffer of the state,
> And the offender's life lies in the mercy
> Of the Duke only, 'gainst all other voice.[22]

The two passages above underscore the ruthlessness of Portia's literal interpretation: its consequence is not only that Shylock loses his case, but he loses all: "You take my house, when you do take the prop/That doth sustain my house: you take my life/When you do take the means whereby I live."[23] Portia's interpretative strategy reduces Shylock to abjection. Moreover, it changes the power balance between appellant and defendant so that Shylock is turned from someone who seeks the protection of the law into a criminal himself.

Chan draws on Portia's example and refuses to stop at winning his case; he goes further and uses the very law on which the judge relies as the means of trapping him. Portia says to Shylock: "For as thou urgest justice, be assur'd/Thou

---

[19] Eagleton, *William Shakespeare*, p. 37.
[20] See, for example, James Shapiro, *Shakespeare and the Jews* (New York: Columbia University Press, 1996) and Harold Bloom, *Shakespeare: the Invention of the Human* (New York: Riverhead Books, 1998), pp. 171–192.
[21] *The Merchant of Venice*, IV.1.307–311.   [22] *The Merchant of Venice*, IV.1.347–355.
[23] *The Merchant of Venice*, IV.1.374–376.

shalt have justice more than thou desir'st"; Chan learns from his predecessor that this excess justice produced by an unswerving reliance on the law can itself be a form of power.[24] As the judge hesitates over how to respond to Chan's argument, Chan says "Think before you speak, [if you insist on killing Foon] [...] I'll also sue you for murder!" In other words, he redirects the force of the law away from Foon and towards the judge. Like Portia, Chan reverses the power balance, so that the judge becomes a potential criminal, and the man originally branded as a criminal regains his freedom.

Beyond the structural parallels between Shakespeare's play and Chan's argument, there is a further point bolstering the view that Chan is following Shylock's case, which is that there is an explicit reference to Shakespeare in *Lawyer Lawyer*. It appears in the final five minutes of the film, and it is strategically placed near the end so that it would be more likely to remain in the mind of the viewer. In the penultimate sequence of the film, the events of which take place one year after the trial, Foon tells Chan that his wife has gone to England to study:

Chan: Really? What is she studying?
Foon: English literature.
Chan: Ah right, as in Shakespeare . . .
Foon: Yes! Wow you're good, you even know Shakespeare?
Chan: The study of Shakespeare is suitable for her. Yes, you can ask me
          anything about Shakespeare . . .

The scene then fades into another one, and as it does so we see Chan continuing to expound upon Shakespeare. At first sight, this scene seems incongruous with the rest of the film: why is there a reference to Shakespeare in the final five minutes of the story, when the playwright had not been mentioned before? However, the scene no longer seems incongruous if we read it in the context of the trial: as a man known for his intelligence and his knowledge, Chan is very worldly and very well read. The scene shows the audience that he is not only familiar with Shakespeare, but that he has an in-depth knowledge of his work; it is likely that he is familiar with *The Merchant of Venice* specifically given that it contains the most famous trial scene in the entire Shakespearean canon. The function of the final sequence is therefore to reveal the inspiration of Chan's interpretative strategy.

I have so far suggested that the trial scene in *The Merchant of Venice* informs and directs Chan's argument in Foon's trial. To put the idea in slightly different terms, I have contended that Shylock's case functions as a precedent on which Chan relies to build his argument. Neil Duxbury has argued that the doctrine of precedent is not, as conventionally understood, premised on the idea that cases bind, but on the more nuanced requirement that "past events be respected as guides for present action" in the common law courtroom.[25] It is

---

[24] *The Merchant of Venice*, IV.1.314–315.
[25] Neil Duxbury, *The Nature and Authority of Precedent* (Cambridge: Cambridge University Press, 2008), p. 183.

precisely in this capacity that Chan draws upon Shylock's case in *Lawyer Lawyer*: the reasoning and the outcome of that case from the past guide the present argument, and it is arguably because Chan sticks to the philosophy of that case so closely that the judge has no choice but to concede to his conclusion. By relying on *Antonio v. Shylock*, Chan can be said to be following an English precedent: Shylock's case functions as a (fictional) precedent which guides and informs his legal argumentation in the (film) trial set in late nineteenth-century Hong Kong. The principle that the law should be given a literal interpretation is derived directly from Shylock's case, and is here applied to Foon's advantage by his lawyer. One can also say that by citing Shylock's case in this way, Chan is also being true to Shakespeare's text, for Portia herself is aware of the value of the play's trial scene as judicial precedent: she notes that the correct judgment must be rendered and the right principle laid down in Shylock's case because "Twill be recorded for a precedent," and if wrongly decided "many an error by the same example/Will rush into the state."[26]

4.4 Citing Shakespeare in Court, Or the Place of English Precedent in Post-Handover Hong Kong

The scene of interpretation in the film takes on legal-historical significance when we situate it in the context of the controversy about the place of English precedent in the postcolonial courts in Hong Kong at the time of its release. Taking our cue from Fonoroff's recognition that the film can be regarded as a critique of the law in Hong Kong around the time of the handover, it is possible to think of the scene as a response to this controversy. Chan's use of Shylock's case as English precedent in his argument in the execution scene can be read as a comment on the proper place of English precedent in the Hong Kong courts after the handover.

Chan draws on an English case in order to save his servant. This continued use of an English precedent in the film can be understood as a response to local critics with strong nationalist sentiments who regarded the common law system as a mode of domination and who advocated its outright rejection. Through Chan, *Lawyer Lawyer* suggests that it is possible for a Chinese lawyer to cite an English precedent and still achieve justice: Chan's wit lies in showing how procedural justice can lead to substantive justice in the common law, and hence shows that there are parts of the English system that are worth keeping. Chan's reliance on Shylock's case therefore seems to suggest that it would be unwise to discontinue the use of English precedent entirely; English case law has served Hong Kong well in the past and is likely to do so in the foreseeable future. It would be rash to jettison English cases in the name of a pro-China nationalist politics.

---

[26] *The Merchant of Venice*, IV.1.219–221.

However, despite Chan's continued use of English precedent, it would be a mistake to see the film as indicative of an attitude of unquestioning or mechanical reliance on English cases. This is so for three reasons. First of all, Chan is by no means uncritical of the English presence in Hong Kong. At the beginning of the film, Chan proposes a truce with his enemies in China: "The nation is under threat because Hong Kong, Kowloon and the New Territories have fallen into the hands of Westerners. We should put aside our differences and join forces against the foreigners." Moreover, when Foon first decides to move from China to the British colony, Chan urges him to stay by saying that "Hong Kong is a colony. It is not for the habitation of real people, it is only for the habitation of Western people." Finally, during the trial he becomes irritated by the judge and the opposing counsel in the Hong Kong court: "Why can't they shut up about their great British Empire? Have they forgotten that they only borrowed Hong Kong from us? They need to return it to us in the future!" This is an explicit reference to the handover of 1997. Chan's impatience with the British presence in Hong Kong, his criticism of English attitudes, and his at times overtly racist remarks betray his deep suspicion of English law and indicate that he would be unlikely to make use of English cases passively or deferentially.

Second, even though Chan relies on the logic of Portia's argument, he in fact makes use of Shylock's case in a highly unconventional way. The normal procedure for citing precedent in the courtroom would of course require the lawyer to name the cases, state the facts, and explain how their legal principles apply to the circumstances at hand. In this instance, however, *The Merchant of Venice* guides and structures Chan's legal argument, but it is never explicitly cited in court. The advantage of this method of introducing precedent in one's argument is that the inspiration for the argument is never revealed, so that it would be much harder for the lawyer on the opposing side to try to set aside Chan's argument through the traditional means of distinguishing a case based on its facts. Given the vast differences between the context of Shakespeare's play in Renaissance Italy and the context of Foon's trial in late nineteenth-century Hong Kong, one can easily imagine the opposing lawyer seeking to distinguish *The Merchant of Venice* as authority by underscoring the circumstantial differences between them. However, since Chan relies on the case without explicitly naming it, the other lawyer must confront the logic and principle of the case in their purest form, without the trappings of the specific facts giving rise to them. He cannot seek to parry the force of Chan's argument by seeking to distinguish Shylock's case. Chan is citing Shylock's case, but he does so in an entirely original way that allows him to capitalize on its core principle of literal interpretation and bypasses the potential problem of having the case distinguished on its facts.[27]

---

[27] Interestingly, this use of cases without direct citation is echoed by the use of comparative jurisprudence in some overseas courts, in which judges at times adopt a legal principle without citing the case. See Christopher McCrudden, "A Common Law of Human Rights? Transnational Judicial Conversations on Constitutional Rights," 20(4) *Oxford Journal of Legal Studies* (2000), 499–532.

Chan's method of using the precedent case is also unconventional for jurisprudential reasons, because when he introduces Shylock's case he is not merely making a legal argument in defence of Foon, but is taking on the colonial legal system itself and undermining it from within. When Portia traps Shylock through her perversely literal reading of the bond, she is bolstering the legal edifice in the play: the legal system is one which is biased against Shylock the Jew in favor of the Christians, and by advancing the interest of the Duke, Bassanio and the other Christians she is on the side of the law. Chan's literal reading, however, is nothing short of a postcolonial strategy of resistance because it draws on an English case to challenge the English colonial legal system. In other words, Chan is using a core element of the system – English precedent – to challenge it. If the judge finds Foon guilty, he would have to contradict his own premise that the letter of the law must be interpreted literally, and this would imply an unjustifiable deviation from past practice and would hence expose an inconsistent judicial attitude at the heart of colonial law. "Your judgment will bring your great British Empire to shame through your own inconsistency" Chan tells the judge, and urges him to do justice and release Foon from the execution stand. Chan therefore uses English precedent not only to advance his own argument, but also to strike at the very rigidity and nepotism in the heart of the colonial-legal project.

The final indication that the film does not advocate a deferential attitude towards English precedent lies in the way Chan refers to Shakespeare in the last scene. Foon has just told Chan that his wife is studying English literature in England, and Chan has revealed his knowledge of Shakespeare to Foon. The entire conversation takes place in Cantonese, and contains a pun. The Cantonese term for Shakespeare is "Sa Si Bei Ah" (莎士比亞), a transliteration of the English word. Within this transliteration, the meanings of the four characters which make up the Chinese word for Shakespeare are purely onomatopoeic; their normal meanings are set aside so that this particular combination of the four characters refers to the playwright and to nothing else. Yet when Chan refers to Shakespeare, he comically – some might say facetiously – changes the last two characters, so that "Sa Si Bei AH" (莎士比亞) becomes "Sa Si Bei LA" (莎士脾罅). "Bei La" (脾罅) in Cantonese refers to the area between one's crotch and one's leg, that narrow area of the body that is usually overlooked and is not regarded as particularly appealing. The effect of this pun, then, is to transform the greatest playwright in English literary history into a random body part, and not a particular elegant part either.

Such word play constitutes another instance of Stephen Chow's signature "Moleitau" humour. Here, the reduction of Shakespeare to an overlooked body part can be seen as a way of undermining the canonicity and the authority of the playwright, a mocking gesture which takes him down from the pedestal of great English literature and places him amongst the silly, the mundane, and the everyday. Chan's appellation of Shakespeare, his transformation of "Sa Si Bei AH" (莎士比亞) to "Sa Si Bei LA" (莎士脾罅) can be interpreted as an indication of how he conceives of Shakespeare: not as an unalterable authority or a great figure to be revered or deferred to, but as an entity which can be linguistically transformed, remolded, even mocked in a Chinese context. Through translation into a different linguistic and cultural frame, the name "Shakespeare" can become funny in ways which Shakespeare himself would not have understood. This treatment of Shakespeare's name can, by extension, give us an indication of the way Chan is prepared to read and cite his plays in general, and Shylock's case in particular: not with great deference or reverence, as if it was an absolute authority which must be strictly followed, but with creativity, lateral thinking, playfulness, even a certain degree of disdain. He is capable of using his plays creatively to suit the new cultural and legal contexts in which he finds himself.

In short, Chan's use of Shylock's case does not suggest an attitude of continued deference to English case law in the Hong Kong courts. His attitude towards English precedent is not one of colonial awe, and he certainly does not regard Shylock's case as being in any way binding on himself or on the judge in Foon's trial. Rather, it is merely a guide or an inspiration for his argument. In Chan's mind, English precedent is one form of argument amongst many rather than an absolute binding authority which he cannot set aside. He does not rarefy English law by regarding it as an endangered species which needs to be protected after the handover, nor does he place it on a pedestal and regard it as having any more force or legitimacy than other laws in the land.

Not outright rejection, and not uncritical reliance: the film seems to present a third way of using English cases in the postcolonial period through Chan's act of interpretation. It suggests that English cases should be retained, but adapted in such a way as to be useful to Hong Kong's postcolonial situation as it confronts new legal scenarios after the retrocession. Chan draws on Shakespeare but evokes his name in a way which is irreverent and even daring by turning him into a body part, and he cites Shylock's case in a way which departs from the traditional mode of introducing cases in court. In a similar mode, Hong Kong lawyers could continue citing English precedent, but be bold enough to do so in new, creative, and even unorthodox ways to enable the legal system in Hong Kong to face the challenges which lie ahead. "Legal case-history is not just a record of past applications of the law, but a tradition of continuous interpretation of it which bears in forcibly on any current act of legal judgement," and the ability to draw on English precedent in new and creative ways is part of this process of "continuous interpretation" which is especially necessary at a time of sovereignty transfer.[28] The scene of interpretation in the film seems to suggest that instead of rejecting or deferring to the

---

[28] Eagleton, *William Shakespeare*, p.36.

colonial past, Hong Kong should take what we have inherited from English law, but always be ready to change it, to treat it with irreverence, to adapt it to the local context, to the local language, and to the local culture in postcolonial period.

Some examples of such an attitude could already be found in the law at the time of the handover. Article 84 of the Basic Law is a case in point. The provision explicitly allows Hong Kong courts to refer to precedents from common law jurisdictions other than England. As the Solicitor General pointed out, after the handover

> Hong Kong courts [. . .] regularly cite and follow, by way of precedent, decisions of the House of Lords, the Privy Council, the High Court of Australia, the New Zealand Court of Appeal, the Indian Supreme Court, the South African Supreme Court, the Supreme Court of Canada and last, but by no means least, decisions of the U.S. Supreme Court and the U.S. Federal District Court.[29]

The drafters of Article 84 and the judges who have interpreted this provision arguably epitomize the creativity and boldness in the treatment of English precedent in the film: Hong Kong lawyers continue to cite English cases in the courts but no longer treat them as inherently more authoritative or persuasive than cases from other common law jurisdictions, and by following a much wider and much more international range of precedents they creatively modify the use of case law to make it suit the new global order in which Hong Kong found itself, resulting in a more cosmopolitan and more fertile legal system.

4.5 Conclusion

Yang Ti-liang, the first Chinese person to serve as Hong Kong's Chief Justice, once noted that the common law in Hong Kong must adapt and evolve after the retrocession: there "must be transformation – a process by which the spirit of the legal system is so mingled with the culture and ethos of the new society that a new system emerges, still largely based on the ancestry whence it came, but evidencing a metamorphosis which has eradicated its foreignness."[30]

In light of the intertwining of law and identity which I have been tracing in this book, this new, localized common law can be read as part of the process of negotiating an identity in a time of constitutional transformation. In the film, Chan's creative use of English precedent means that he is able to achieve a just outcome in a way which no English lawyer without knowledge of the Chinese language could have done, because he brings Portia's literal interpretation to bear on the *Chinese* phrase for "death by hanging" in the Penal Code. As such, it reflects a vision of Hong Kong law, and Hong Kong identity, which retains

---

[29] Fung, "Paradoxes of Hong Kong's Reversion: The Legal Dimension," p. 109.
[30] Cited in Lau Chi-kuen, *Hong Kong's Colonial Legacy* (Hong Kong: Chinese University Press, 1997), p. 131.

"the ancestry whence it came," but which also undergoes "a metamorphosis" that makes it distinctly local. Chan's strategy seems to suggest that Hong Kong lawyers should continue to make use of English case law, but they must not be afraid to allow it to be reworked, recontextualized, and reinterpreted, so that it can evolve together with Hong Kong as the city moves into a new era.

5

A Matter of National Security:
Tammy Cheung's *July*

One of the key constitutional challenges that emerged in Hong Kong after 1997 centered on the introduction of laws relating to national security, and it triggered the first major post-handover mass demonstration in the territory. Under the laws of mainland China, "national security" can be used to justify a wide range of government intrusions into private life, including the arrest and detention of individuals suspected of engaging in anti-government activities or having links to foreign political organizations. Moreover, the Chinese state suppresses overt criticism of the Communist Party and even the possession of publications it deems too critical of its policies in the name of security. In the years leading up to the retrocession, it was obvious that the introduction of China's national security laws into Hong Kong after 1997 could spark a crisis in confidence about the future of freedoms and rights in the city, but it was equally evident that China would not allow Hong Kong to become a zone where activities that threatened the overall safety of the nation would be tolerated.

Article 23 of the Basic Law is designed to provide a solution to this conundrum: under this provision, China's laws on national security-related offences law will indeed not apply directly to Hong Kong, but the post-handover administration is specifically obligated to introduce local legislation to protect national safety. In other words, Hong Kong will have laws to protect national security, but such laws will be passed by the territory's own legislature so that they can be drafted in accordance with the higher level of protection for individuals under the common law. Article 23 is therefore designed to reflect the overarching constitutional principle of "One Country, Two Systems": Hong Kong is an inalienable part of China and must enact laws to protect the nation's overall security and integrity (One Country), but it will have autonomy on all matters relating to the drafting, timing, and passage of national security legislation (Two Systems).

In 2002, five years after the handover, the Hong Kong government moved to enact such legislation. A number of legal scholars have noted that, as a matter of law, the final bill that it put forward the following year, known as the National

Security (Legislative Provisions) Bill 2003, was not unreasonable.[1] However, the government underestimated the intensity of resistance to the legislation. Part of the reason for the resistance was the specificity of the legal issue: the term "national security" conjured up in the minds of many Hong Kongers the Central authorities' use of it as justification for some of the worst human rights violations in the mainland. A coalition of non-governmental organizations in Hong Kong issued a joint statement warning that the law would create a "white terror," and that the local authorities could also begin using national security as a "pretext to silence different opinions, suppress development of our civil society, and deprive Hong Kong people of their basic human rights protections."[2] In other words, the NGOs feared that the law would constitute a significant, and irreversible, step towards the introduction of mainland Chinese legal norms and practices into the city. Voices from across the political spectrum and from different parts of society also emerged to warn of the law's potential impact on human rights and to urge caution against overly hasty legislation. The longstanding ambivalence towards China from the pre-handover years hardened into a more explicit mentality of resistance on the back of these concerns. Yet the government seemed determined to push through the legislation. The Article 23 controversy culminated in a high-profile protest: despite the sweltering heat and the stifling humidity of the summer, around 500,000 people gathered on July 1, 2003 and marched from the commercial area of Causeway Bay to the business hub of Central to express their discontent. The reaction against the proposed law stunned the government and also led to a defection by the Liberal Party, one of its staunchest supporters in the legislature. As a result, the government lost the majority it needed to pass the national security bill. It then introduced a number of concessions on the scope of the proposed laws in an attempt to address the protestors' demands, and when that failed it shelved the bill indefinitely.

The 2003 protest was a monumental event in Hong Kong's constitutional history. One person who recognized its monumentality was Tammy Cheung, whom Ian Aitken and Michael Ingham call "the leading Hong Kong-resident documentary filmmaker" in their history of Hong Kong documentary film.[3] Cheung was born in Shanghai and grew up in Hong Kong. She learned the craft of documentary film making in Canada, and established the Chinese International Film Festival in Montreal while she was studying film at Concordia University. She started making documentaries not long after she returned to Hong Kong from her studies, and her work engages directly with

---

[1] See, Carole J. Petersen, "Introduction," in *National Security and Fundamental Freedoms: Hong Kong's Article 23 Under Scrutiny*, edited by Fu Hualing, Carole J. Petersen and Simon N. M. Young (Hong Kong: Hong Kong University Press, 2005), pp. 1–10 (p. 10).

[2] Angela Li, "Coalition Warns Article 23 Rules Will Create 'White Terror'," *South China Morning Post*, September 20th, 2002.

[3] Ian Aitken and Michael Ingham, *Hong Kong Documentary Film* (Edinburgh: Edinburgh University Press, 2014), pp. 185–186.

a wide range of social issues, including race, gender, education, old age, and the fight for democratic government.

Cheung was worried that, without a proper record, the events of July 1, 2003 would eventually fade away from collective memory. She therefore made her way to the march with three cameras and a small crew, and captured what happened that day on camera. The result is *July* (七月; 2004), which she describes as a "report" of what she saw at the protest site.[4] The film critic of the *Ming Pao Daily News* calls the documentary a "rare, independent testimony"[5] of the demonstration, and the *Hong Kong Economic Times* even predicts that it will in time become "proof of Hong Kong history."[6] The impulse to faithfully record history, to convey the impact of resistance, and to commit an event to cultural memory, raises interesting questions for the law-and-film scholar, as well as for scholars of Hong Kong constitutional law. What might it mean for a film to "report" or "bear testimony" to a constitutional controversy? How can it impart to the audience the sense of urgency that motivated demonstrators to take to the streets, or communicate the sense of togetherness that emerged at the event, or enable us to feel the energy that was in the air as the protestors marched side by side? In short, in what ways might film make a contribution to our understanding of the Article 23 controversy in a register different from that of history books or constitutional law scholarship? These are the questions which I will explore in this chapter.

In Section 5.1, I will provide an overview of the events that led to the 2003 protest. In Section 5.2, I will draw on the work of geographer Ben Anderson to develop a vocabulary for investigating, describing, and analyzing the atmosphere of the demonstration, or the sensorial dimension of being part of the movement. Moreover, I underscore how the demonstration consolidated and intensified a sense of Hong Kong identity amongst the participants, and I will delineate the connections between the act of protesting and sentiments about home and belonging. In Section 5.3, I offer a detailed analysis of *July* to consider how the film not only captures the atmosphere of protest, but co-opts its viewers as part of the movement by breaking down the divide between viewing and being viewed, observing and participating, and witnessing and belonging. I contend that the uniqueness of Cheung's film lies in the way it interpellates the audience as Hong Kongers by cinematographically bringing them into the fold of the community of protestors.

---

[4] Esther M. K. Cheung, Nicole Kempton, and Amy Lee, "Documenting Hong Kong: Interview with Tammy Cheung," in *Hong Kong Screenscapes: From the New Wave to the Digital Frontier*, edited by Esther M. K. Cheung, Gina Marchetti, and Tan See-kam (Hong Kong: Hong Kong University Press, 2011), pp. 151–165 (p. 155).

[5] "Witnessing the July 1 Protest Amongst the Crowds: the Independent Documentary Film 'July'," *Ming Pao Daily News*, December 29th, 2003.

[6] "July 1 Reappears in *July*," *Hong Kong Economic Times*, December 3rd, 2003.

5.1 The Law and Politics of Article 23

Article 23 of the Basic Law states that:

> The Hong Kong Special Administrative Region shall enact laws on its own to prohibit any act of treason, secession, sedition, subversion against the Central People's Government, or theft of state secrets, to prohibit foreign political organizations or bodies from conducting political activities in the Region, and to prohibit political organizations or bodies of the Region from establishing ties with foreign political organizations or bodies.[7]

There are three elements about Article 23 that are worth underscoring from the outset. First, even though it was described by both Hong Kong and mainland government officials, as well as the general public, as a provision on "national security," strictly speaking the provision concerns the criminalization of six inter-related, but distinct, activities: treason, secession, sedition, subversion, the theft of state secrets, and illicit activities by political organizations. Second, the obligation to enact laws protecting national safety is clearly stated in the Basic Law and is not externally imposed by either the post-handover local administration or the mainland authorities. Third, Article 23 clearly states that Hong Kong shall enact such laws "on its own." In other words, the wording of the relevant legislation, as well as the method and timing of its introduction, will be determined by the Hong Kong government without interference from across the border.

The Hong Kong government seriously mishandled the introduction of the bill for national security, and its misjudgment had grave consequences for the reception of the idea of national security laws in the territory. One way of understanding such consequences is through the metaphor of "walls of law" which Carol Jones has posited as a way of conceptualizing post-1997 Hong Kong law and politics. Jones contends that the constitutional order in Hong Kong is premised on the erection of figural "walls of law" that demarcate, separate, and protect the city from the mainland. She identifies the Sino-British Joint Declaration, the Bill of Rights, and the Basic Law, together with institutions such as the Court of Final Appeal as well as the idea of the rule of law itself, as legal ramparts that shield the city from the intrusion of mainland legal norms and practices. The walls of law are critical to ensure Hong Kong's autonomy and distinctiveness because they shield the city from China's authoritarian approach to law and order, despite the fact that it is under Chinese sovereignty.[8] Through an attentive reading of Chris Patten's political discourse, Jones further identifies Hong Kong's last governor as one of the key figures advancing this conception of the city as a *mondo juralis* protected by

---

[7] Article 23, *Basic Law of the Hong Kong Special Administrative Region of the People's Republic of China.*

[8] Carol A. G. Jones, *Lost in China? Law, Culture and Identity in Post-1997 Hong Kong* (Cambridge: Cambridge University Press, 2015), p. 41.

legal ramparts: she points out that iterations of terms such as "rule of law," "independent judiciary," "level playing field," and "fair and equitable treatment for everyone" in his public speeches contribute to promoting law as a "scaffolding" upon which not only the city's autonomy but its inhabitants sense of selfhood are built.[9] Crucially, these walls are not meant to be impervious. As Carole Petersen points out, the Basic Law establishes a number of necessary "connecting doors" between the legal systems of Hong Kong and China, such as Article 18 (which provides for the application of national laws through Annex III of the Basic Law) and Article 158 (which gives the National People's Congress Standing Committee the power of final interpretation of the constitutional document).[10] Article 23 clearly constitutes one of these connecting doors, insofar as it provides a constitutional basis for the proscription of activities that undermined the security not only of Hong Kong but of China as a whole. However, the Hong Kong authorities introduced the legislation at such a time, and in such a way, as to make it seem less like Petersen's connecting door and more like what Jones calls a "breach" in the walls of law, or a threat to the fundamental freedoms in Hong Kong that emanated from across the border. With "the grace of a battle tank at full throttle with guns blazing," the government made the criminalization of activities listed in Article 23 seem like an invasion from across the border.[11]

In terms of timing, Hong Kong in the first few years of the twenty-first century was marked by falling house prices, negative equity, and concerns about the lack of affordable housing. The mood was made worse by the health crisis triggered by the onset of the viral disease known as Severe Acute Respiratory Syndrome (SARS). Hundreds of people had to be isolated in their homes to prevent contagion, and many people died in the local hospitals. Moreover, in the background of the financial and public health problems was the simmering discontent at the slow pace of democratization which, as we will see in the next chapter, also gave rise to a rich set of cinematic engagements.[12] The overall public sentiment was therefore already marked by anxieties over politics, the economy, and the administration's ability to contain an epidemic. In addition to these more general factors, the government's decision to introduce the law specifically in late 2002 seemed less an autonomous decision than a reaction to an implied directive from China. As the veteran journalist Chris Yeung astutely observed, the issue suddenly became "top priority" for the Hong Kong government after Chinese President Jiang Zemin expressed a wish to see greater local efforts to safeguard national security in a speech at

---

[9] Jones, *Lost in China?* p. 42.   [10] Petersen, "Introduction," p. 16.

[11] Kevin Sinclair, "Focus on the Law, Not the Process," *South China Morning Post*, December 11th, 2002.

[12] For a helpful overview of the context, see Joseph Y. S. Cheng's introduction to *The July Protest Rally: Interpreting a Historic Event*, edited by Joseph Y. S. Cheng (Hong Kong: City University of Hong Kong Press, 2005), pp. 1–27.

the fifth anniversary of the handover.[13] The Hong Kong government's sudden enthusiasm for the law sharply contrasted with its "seemingly relaxed attitude" prior to President Jiang's speech. He urged the government to proceed carefully as Hong Kongers remained "hyper-sensitive" to any laws that threatened to blur the legal distinctions between the city and the mainland.

In terms of process, the Hong Kong government sparked concerns about the influence of the mainland by openly admitting that it was consulting the Chinese government on Article 23.The government usually conducts a public consultation to gather and incorporate societal views on its proposals on law and policy before proceeding to the drafting stage, but in this instance it added an extra step of speaking to Beijing about the legislation. A legislator wondered aloud how genuinely the local government was taking Hong Kongers' concerns about the law into consideration if it had "already consulted the Beijing government about it."[14] Martin Lee, a barrister and the chairman of the Democratic Party, expressed outrage that "a consensus had been reached with Beijing on both the timing and general principles of the proposed legislation before it was even finalised."[15] Such overt interactions between the local and the Chinese authorities deepened the impression that the "walls of law" have been breached, and that Beijing was directly influencing the drafting of laws which Hong Kong is constitutionally mandated to enact "on its own" under Article 23. As Lee starkly pointed out, "the most important point, which seems to have been missed by [the local government], is that the central government, or any other organ of power in the mainland, is not to be consulted at all."

Even though the Hong Kong government did conduct a local consultation exercise on the proposed legislation, the exercise actually had the effect of deepening the suspicion that new laws were a *fait accompli*. Not only did individual officials seem dismissive of criticism, but the consultation period of a mere three months suggested that the whole administration was merely going through the motions of consultation. There was also evidence that more critical responses to the legislative proposals were misclassified as "unclear" responses which the government could then discard. For instance, the Article 23 Concern Group, a pressure group comprising a number of prominent constitutional law and human rights experts, denounced the consultation as a "sham" when it discovered that its own "clear and unambiguous" submission against the proposals was placed in the "unclear" category.[16] The entire exercise seemed to confirm that the government did not care to hear the voices of opposition because they were not in accordance with the voices of the

---

[13] Chris Yeung, "Urgency Appears to Be the Watchword Where Once There Seemed No Rush," *South China Morning Post*, September 25th, 2002.

[14] Angela Li, "Beijing Views Sought on Subversion Law," *South China Morning Post*, September 10th, 2002.

[15] Martin Lee, "Why It Was Wrong to Consult Beijing on Article 23," *South China Morning Post*, November 13th, 2002.

[16] Ambrose Leung, "Consultation Profess Just a Sham, Says Pressure Group," *South China Morning Post*, January 30th, 2003.

Central authorities in whose shadow it operated. In the aftermath of the public consultation, one concerned Hong Kong resident speculated that the officials of the Special Administrative Region either had "something to hide" or was already "dancing to another's tune."[17]

In the months leading up to the protest, many Hong Kongers increasingly felt that their city was under siege, and that the way of life as they knew it, as well as the rights and freedoms which make it possible, would be severely undermined should the laws be passed. The Hong Kong Bar Association called the government's draft legislation "alarming," and the Human Rights Monitor issued a statement highlighting that it posed a "very serious threat" to freedom of speech in the territory.[18] In Westminster, British Members of Parliament raised concerns that the laws could contravene international human rights law and bring its former colony under the "heavy hand" of the Chinese authorities.[19] A local caller on a radio phone-in programme expressed the thoughts of many at the time: "I'm very frightened, very frightened."[20]

5.2 The Atmosphere of Protest

At the heart of the constitutional controversy about national security and the 2003 protest it sparked was the sense of a city under siege. By introducing its proposal at a particularly uneasy moment in Hong Kong society, and by attempting to push through legislation despite grave reservations within the territory, the Hong Kong government created the impression that the proposals in the national security bill constituted a "breach" in the "walls of law," or an intrusion from across the border which will undermine the rights and liberties setting the *mondo juralis* of Hong Kong apart from the rest of China. One concomitant effect of this conception of national security legislation is an intensification of the sense of Hong Kong identity amongst the protestors: since they imagined the territory as a place under attack, or a fort whose ramparts were about to be demolished, they came to regard themselves as a united group that was defending its city against "mainlandisation."[21] According to an *Economist* survey, it was around the time of the Article 23 controversy that the number of young people in Hong Kong who identified themselves as unequivocally "Chinese" began to fall.[22] Jones posits that "the

---

[17] John Shannon, "Calm People's Fears with White Bill," *South China Morning Post*, December 18th, 2002.

[18] Ambrose Leung, "Constitutional Crisis Fear Over Security Laws," *South China Morning Post*, December 10th, 2002.

[19] Marc Lopatin, "MPs Voice Rights Fears on Article 23 in a Westminster Debate," *South China Morning Post*, November 27, 2002.

[20] Chris Yeung, "Article 23 to Test Hong Kong's Autonomy," *South China Morning Post*, September 28th, 2002.

[21] Jones, pp. 10–17.

[22] "Almost Nobody in Hong Kong under 30 Identifies as 'Chinese'," *Economist*, August 26th, 2019.

[...] fight brought together otherwise disparate social groups in a common cause, defence of freedom and the rule of law."[23] Legal scholar Albert Chen also observes that the demonstration of 2003 "served to forge an identity for Hong Kong."[24] The *feeling* of solidarity, community, and belonging amongst the protestors is an integral, and some might even say definitive, part of the protest, but it has often been elided in the historical, legal, or even socio-legal analysis of Article 23, in part because it is so difficult to analyze: how does one even begin to articulate the *sense* of identity which arose and deepened in the course of the events in 2003? Through what vocabulary, register, or mode of examination can one investigate the ways in which the movement intersected with the coalescence of forms of selfhood? This section provides a framework of analysis through a close reading of descriptions of the event by some of the demonstrators in light of recent interdisciplinary work on atmosphere.

One point of entry is the observations of the journalist Luisa Tam. Tam writes: "Those who took part in the July 1 march must have felt an intense rush to be part of such an emotional solidarity movement, and been thrilled by the shared political participation."[25] Tam's description underscores that the sense of togetherness – that "shared" sense of participation in the common cause of defending one's home – arose from a series of affective associations: "the intense rush" of involvement, the "emotional" impact of a communal struggle, and the thrill of standing in unison with fellow Hong Kongers. Writing from a more academic standpoint, the sociologist Agnes Ku describes the protest as a "collective experience of catharsis," again indicating that the feeling of being a Hong Konger that arose from participation (a "collective experience") is primarily a sensorial rather than cognitive one ("catharsis").[26] The challenge, then, is to find an analytical register which adequately captures the affective charge in the *atmosphere* of the protest, that feeling of bondedness that defines participation.

Ben Anderson's work on atmosphere provides a helpful frame of analysis. Anderson begins by noting that atmospheres are "material phenomena, but their materiality is strange."[27] In other words, the affective forces of the atmosphere are emphatically real rather than imaginary. However, this materiality is strange because it is not easy to define its boundaries or pinpoint its nature; it "exceeds rational explanation and clear figuration." Anderson observes that atmosphere can be thought of as a "more" than the events, people, or objects of the material world; it can be thought of as an aura,

---

[23] Jones, p. 173.

[24] Albert Chen, "A Defining Moment in Hong Kong's History," *South China Morning Post*, July 4th, 2003

[25] Tam, *South China Morning Post*, July 8th, 2003.

[26] Agnes Ku, "Civil Society's Dual Impetus – Mobilizations, Representations and Contestations Over the July 1 March, 2003," in *Politics and Government in Hong Kong: Crisis under Chinese Sovereignty*, edited by Ming Sing (Abingdon: Routledge, 2009), pp. 38–58 (46).

[27] Ben Anderson, *Encountering Affect: Capacities, Apparatuses, Conditions* (Surrey: Ashgate, 2014), p. 140.

a mood, or an ambiance, and it is precisely this "more" which acts upon the participants and generates their sense of shared identity. Moreover, "atmospheres may emanate from bodies but they are not reducible to them": the intensity of affect comes from being in the same space as 500,000 other people, but it is more than the sum total of those bodies and so is not reducible to them.[28] Legal scholar Illan rua Wall describes such atmospheres as the "crowdness of the crowd," that powerful "ephemeral experience" of being in a political rally or social movement that is nonetheless not reducible to any tally of its participants or their acts.[29]

One reason why atmospheres are so analytically elusive is that they are "never still, static, or at rest."[30] Instead, they are "always forming and deforming, appearing and disappearing." In the context of the 2003 protest, one can say that the atmosphere varies depending on factors such as the precise location of the people, the time of the day, or the occurrences in the surroundings. Atmospheres are always "unfinished," they are "always in a process of emerging and transforming."[31] The co-existence, fluidity and flux of different atmospheres at an event like the 2003 protest means the overall effect or unity is a "precarious achievement"; in that it coalesces but eludes unproblematic linguistic capture or representation.[32]

Following Anderson, it is possible to think of the atmosphere of the 2003 protest as one of the forces creating that sense of Hong Kong identity. Terms like "catharsis," "rush," "emotional," and "thrilled" can be understood as attempts at grasping at that elusive intensity that touched the participants and gave them a feeling of common selfhood. Reading the reflections of the participants in light of Anderson's work, it is striking how consistently they attempted to convey the importance of the atmosphere of protest to the connection they felt, they had with the people around them. Writing about his own experience of events, the political commentator Ma Kit-wai notes:

> What I couldn't predict was that the July 1 protest gave rise to a new energy [...] It is as though you could feel that these strangers around you felt the same way as you, that they shared an identical anger as you [...] You felt that these were people who spoke in the same voice as you, a group of new Hong Kongers [...] These political heroes are not Martin Lee or the Lee Cheuk-yan [a legislator], but the nameless Hong Kongers who have come from all over.[33]

This is a passage that repays close scrutiny. For Ma, the galvanizing force of the protest is a "new energy" that can be said to form the atmosphere of the protest. Yet the linguistic label of "energy" does not quite succeed at grasping its true nature: the atmosphere is then described as more of a shared experience of

---

[28]   Anderson, *Encountering Affect*, p. 160.
[29]   Illan rua Wall, "The Law of Crowds," 36 *Legal Studies* (2016), 395–414 (409).
[30]   Wall, "The Law of Crowds," 141.   [31]   Wall, "The Law of Crowds," 145.
[32]   Wall, "The Law of Crowds," 159.
[33]   Ma Kit-wai, "The New Hong Kongers," *Ming Pao Daily News*, July 26th, 2003.

grievance, then as a common anger, and then as a common voice. The atmosphere is unassimilable into the mere physical presence of these "strangers" around the participant; it emanates from their presence but is not reducible to it. It is this ephemeral, elusive, amorphous intensity that forms his sensation of bondedness with all the other "nameless Hong Kongers." Ultimately, it was the force of this mood or aura that gave rise to the "new Hong Kongers," who shed the stereotype of the politically apathetic *homo economicus* concerned only about how much they make on the stock market to become "political heroes" fighting for their freedoms and their city. The July 1 protest turns out to be significant in the city's constitutional history not only because it was the first major mass demonstration since the handover, nor because of the legal or political salience of national security, but because it was an event that spoke directly to the *sense* of being part of a community of Hong Kongers. The recollections of another protestor echo Ma's observations:

> Today is the July 1 rally, and 500,000 people are on the streets. Everyone is very orderly, they brought their young and their elderly, we all felt the same way, and I was right there, I could feel the unity of Hong Kongers.[34]

The passage again underscores the link between the elusive, ephemeral, but nonetheless stirring atmosphere of the crowd and the formation of collective identity. The description starts with factual elements: the people, the date, the time. The register then shifts: "the unity of Hong Kongers" arose less from this matrix of facts and figures and more from the atmospheric force of being "right there" in the crowd; it is that sense of *thereness* that creates the sensation of common identity, or the communal "we" who "all felt the same way." The Chinese term in the passage for "we all felt the same way" is "萬眾一心," which literally means "ten thousand people, one heart." He *felt* as if everyone's heart was beating to the same rhythm, and it was this sensation that created the feeling of solidarity that so moved him.

It is with this communal "we" and with considerations of community, solidarity, and identity in mind that I now turn to *July*. As a "report" or a "testimony" of the 2003 protest, the film needs to present more than the statistical or more easily verifiable aspects of the event, such as the age, gender, or class of the people who took part or the duration of the march. To be a meaningful record, it needs to communicate the affective charge of the demonstration, to register the unique atmosphere of being in a crowd of 500,000 people on an almost unbearably hot summer's day, and to express the sense of identity arising from the belief that one is defending one's homeland against a breach in the walls of law. In other words, for *July* to function as a documentary of the 2003 protest, it needs to bring the viewers into the folds of the community of protestors, to interpellate them as part of the

[34] Anonymous, "That Day," *Hong Kong Economic Times*, July 7th, 2003.

march, to make them share that sense of being "right there" so that they, too, feel "the unity of the Hong Kongers."

5.3 Documenting a Constitutional Controversy

To document the protest, then, a film needs to provide not only a visual account of how it unfolded, but also a sense of how it felt to be there. To put the idea slightly differently, it needs to throw into question the distinction between observation and participation. Cheung, like the American documentarian Frederick Wiseman whom she names as one of her major stylistic influences, is known for an observational approach to documentary filmmaking, whereby a filmmaker supposedly observes and records events from behind the camera without directly intervening in their development. As Bill Nichols remarks in his classic work on documentary film, the observational mode of representation "hinges on the ability of the filmmaker to be unobtrusive."[35] The camera eye sees its subject like a "fly on the wall," without the filmmaker's explicatory exposition or interaction with the people being filmed, and it is this non-intervention which to a great extent allows us to "imagine the screen pulled away and direct encounter possible."[36] Yet as Nichols also emphasizes, the idea of a purely objective observational, and hence non-participatory, camera is an illusion: by creating shifts in time, location, or perspective through the editing process, the filmmaker can implicitly make known their position on the subject of the documentary. Gina Marchetti similarly points out that direct cinema like that of Wiseman can "go beyond witnessing to advocacy," and that Cheung's own sympathy for the 2003 movement is made "quite clear" through her selection and juxtaposition of images.[37] I contend that while there is little doubt that the vision of the demonstration which *July* presents to the audience is the filmmaker's own sympathetic one, the blurring of the distinction between observation and participation in the film goes beyond the conveyance of her perspective: it also develops a fuller, more multi-dimensional spectatorial position that actively brings viewers into the folds of the movement. In other words, *July* enacts what Stella Bruzzi calls a "pact" between documentary, reality, and the spectator by creating the filmic conditions for the audience to share the thrill of participation, the affective bonds of community, and the sense of belonging to Hong Kong that were at the core of the protest.[38]

One way in which this process of interpellation takes place is through Cheung's dynamic, but subtle, camera work. At times, the camera is placed

---

[35] Bill Nichols, *Representing Reality* (Bloomington: Indiana University Press, 1991), p. 39.
[36] Nichols, *Representing Reality,* p. 43.
[37] Gina Marchetti, "Hong Kong as Feminist Method: Gender, Sexuality, and Democracy in Two Documentaries by Tammy Cheung," in *Hong Kong Society in the New Millennium: Hong Kong as Method,* edited by Chu Yiu-wai (Singapore: Springer, 2017), pp. 59–77 (68–69).
[38] Stella Bruzzi, *New Documentary: A Critical Introduction,* 2nd ed. (Abingdon: Routledge, 2006), p. 6.

to the side of the demonstration; it could be on the sidewalk, next to an entrance as people move into an arena, or on the other side of a barricade. Such camera angle positions us in proximity with, but not within, the demonstration, and therefore as people who look on from the outside. At other times, the camera is placed squarely within the crowd, when the crew is marching along with the other protesters. In these instances, the camera positions us in the midst of the march and therefore as an integral part of the events that unfold. These unannounced shifts in the cinematic spatial position and point of view quietly bring us back and forth between a more purely visual experience of observation and the more sensorial experience of participation.

One segment in the film epitomizes such cinematographic effects. It takes place inside what appears to be a shopping complex in the busy commercial district of Causeway Bay. A giant screen hangs overhead, and the protestors are watching the rolling coverage of the demonstration on the news. They are therefore watching themselves in the television footage. In this segment, the camera is placed inside the crowd; we see not just the giant TV screen but the back of the heads of the people who are standing in front of the camera. Moreover, the lens is set at eye level and is tilted upwards, so that we are watching the reportage from the position of the participants. When the news anchor announces that a record number of people are taking part in the on-going march, a loud cheer breaks out and cheer seems to come from all sides at once because of the camera position. At one point in the TV footage, an on-site reporter stares confusedly at us because faulty reception prevents him from hearing the questions of the news anchor in the studio, and we can hear laughter coming from the people around us. A woman is so amused by the reporter's predicament that she claps her hands animatedly and jumps up and down. Since she is standing close to the camera she appears enlarged on our screen, thereby creating an impression of side-by-sideness with the viewers. The *mise-en-abyme* here simultaneously underscores the different subject positions in the film and interrogates the boundaries between them: the people on our screen are observers insofar as they are watching the news on their screen, but they are also participants insofar as what they are watching is footage of themselves. In terms of our own engagement, our gaze is simultaneously that of an observer observing the protesters observe themselves, and that of a participant positioned amongst them in this moment of looking, cheering, laughing, and community building. This segment captures the way in which *July* incessantly troubles the divide between here and there, between us and them, and between on screen and off screen.

The nature of a documentary like *July* thus also stands to be illuminated by the work of the film theorist Vivian Sobchack. Sobchack argues that cinema works not only visually, but by mobilizing all of our senses. Focusing on the opening scenes of Jane Campion's *The Piano* (1993), she details how her fingers registered what was happening on screen before her eyes were able to make out what was being shown. From this example, she contends that, as viewers, we respond to moving images not only through our eyes but through the "undifferentiated" senses of our entire body, and that a film can immerse our bodies in its world through an effective use of elements such as editing, sound, and close ups.[39] To phrase her idea slightly differently, an encounter with film potentially raises questions not only about what it means to "*look* at bodies" but to "*live* one's body."[40] With films that bring about this form of cinematic experience, the divide between the bodies on the screen and the bodies in the cinema becomes "vacillating" and "ambivalent."[41] Sobchack posits that the relationship between audience and film is characterized by "an irreducible and dynamic relation structure of reversibility and reciprocity" rather than by any absolute divisions.[42] Her phenomenological account underscores that our encounter with film is an "embodied" one that involves more than our visual capacities.[43] Her emphasis on the difference between "experiencing a movie" and "merely 'seeing' it" sheds light on *July* which, through its cinematography, not only shows the audience the events of 2003, but places them within the fold of the events.[44]

Three sequences, taken from the early, middle, and later parts of the film, serve as exemplary moments of the ways in which *July* reconfigures the distinction between audience and protestors. The first sequence plunges us into the demonstration by bringing us into confrontation with two men who are visibly angry with the protestors. While the public was overwhelmingly against the legislation, there remained those who were in favor of it.[45] The first man seems to think that all the demonstrators are traitors to the nation: "You are but flies, buzzing about over the heads of thirteen billion Chinese citizens. You dare dream of overthrowing China?!" He is so angry that his eyes pop and his veins are visible in the shot. The camera cuts to a young person who walks straight past as he speaks, and it becomes evident that this is a listless, rambling old man who is talking to himself in Victoria Park. However, we do not have a luxury of walking away from his tirade. We become his captive audience, and have to endure his scolding as he accuses us of being "shallow," "naïve," and "absurd." The second man blames his personal economic woes on the demonstrators, and berates them for jeopardizing the city's financial recovery. He seems to think that the protest will undermine the Hong Kong economy: "I'm telling you, I'm unemployed. Hong Kong's economy is just recovering. Why are you doing this? Why are you doing this??" As he speaks, he looks directly into the camera, creating the impression that he is chastising us directly. He then walks away, but, unable to contain his anger, he walks directly up to the

---

[39] Vivian Sobchack, *Carnal Thoughts: Embodiment and Moving Image Culture* (Berkeley: University of California Press, 2004), p. 75.
[40] Sobchack, *Carnal Thoughts,* p. 2.   [41] Sobchack, *Carnal Thoughts,* p. 73.
[42] Sobchack, *Carnal Thoughts,* p. 78.   [43] Sobchack, *Carnal Thoughts,* p. 3.
[44] Sobchack, *Carnal Thoughts,* p. 66.
[45] Klaudia Lee, "Most People Oppose Security Bill, Poll Shows," *South China Morning Post,* June 28th, 2003.

camera again. This time, he moves closer, so that his face is magnified on the screen. As he gesticulates indignantly, his hand appears right in front of our eyes. This form of direct address creates a feeling of uncomfortable proximity, as if this man was insisting on holding us personally responsible for his misfortune. We are the receivers of his angry glare at the end of the sequence, as well as of his lingering look of distain as he slowly takes his leave. From these first moments which address the audience directly, the film takes us out of the position of disinterested onlookers and brings us directly into the realm of the protest. The camera eye positions viewers as one of "us" in the demonstration, in contradistinction to an antagonistic and berating "them" outside of it.

In the second sequence, the protestors are waiting to enter Victoria Park, which is occupied to its maximum capacity and cannot accommodate any more people. The police have set up barricades, and they usher protestors to one side of these barricades in an attempt to maintain order. On the other side, one of the organizers of the protest is negotiating with several police officers over the pace of demonstrations. The crowd has been waiting to enter Victoria Park for a long time, and tempers are getting short. There is clearly a feeling of agitation in the air. In the first part of the sequence, the camera is placed on the sidewalk, filming the demonstration from the side as the participants file past. Cheung does little to hide the presence of the crew: many of the protestors walking past stare curiously at the camera, and some of them wave and smile. At one point, a man and his son strike a pose by putting their arms around each other and making a "V" sign with their hands. The participants are aware of the camera's presence, and that someone who is not taking an active part in the march is filming them. Their acts and gestures consciously directed at the camera lens remind us that we are external observers to the events. A second shot, taken from a point above the crowd, shows the scale of the march and conveys how congested the streets had become by the afternoon. By giving us a view in a shot could not have been taken by someone positioned within the march itself, it again reinforces the status of the audience as external observers. Moreover, by showing the sheer size of the crowd that has to remain bottlenecked on the street until the police give the signal to continue, the shot also suggests just how jittery everyone is becoming.

With the next shot, we are suddenly placed in the middle of the march. The change in point of view creates an immediate sense of immersion in the on-screen world. The shot is taken from the protestors' side of the barricade, and we witness the organizer's conversation with the police. From that perspective, we are positioned close to the metal barriers, and side by side with numerous other demonstrators. The camera then cuts rapidly to capture the reactions of various people in the crowd. These rapid cuts, with each shot capturing the reaction of a different person, mimic what we would have seen if we had been turning our heads in the middle of the street. One person repeatedly yells "I've been waiting for three hours!"; another laments "It's all blocked over there!"; a police officer implores "Don't go backwards, it's against the regulations!";

a man wearing a black t-shirt angrily says "These communists! They won't tolerate anti-government protestors like us!"; an old man wails "I'm thirsty and I need to pee!." At one point, a jovial young man with glasses and a big smile on his face jokingly says "I bet you anything that even if we had 400,000 people here, the official figures are going to state that only 20,000 came!." Amidst these reactions, we can hear cries of "No Article 23!." These reactions, from people who have been waiting for hours in the summer heat, are constitutive of the atmosphere of protest, and their compilation and juxtaposition in the film create the impression that these are voices from across different segments of Hong Kong society – from men and women, the young and the old, the cantankerous and the cheerful – that are finally making themselves heard through the demonstration. Towards the end of the segment there is a sudden cheer, as the road becomes unblocked and people start moving towards Victoria Park again. Since sound editing is kept to a minimum, the voices close to the camera are louder while those further away are fainter, just as they would have been at the scene of the demonstrations. Moreover, as the camera cuts amongst different parts of the crowd, its distance from the protestors changes: sometimes it zooms in on them so that they become larger on the screen, and at other times it zooms out so that they seem further away. The camera is tilted at times, so that we see the demonstrators at an incline in a number of shots. The camera movements combine to bring across the sensorial mixture of chaos, frustration, but also laughter and exhilaration that form the ambiance on the streets at that point in the protest.

In the third sequence, the march reaches Hong Kong's Central Business District. Night has fallen, and one of the organizers stands on a bridge and looks on as wave after wave of protestors come pouring into the city center with their anti-government and anti-national security legislation placards. In this sequence, our spectatorial position is further complicated. In the first few shots, the camera is placed behind the organizer as he surveys the scene from a bridge. We therefore adopt the point of view of someone leading the protest and directing the mood of the crowd; when he says "Please give a round of applause to yourselves!," a cheer predictably rings out. As the demonstrators flow in, euphoric and triumphant from a turnout that far surpassed their own expectations, they resemble what Bill Nichols calls "agents of history" who have all played a part in changing the course of Hong Kong's constitutional development and in defending the city against the erosion of its liberties. The point of view then shifts, and in the next few shots the camera is positioned at street level. However, unlike in the previous sequences, the camera is placed in front, and at times to the side of, the incoming crowd. In that more tangential position to the demonstrators, the camera appears to be documenting the protest in a more detached manner. Yet by this point, the success of the movement is so apparent that even this more observational mode seems to be inflected by the rapturous atmosphere: we hear laughing, cheering, and shouts of encouragement, and we also hear someone excitedly proclaim that together we have succeeded in "turning over a new leaf in Hong Kong history."

The point of view then shifts again, back to that of the protestors. As the procession moves towards Hong Kong's iconic Legislative Council Building, we see the core message of the demonstration reflected in its placards: "Protect Human Rights, Love Freedom," "Article 23 = Fear and Silence," and also "We Love Hong Kong! No to Article 23!." The final slogan, repeated several times by the crowd, underscores the link between identity and resistance to the new legislation: in the eyes of the protestors, having an affective attachment to the territory as one's home meant protecting it from the intrusion which the national security bill represented. The music further reinforces their sense of identity: the anti-government slogans are set to the tune of Anita Mui's "Dr IQ" and Leslie Cheung's "Monica," both of which are well known to Hong Kongers but would have presumably been unfamiliar to people who did not grow up amidst the territory's pop culture. The camera shows the protestors singing along to the tunes as they marched. The cheering, the slogans, the applause, the music, and the shouts of encouragement combine to create the exuberant atmosphere of the latter part of the demonstration, which the film capture and convey to the audience through its cinematography.

5.4 Conclusion

The constitutional controversy over Article 23 led to a strong public reaction in Hong Kong and brought 500,000 people onto the streets in protest. The very idea of national security came to be construed by many Hong Kongers as a threat to their fundamental rights, and fueled suspicions that Beijing intended to use the laws which the government was proposing as a pretext for extending its control over Hong Kong. In face of fierce societal opposition, the government backed down and shelved its plans for legislation. At the time of writing, the government has still not attempted to re-open the issue. Cheung's documentary provides a valuable record of the 2003 protest, and conveys a sense of the fears, passions, and affective attachments that were interwoven into demonstration.

Yet the government's inaction does not mean that fears have subsided. Moreover, the demonstration, which succeeded in making the local administration withdraw the proposed legislation, also had the impact of making Beijing tighten its overall grip on Hong Kong: Chinese leaders responded to what they regarded as the destabilizing forces of protest by emphasizing "more central government engagement and involvement in Hong Kong's political development" and by placing more weight on "One Country" over "Two Systems."[46] In this light, the movement perhaps had the paradoxical effect of placing the need

---

[46] Jie Cheng, "The Story of a New Policy," 15 *Hong Kong Journal* (July 2009) www.hkbasiclaw.com/ Hong%20Kong%20Journal/Cheng%20Jie%20article.htm.

for national security laws in Hong Kong more firmly on the mainland's agenda. Even though Article 23 does not specify a timetable for legislation, it does impose an unequivocal constitutional duty on the local government to pass the necessary laws at some point. The issue of national security lingers, and periodically erupts into Hong Kong's political discourse. In the aftermath of Occupy Central, a deputy to the National People's Congress re-ignited the controversy by suggesting that if Hong Kong did not show a commitment to legislate on its own, then China should impose its own, tougher, laws on the city.[47] He even noted that he would try to table a motion in the National People's Congress for the mainland's laws on national security to apply to Hong Kong. His remarks brought to the surface anxieties that have been latent since 2003. These anxieties became reflected in *Extras*, the short film directed by Kwok Zune which opens the anthology film *Ten Years* (2015) with which I began this study.

In *Extras*, a group of mainland Chinese and pro-Beijing local politicians conspire to stage a terrorist attack. Their plan is to plant two "terrorists" in a public event to murder two local politicians; if the public can be made to believe that terrorists are threatening the safety of Hong Kongers, then public support for the law will surge. The "extras" in the title of the film are the two men who have been hired to carry out the attack. They agree to carry out the assassination to make some quick money, but in the end they both are shot by the police in the course of the attack. The meeting of the conspirators is headed by a mainland Chinese official, whose ethnicity is foregrounded by his Chairman Mao-style suit and his use of Mandarin. Their initial plan was to kill only one of the politicians. When deliberating over which of the two politicians to kill, the group leader says: "we need to create panic [. . .] so tell me, who should we kill to generate a bigger reaction?" The plan changes when he receives instructions from the Chinese government's Liaison Office to assassinate both politicians; after he puts his phone back in his pocket, he walks into the meeting room again and he explains to his fellow conspirators that taking out both politicians is a wiser course of action because it will "create as much chaos in Hong Kong as possible, and to instill as much fear in Hong Kongers as possible." He also reminds the group that they will be rewarded when the laws are successfully passed. The ending suggests that the plan is a success; the film closes with excerpts from the news coverage of the attack, in which the Liaison Office states that it has become imperative to enact national security legislation as soon as possible.

Like the other parts of *Ten Years*, this short film, in which mainland and local officials are imagined to meet in secret to plot assassinations and create disorder in the territory, is crudely hyperbolic, and its portrayal of mainland Chinese officials is unabashedly caricatured. Yet this crude, hyperbolic, and

---

[47] Jeffie Lam, "National People's Congress Deputy Stanley Ng Renews Calls to Enact Hong Kong National Security Law," *South China Morning Post*, January 22nd, 2015.

caricatured imagination of events speaks precisely to the fears about the breach in the walls of law which have become part of the way in which national security is understood in Hong Kong. In *Extras*, the walls have crumbled and the destruction of Hong Kong's liberties are planned and executed within the city's legal and physical boundaries. The film's imagination of the lengths to which China will go to enact the law, and of the self-interest, corruption, and underhanded maneuvers associated with the people involved in the conspiracy, reflects deep-seated anxieties about the breakdown of the *mondo juralis* without which a distinctive Hong Kong identity would not be possible. From *July* in 2003 to *Extras* in 2016, Hong Kong cinema has reminded us that the apprehension and even dread surrounding national security controversy has not lessened, and that the issue will likely become more, not less, volatile as we move towards the inevitable moment of legislation.

6

Choosing the Leader:
Chief Executive Elections and Hong Kong Gangster Films

The selection of Hong Kong's leader, the Chief Executive, constitutes one of the most important and longstanding constitutional controversies in the city. On the one hand, many Hong Kongers demand a democratic electoral system that will allow them to choose their own leader; but on the other, the mainland Chinese government insists on a framework in which only those who are loyal to it may be elected to run the city. In other words, Hong Kong's demand for genuine universal suffrage is in tension with Beijing's insistence on a selection mechanism dominated by a limited group of electors. At the core of the debate over elections is the question of the extent to which mainland China can exert political control over Hong Kong: if only someone acceptable to the Chinese government is allowed to become the city's leader, then one needs to ask how much say Hong Kong actually has over its internal affairs. Moreover, the promise of universal suffrage is a core part of "One Country, Two Systems," and attempts by the mainland Chinese or Hong Kong government to limit local democratic development quickly become perceived as political tactics to push Hong Kong towards the single-party system in the mainland, and hence as a threat to the territory's autonomy and pluralistic way of life. Between 2004 and 2014, the Standing Committee of China's National People's Congress, or the NPCSC, handed down an Interpretation and a series of Decisions that progressively tightened Beijing's control over the outcome of Chief Executive elections. How its top official is to be chosen constitutes one of the most difficult legal and political questions in postcolonial Hong Kong. Ultimately, it was the impasse over electoral reform that led to the Occupy Central movement.

Given its centrality, it is unsurprising that the question also has great cultural import. References to electoral reform abound in radio talk shows, television programmes, and satirical theatre, but it arguably receives the most sustained cultural engagement in the Hong Kong's gangster or "triad" films.[1]

---

[1] For an examination of the treatment of the question of electoral reform in Hong Kong theatre, see Marco Wan, "A Ghost Story: Electoral Reform and Hong Kong Popular Theatre," in *Administering Interpretation: Derrida, Agamben, and the Political Theology of Law*, edited by Peter Goodrich and Michel Rosenfeld (New York: Fordham University Press, 2019), pp. 272–290.

A triad is a branch of an organized crime syndicate that supposedly originated in Ancient China as a secret society rebelling against the Qing government, and triad films constitute an immensely popular genre amongst local and international film-goers. Scholars of U.S. film history have demonstrated that American gangster films are intertwined with legal concerns. For instance, Ron Wilson has shown that many U.S. gangster film narratives "originate from [...] true-crime narratives of newspapers and tabloid publications," and Jonathan Munby has posited that the classic gangster films of the 1930s such as *Little Caesar* (1930), *The Public Enemy* (1931), and *Scarface* (1932) can be understood as dramatizations of ongoing tensions about core constitutional issues like racial equality and citizenship.[2] In this chapter, I take my cue from scholars such as Wilson and Munby to argue that triad films in post-handover Hong Kong can be understood as a genre that consciously engages with the law and politics of Chief Executive elections. In Johnnie To's *Election* (黑社會; 2005), for instance, a police officer jokingly says to his colleague that "the triad was electing its leader way before we started electing our Chief Executive," and such seemingly throwaway lines signal a self-awareness of the interpenetration between popular culture and constitutional law. By refracting the process of leadership selection in Hong Kong society through the process of leadership selection in the criminal underworld, triad films explore what Martha Nochimson calls the "dark side" of a key constitutional controversy.[3]

In Section 6.1, I examine the reactions which the NPCSC's pronouncements on Chief Executive elections generated in Hong Kong. Part of these reactions arose in the world of cinema, and in Section 6.2 I explore how a group of triad films incorporated the terms and structures of the public discourse about elections into their narratives. As film scholars have long noted, gangster films are an inherently violent genre, yet there has been relatively little discussion of the relationship between on-screen depictions of violence and the law in the Hong Kong context.[4] In Section 6.3, I offer a detailed analysis of an iconic triad film, Herman Yau's *The Mobfathers* (選老頂; 2016), in light of the writings of the jurist Robert Cover to consider the relationship between the law of elections and filmic representations of violence. Through an examination of disputes over the electoral system, as well as the films that have emerged in their wake, I hope to show how a distinctively Hong Kong genre registers the sense of helplessness, frustration, and anger that many Hong Kongers felt about their inability to choose their own leader.

---

[2] Ron Wilson, *The Gangster Film: Fatal Success in American Cinema* (New York: Wallflower Press, 2015), p. 3 and Jonathan Munby, *Public Enemies, Public Heroes: Screening the Gangster from* Little Caesar *to* Touch of Evil (Chicago: University Of Chicago Press, 1999), p. 27.

[3] Martha Nochimson, *Dying to Belong: Gangster Movies in Hollywood and Hong Kong* (Malden: Blackwell, 2007).

[4] For discussions of representations of violence in U.S. cinema, see *Screening Violence*, edited by Stephen Prince (New Brunswick: Rutgers University Press, 2000) and *Violence and American Cinema*, edited by J. David Slocum (New York: Routledge, 2001), pp. 1–37.

6.1 China's Tightening Grip

The controversy over how Hong Kong's Chief Executive should be chosen began in the 1980s, not long after it became clear that colonial rule would come to an end, but it intensified in the first decade and a half of the twenty-first century. One reason for the intensification is the interventions by the NPCSC through which Beijing asserted increasing control over the territory's electoral process. To understand the complexities of the election controversy, as well as the cinematic responses to them, it is necessary to begin with the Basic Law's provisions relating to the methods for selecting the Chief Executive. The key provisions are Article 45, which sets out broad guidelines for post-handover arrangements, and Article 7 of Annex I, which stipulates how the method of leadership selection after 2007 can be amended. Hong Kong was not a democracy when it was returned to China in 1997, but the wording of its constitutional document suggests that the drafters envisaged a slow but steady evolution into a democratic regime after the handover: Article 45 states that the "ultimate aim" is for Hong Kongers to elect their leader based on "universal suffrage." In other words, the Basic Law explicitly provides for democratic elections. To prevent disruptions to the political system, the transition is to be based on "the principle of gradual and orderly progress" and be "specified in light of the actual situation" of the city. As the city moves towards democracy, the method for choosing the Chief Executive will need to be amended. The text of Annex I, Article 7 stipulates a three-step procedure for such amendments: proposed changes need to (i) "be made with the endorsement of a two-thirds majority of all the members of the Legislative Council," (ii) secure "the consent of the Chief Executive," and (iii) "be reported to National People's Congress Standing Committee for approval."

There are three contentious, and overlapping, areas relating to the electoral framework that converge on the meaning of Article 45 and Annex I, Article 7: (i) the pace of democratization; (ii) the qualities required of the Chief Executive; and (iii) the role of the nominating committee which vets the candidates running for the top office. In each of these areas, Beijing tightened its grip on the selection mechanism through the NPCSC. Let us take these areas one by one.

First, the pace of democratization. In 2004, the NPCSC issued an Interpretation of Annex I, Article 7 which significantly increased its influence over the pace of democratization in Hong Kong. The Interpretation states that before the Hong Kong government proposes any amendments that could further democratize Hong Kong, the Chief Executive "shall make a report to the standing committee of the National People's Congress as regards whether there is a need to make an amendment," and that the NPCSC shall "make a determination" as to whether such an amendment is necessary.[5] As a number

---

[5] *The Interpretation by the Standing Committee of the National People's Congress of Article 7 of Annex I and Article III of Annex II to the Basic Law of the Hong Kong Special Administrative Region of the People's Republic Of China, Paragraph Three (April 6th, 2004).*

of commentators noted at the time, the 2004 Interpretation turned the amendment procedure from a "three-step" process in the Basic Law to a new "five-step" process.[6] For an amendment on elections to pass after 2004, (i) the Chief Executive had to make a report to the NPCSC, (ii) the NPCSC would then make a determination as to whether the amendment was necessary, (iii) the proposed amendment had to receive the support of two-thirds majority in the Legislative Council, (iv) it had to receive the consent of the Chief Executive, and (v) it had to be reported to the NPCSC for approval. Only the last three steps are in the text of the Annex; by adding the first two steps, Beijing gave itself a determinative and even final say on when, if ever, Hong Kong could become fully democratic that was not provided for in the wording of the constitutional document. Moreover, by stating that it will make a determination under step two in accordance with "the principle of gradual and orderly progress" and "in light of the actual situation" in the territory, the NPCSC made explicit its intention to exercise its power as the ultimate arbiter of the meaning of Article 45 rather than leave that role to the local courts. In the Decision handed down the same year, the NPCSC stated that the next election, in 2007, would not be by universal suffrage.[7]

The Interpretation and Decision of 2004 generated a strong reaction in Hong Kong. For some, they merely restated the powers which mainland China always had over the city: as a delegate to the Chinese People's Political Consultative Conference put it, "from the very beginning" these were already "the rules of the game."[8] For others, however, Beijing's high profile intervention was a naked attempt to screen out candidates it deemed undesirable because it was worried, some might say paranoid, that a fully democratic system could lead to the rise of "someone with foreign ties" or who held "hostile views" against the Central government.[9] The veteran political commentator Chris Yeung observed that many Hong Kongers felt "disappointed, angry and helpless about the Decision and the way it was made."[10] The editorial of the *Ming Pao Daily News* expressed the local reaction in more emotive language when it lamented that the Interpretation "shattered Hong Kongers' 'Dream of Universal Suffrage'."[11] Since the NPCSC Decision made clear that there will be no universal suffrage in 2007, those who tried to

---

[6] See, for instance, "Hong Kong Now Needs to Play a More Sophisticated Game," *South China Morning Post*, April 7th, 2004 and Fan Chong-lau, "A Political Reform Decision Where the Costs Outweigh the Benefits," *Hong Kong Economic Journal*, April 30th, 2004.

[7] *Decision of the Standing Committee of the National People's Congress on Issues Relating to the Methods for Selecting the Chief Executive of the Hong Kong Special Administrative Region in the Year 2007 for Forming the Legislative Counsel of the Hong Kong Special Administrative Region in the Year 2008 (April 26th, 2004).*

[8] Lai Nai-keung, "Welcome Beijing's Initiative," *South China Morning Post*, March 30th, 2004.

[9] Wong Chuk-kei and Tsang Shu-kei, "Conceptual Changes in the Post-Interpretation Era," *Hong Kong Economic Journal*, April 17th, 2004.

[10] Chris Yeung, "Decision Makes a Mockery of the Promises to Consult the Public," *South China Morning Post*, April 27th, 2004.

[11] Ming Pao Journalists, *Ming Pao Daily News*, April 29th, 2004.

move on from the disappointments of 2004 pinned their hopes on the election two terms down the track, in 2012. However, they were again disappointed when the NPCSC handed down a Decision in 2007: in that Decision, the Standing Committee ruled out universal suffrage for 2012. It also equivocated on whether democratic elections would be possible in 2017 by stating that the Chief Executive election that year "may" – not "shall" or "will" – be conducted by universal suffrage that year. One respected politician started wondering whether he would see democratic elections in his lifetime,[12] while another observer lamented that Beijing would not allow genuinely democratic elections because it was "still worried that Hong Kongers would pick someone anti-China" to be their leader.[13] As the horizon of democratic elections moved further and further away, from 2004 to 2007, then from 2007 to 2012, and finally from 2012 to 2017, worries about Beijing's control over the leadership selection process mounted, as did doubts about the sincerity of its promise to maintain a high degree of autonomy in Hong Kong.

The second contentious area concerned disputes over the necessary qualities of candidates running for election. The Standing Committee's 2014 Decision states that Beijing will only appoint someone "who loves the country and loves Hong Kong."[14] In other words, China will only allow 'patriots" to lead Hong Kong, and anyone who holds political beliefs that diverge from those of the Central government will be screened out. The imperative to "love the motherland" which, as we saw in Chapter 1, emerged in the 1980s, had become a basic requirement for public office by 2014. While Deng Xiaoping had noted at the time of the Sino-British negotiations that Hong Kong's top officials had to be patriots, the stark insistence on patriotism as a prerequisite in the Decision still came as a shock to many people.[15] As legal scholar Surya Deva warned, the stipulation in the 2014 Decision meant that Beijing wanted nothing more than "a dummy chief executive" who would neither criticize nor question the mainland Chinese government.[16]

The third contentious issue concerns the nominating committee. Article 45 provides for a mechanism whereby a committee nominates candidates to run in the election, and Hong Kongers then elect one of the nominated candidates through universal suffrage. In the interim period between the handover and the envisaged achievement of universal suffrage, the Chief Executive is elected

[12] Lo Man-see and Yeung Hui-fung, "Szeto Wah, Who Will Be 86 in Ten Years: "I Don't Expect to See Universal Suffrage in My Lifetime," *Ming Pao Daily News*, December 30th, 2007.

[13] Sek Kei, "Another Ten Years Is too Long," *Ming Pao Daily News*, December 30th, 2007.

[14] *Decision of the Standing Committee of the National People's Congress on Issues Relating to the Selection of the Chief Executive of the Hong Kong Special Administrative Region by Universal Suffrage and on the Method for Forming the Legislative Council of the Hong Kong Special Administrative Region in the Year 2016 (August 31st, 2014).*

[15] Deng Xiaoping, "One Country, Two Systems" (June 22nd–23rd, 1984), in *Deng Xiaoping on the Question of Hong Kong*, pp. 6–12 (11).

[16] Surya Deva, "Hong Kongers Will Not Accept Beijing's Idea of a Patriot," *South China Morning Post*, August 26th, 2014.

by members of an Election Committee.[17] The Basic Law explicitly stipulates that the nominating committee has to be "broadly representative" so that views from different strata of Hong Kong society are represented in the nomination process. The inclusion of a nominating committee in the drafting of Article 45 was meant to be a compromise between mainland Chinese oversight and Hong Kong autonomy: Beijing would have some degree of influence over the candidates running for local election through the committee, but the influence would be counterbalanced by the fact that the committee is representative enough to include members who do not necessarily see eye-to-eye with Beijing. For many years, there has been simmering discontent over the composition of the nominating (and election) committee. Critics have long noted that, despite the wording of the Basic Law, the committee structure entrenches a "small-circle election" which excludes the majority of the population from the leadership selection process.[18] The committee was expanded from its initial 800 members to 1,200 members in 2010, but in the eyes of critics this hardly addressed the democratic deficit in a city of over seven million people.

When democracy did come to Hong Kong, it came in a much diluted form and therefore as a disaster. The 2014 Decision reiterated that Hong Kong may have universal suffrage in 2017, in the sense that Hong Kongers would all have a vote in the electoral process. However, it also stipulated that the nominating committee could nominate no more than two to three candidates to run for Chief Executive, and crucially, that all candidates must have the endorsement of more than half of the nominating committee.[19] Given the large number of pro-Beijing members on this committee, such a high nomination threshold meant that candidates who were not supported by the Chinese government would effectively be ruled out, even if they had wide support from the local Hong Kong electorate.

In the local Chinese-language press, the Decision was frequently described as effectively "lowering the gates" on Chief Executive election: the high nomination threshold, the limited number of nominating committee members, and the small number of candidates allowed collectively constituted three "gates" that barred anyone not favored by Beijing from running for the post.[20] The 2014 Decision therefore worsened the problem of small-circle elections by drastically restricting the range of their possible outcomes. By imposing severe constraints on Hong Kongers' ability to choose the Chief Executive, the Decision came across as a means of curtailing Hong Kong's autonomy, and the anger in the city was palpable. In the words of one commentator: "I don't

---

[17] Article 1, Annex I: Method for the Selection of the Chief Executive of the Hong Kong Special Administration Region, *Basic Law of the Hong Kong Special Administrative Region of the People's Republic of China*.

[18] Nikki Sun, "1,000 March In Protest Against Small-Circle Vote on Eve of Hong Kong Leadership Election," *South China Morning Post*, March 25th, 2017.

[19] *Standing Committee 2014 Decision*.

[20] "National Congress Lowers Gate on Political Reform; Democrats Furious," *Hong Kong Economic Journal*, September 1st, 2014.

even want my vote. [...] What's the point of voting if I can only choose between Lackey A and Lackey B?"[21] Another political commentator similarly observed that the requirement that the Decision "filled people's hearts" with "anger, despondence, despair."[22] As we will see, some of the sentiments became registered in the triad films of the period.

6.2 Screening Elections

One of the most notable aspects of post-handover triad films is the narrative structure many of them share. They depict the crime syndicate as an organization with leadership changes at periodic intervals, and as the story opens the time has come for a new leader to be chosen. A Council of triad elders, evoking the nominating committee, comes together to decide who the new leader will be, and no one else in the syndicate has any say in the selection process. The Council's decision is then contested by key triad members who are excluded from the committee, in a narrative that reflects the territory's widespread discontent with the restrictive electoral process. While the exact resolution of the conflict between political control and individual choice varies, the films' endings all tend to entrench a system in which the outcome is dictated by a small number of electors.

Johnnie To's *Election* (2005) provides an illuminating instance of the portrayal of the nominating committee in the form of the Council of elders. By setting the Council meeting in a poorly lit apartment, the film conveys the idea that the leadership decision is made in the shadows. The meeting is presided by Old Teng, the patriarch of the crime syndicate, and as the elders discuss the merits of their preferred candidates the camera zooms in on him pouring tea. The film portrays tea drinking as a communal experience within the Council, or a process through which the members bond and overcome their differences. As Old Teng sips his tea, he observes that the method of choosing a leader on the basis of a decision by the senior members of the syndicate, rather than through open or democratic procedures involving the whole triad community, has been in place since he was a young man, thereby underscoring that this is a time-honored way of guaranteeing the continued stability and success of the organization. This closed-door process appears to be blessed by the Chinese deities for good fortune, whose statues are prominently displayed at the center of the shot. Through its visual cues and its dialogue, *Election* seems to suggest that a system whereby a small group makes succession decisions, without the input of the wider populace, is aligned with furthering "stability," "social harmony," and "prosperity," goals which are repeatedly emphasized by the Chinese authorities and which they evidently regard as being at risk of being undermined if a candidate which Beijing could not control were to emerge as

[21] Chan Sik-chi, "I Don't Want This Vote," *Ming Pao Daily News*, September 2nd, 2014.
[22] Leung Mei-yee, "Time to Wake Up," *Ming Pao Daily News*, September 4th, 2014.

Hong Kong's leader.[23] However, the sequel to *Election* complicates this cinematic depiction of the electoral process. In *Election 2* (黑社會:以和爲貴; 2006), the Council is portrayed as being increasingly out of touch with the needs of the syndicate. In that film, the Council generates resentment within the triad community and brings about its own demise, first by forcing someone with no desire to become triad leader to occupy the position, and second by being completely unresponsive to the other members who are eyeing the top position. In the sequel, it is to a great extent the Council's insistence on selecting the triad leader on their own, behind closed doors, that causes a loss of stability, harmony, and prosperity. The director has underscored that the two films are meant to be approached as a single unfolding of events, and that he needed "more than two hours to finish telling the story." The combined narratives of the two films suggests that a mechanism restricting the process of choosing a leader to a small circle of electors is ultimately not a viable one.

Herman Yau's *The Mobfathers* (2016) registers Hong Kongers' frustration with the restrictive electoral framework the NPCSC imposed on the city even more explicitly. The Council meeting, convened by the Mobfather, again takes place in the shadows, this time in the private room of a nightclub run by the syndicate. Terms that make reference to the election controversy are interspersed in the dialogue: the Mobfather himself refers to the Council as the "nominating committee," a candidate questions whether the elders have "lowered the gates" on him, and, in a parodic reference to the language of patriotism in the 2014 NPCSC Decision, the Mobfather notes that the new triad leader can be a "schmuck" as long as he "loves the syndicate and loves us."

A triad member named "Chuck" decides to run in the election for the head of the organization. When he first expresses his interest in running to the elders, the Mobfather tells him starkly: "Only we can decide who can be candidates in this election. It is not up for you to say." Later on, an increasingly disgruntled Chuck challenges the system by pointing out its lack of representation in front of the entire crime syndicate. Addressing his fellow triad members, he says:

> Don't you all see that there is a problem? There are so many of us in the organization. Why is it that so few people have the right to vote for the next Mobfather? [. . .] We should all have the right to vote! [. . .] My brothers, the new Mobfather can directly affect the interests of every single one of us. How can it be that none of us have a vote when it comes to deciding who he will be? I'm asking you now: do you want the right to vote?

The film's references to the election controversy can be heavy-handed and even crude at times, as they seem to be in this instance, but they are all the more

---

[23] See, for instance, "The Practice of the 'One Country, Two Systems' Policy in the Hong Kong Special Administrative Region" issued by the Information Office of the State Council (June10th, 2014).

unmistakable for being so. Through its critique of the leadership selection mechanism in the criminal underworld, Yau's film not only comments directly on the problems with the Hong Kong electoral system, but articulates the widespread dissatisfaction and frustration with Beijing's interventions. At the end of the sequence, the entire syndicate is clamoring for the right to vote, and the camera slowly pans to show a room of triad members shouting "I want a vote! I want a vote!." In a line that references the mounting anger towards the unrepresentative nature of the real-life electoral system, Chuck says to the Mobfather: "You can reject me, but can you reject the times?." Given the reaction of the triad members, the Mobfather has no choice but to announce that the system will be changed, and that the next triad leader will be elected through a system of "one person, one vote."

The narrative is told from Chuck's point of view, such that the audience is led to believe, along with Chuck, that the system has truly changed: in a voiceover, Chuck proudly says to the viewers: "I think I changed history." However, the reform turns out to be illusory, because of the Mobfather's secret maneuvers to turn an otherwise orderly election into a violent contest. He arranges the murder of Chuck's wife, knowing that Chuck will assume that the culprit is Wolf, the other contender in the election. Devastated by the death of his wife, Chuck vows revenge and starts a bloody gang fight against Wolf and his supporters. As the Mobfather accurately predicts, both Chuck and Wolf perish in the fight. Everything unfolds according to the Mobfather's master-plan. When asked what he will do now that both contenders for the position of triad leader are dead, the Mobfather smiles and says "*I* will become the triad leader." The earlier promise of "one person one vote" is an empty one, and he never intended to hand over the reins to any of the candidates. The Mobfather's ruses in Yau's film can be read as a reflection of the view that China will never relinquish control over Hong Kong, and that its promises of democracy are empty.

Daniel Chan's *Triad* (紮職; 2012) constitutes another instance of how Hong Kong gangster films form part of the cultural imaginary of how elections are conducted in the city. In that film, the elders arrange to have the contenders murdered so that they can install someone more obedient to them as the new triad leader. The determinative role of the elders is only revealed in the final sequence: they are playing the Chinese gambling game of mahjong, and one of them says: "These youngsters all talk about change. If we allow change to happen, then what will happen to us? Don't be stupid!" *Triad* compares elections to mahjong, with the four elders in firm control of the rules of the game. Its ending hints that the system is unlikely to change in the future, as one of the players gleefully says "Let's continue playing!" while shuffling the mahjong pieces.

It is perhaps the ending of *Election 2* that most poignantly captures Hong Kongers' attitude towards mainland Chinese control of the electoral system. The newly elected triad leader, Jimmy, is eager to start a family and a new life with his pregnant wife. He is therefore determined to be leader for only one term. In the final scene, however, an official from China tells him that in order for his businesses on the mainland to succeed, he must remain as the triad leader for as long as the Chinese government wants him to do so. The official notes:

> It's not that we don't respect the election system. It's just that we are worried that the person who gets elected after you will [. . .] upset the societal order. This is something we do not want to happen. You are someone we can trust. [. . .] With you at the helm, Hong Kong will be a better place. Hong Kong will have more stability and prosperity.

The Chinese official here is stand-in for Beijing, and his views are clear: elections are fine, as long as the Central government controls the results. The references to "stability" and "prosperity," lifted from the NPCSC discourse, explicitly establish a parallel between the Central authorities' control over Jimmy in the film and their control over Hong Kong in real life. The language of the exchange is also significant: Jimmy's heavily accented Mandarin accentuates his identity as a Hong Konger, while the official's polished Mandarin aligns his voice with that of the Chinese government. Jimmy is clearly horrified at the prospect of being the head of the crime syndicate indefinitely. He repeatedly punches the official in anger, and as he does so he shouts "I don't want to be a gangster! I don't want to be a gangster!." At the end of the sequence, he collapses onto the ground, exhausted, while the official stands over him and says "Thank you for your cooperation." Those final words make clear that Jimmy does not have a say in the outcome of the next round of elections; he will be the next triad leader whether he likes it or not. The punches that he repeatedly throws are a visual representation of the anger about China's control over Hong Kong's electoral system amongst many local viewers, while his collapse onto the ground and the close of the sequence reflect their sense of despair and helplessness in face of the political reality. In contrast to Beijing's official assessment that the NPCSC's 2014 Decision marked the culmination of "a historic progress in Hong Kong's democratic development," Hong Kong cinema suggests, imagistically and from the margins of constitutional debate, that the reality is perhaps not quite as rosy the authorities describe.[24]

6.3 Violence and the Image

All of the films discussed in the previous section have large amounts of graphic violence; gang fights involving knives, steel rods, and mallets, as well as the bloodshed that inevitably follows from those fights, are an integral part of their narratives. Yet to date there has been little consideration of the relationship between law and the representation of violence in triad films. In this section,

---

[24] *Explanations on the Draft Decision of the Standing Committee of the National People's Congress on Issues Relating to the Selection of the Chief Executive of the Hong Kong Special Administrative Region by Universal Suffrage and the Method for Forming the Legislative Council of the Hong Kong Special Administrative Region in the Year 2016* (August 27th, 2014).

I offer a close reading of *The Mobfathers* to argue that Yau refashions the trope of violence into a visual expression of the impact of Bejing's legal interventions on Hong Kong. A seasoned and prolific director and cinematographer, Yau has a long-standing interest in the law. His *From the Queen to the Chief Executive* (等候董建華發落; 2001) mixes fiction and real-life news footage to advocate for the release of a young prisoner who had been detained with the possibility of a royal pardon under the colonial justice system, but who was forgotten by both the British and the Chinese governments when Hong Kong returned to China.[25] He also directed the courtroom drama *No Justice for All* (真相; 1995) prior to the handover. What makes *The Mobfathers* stand out stylistically amongst other post-handover gangster films is its manipulation of narrative time through a highly aestheticized representation of violence; Yau not only presents carefully choreographed scenes of gang fighting, but often deliberately disrupts their tempo by retarding, suspending, or elongating the action cinematographically. The violence here can therefore be said to draw attention to itself and to call out for interpretation.

Two instances from *The Mobfathers* will give a sense of the film's rhythm and its aesthetics of violence. The first instance is from the opening sequence, in which Chuck and his men are locked in an altercation with another gang member and his supporters. As Chuck explains in a voiceover, a fight is about to break out, and he ponders over how the whole dispute came about in the first place. This confrontation sets the tone of the fight scenes in the remainder of the film: it is fast paced, and the men attack each other with smooth, fluid movements reminiscent of a martial arts movie. The swift rotations of the camera from side to side, together with the multiple cuts in the sequence within a short span of time, create a sense of dynamism. The amplification of the yelling, the shouting, and the sound of knives slicing through bodies during the fight also adds to the film's dynamic quality. This kinetic overflow is then disrupted when, at one point in the fight, Chuck brings his blade down on an attacker: the camera shows his bodily movement in slow motion, and the action then comes to a halt as the frame freezes. The still image of Chuck remains on the screen for several seconds, before the camera cuts to his wife at home. The still image brings about a temporal disruption in the viewing experience, or a condition of stasis giving rise to both a critical distance between the viewers and the violence being screened and a moment in time for them to reflect, along with Chuck, upon why and how the state of affairs came out.

---

[25] See Anne S. Y. Cheung, "What Law Cannot Give: From the Queen to the Chief Executive," in *Law and Popular Culture*, edited by Michael Freeman (Oxford: Oxford University Press, 2005), pp. 425–447 and Mike Ingham, "Hong Kong Cinema and the Film Essay: A Matter of Perception," in *Hong Kong Screenscapes: From the New Wave to the Digital Frontier*, edited by Esther M. K. Cheung, Gina Marchetti, and Tan See-kam (Hong Kong: Hong Kong University Press, 2011), pp. 175–195.

The second instance from the film is the murder of a man known as Cola who, in addition to Chuck and Wolf, is a candidate running for the position of triad leader. Cola's candidacy is short-lived as he is brutally murdered halfway through the film: an assassin, posing as a street cleaner, hits Cola on the head with his shovel as he walks past him on the street. Two men who had been trailing Cola then attack him with knives. As Cola bleeds profusely on the ground, the street cleaner steps forward and decapitates him with the shovel. At this point, the camera zooms in on the dying man: the colors in the shot are carefully calibrated, with the metallic gleam of the shovel cutting into Cola's neck and the deep redness of the spurting blood forming a tonal contrast with the victim's black attire and the dark gray tar of the street. The camera lingers over the image of Cola's corpse, again interrupting the narrative unfolding of events and creating a space for viewers to ponder over this act of violence. Who arranged Cola's murder, and for what reason? Later in the film, when it is revealed that the Mobfather is behind the death not only of Cola but of the other candidates in the race, this lingering image of the decapitated Cola appears for a second time on the screen. Its reappearance creates a visual link between Cola's death and the man who orchestrated it behind the scenes, and seems to suggest that violence is inextricable from a system that enables someone like the Mobfather to assert absolute control.

To investigate the jurisprudential significance of these sequences, it is instructive to place the film and the election controversy in dialogue with the work of Robert Cover, the theorist who has most overtly foregrounded the relationship between violence and the law. Cover argues that the meaning of legal provisions cannot be determined from a reading of the text alone. Rather, meaning is determined within what Cover calls a *nomos*. A *nomos* is "a normative universe," a set of "narratives that locate it [law] and give it meaning."[26] In other words, a *nomos* is the discursive context which supplies the law with "history and destiny, beginning and end, explanation and purpose."[27] To interpret the law is not simply to understand the linguistic content of specific provisions or precepts, but to ascertain its significance and scope within the narratives which embed it. Central to the *nomos* is the idea of "commitment": we live and stand by our acts of legal interpretation because those acts are made in light of the moral values and assumptions that are integral to how we "create and maintain a world of right and wrong, of lawful and unlawful, of valid and void."[28] As such, law is "not merely a system of rules to be observed, but a world in which we live."[29] The act of legal interpretation always takes place within a normative universe.

---

[26] Cover, "Nomos and Narrative," in *Narrative, Violence, and the Law: The Essays of Robert Cover*, edited by Martha Minow, Michael Ryan, and Austin Sarat (Ann Arbor: University of Michigan Press, 1993), pp. 95–173 (95).

[27] Cover, "Nomos and Narrative," *Essays*, p. 96.

[28] Cover, "Nomos and Narrative," *Essays*, p. 95.

[29] Cover, "Nomos and Narrative," *Essays*, p. 96.

Crucial to Cover's argument is the recognition that there exist multiple *nomoi* within the state. He contends that while the political authorities approach the law on the basis of discourses constituting their *nomos*, different communities may have their own set of narratives, or may inhabit normative worlds with different priorities, divergent norms, alternate conceptions of selfhood, or conflicting ideas about their place in history. There is therefore not a single *nomos*, but different *nomoi*, within a state. Cover cautions that "we ought not lightly to assume a statist perspective" when approaching the law, for to do so could entail dismissing other *nomoi*, and hence other understandings of the law, as "particular" or peculiar, and therefore as simply illegitimate. Rather, we should consider seriously the terms of different normative domains, or, in Cover's own words, "we ought to stop circumscribing the *nomos*; we ought to invite new worlds."[30]

In light of Cover's argument, the conflict between the normative vision of those supporting Beijing's electoral framework, and those who so vehemently oppose it, can be said to constitute a clash between two different *nomoi*. The NPCSC's approach to the Basic Law's provisions on Chief Executive elections is tied to a normative universe in which Hong Kong's stability and prosperity, understood as the elimination or pre-emption of challenges to China's sovereignty over it, are of paramount importance. As explained by Li Fei, the Deputy Secretary General of the Standing Committee, at stake are the "sovereignty, security and development interests of the country," as well as the prevention of "all sorts of possible risks" to Hong Kong's "long-term prosperity and stability."[31] Democracy, whereby the people of Hong Kong may choose a leader who could potentially challenge the Communist Party's authority, is regarded as one such risk, and he starkly states that "those who oppose the Central government will never be Chief Executive."[32] An interpretation premised on the *nomos* of the Chinese authorities and pro-Beijing figures in Hong Kong privileges the state over the individual, party control over Hong Kongers' right to political participation, and national development over the Special Administrative Region's autonomy. Ultimately, theirs is a nomos made up of a set of narratives placing "One Country" before "Two Systems."

Hong Kongers who demand democratic elections inhabit a different *nomos*. In their normative world, what is paramount is for the inhabitants of the territory to have the ability to decide who the next Chief Executive will be, without interference from the government authorities. They abide by a set of narratives underscoring that freedom, individual choice, and autonomy are the best means of enhancing prosperity and stability. For them, the outcome of the elections should be firmly in the hands of the people of Hong Kong. Audrey

---

[30] Cover, "Nomos and Narrative," *Essays*, p. 172.   [31] *Instrument 24: Explanations.*
[32] "Those Who Oppose the Central government Will Never Be Chief Executive: Li Fei Urges People Not to Sacrifice Themselves," *Ming Pao Daily News*, September 2nd, 2014.

Eu, a legislator and barrister vocal in the election debate, sums up this position when she notes that while a democratic system "will not guarantee the perfect or the best person" to lead the territory, "having a say in choosing your own leader is surely better than having one thrust upon you."[33] The idea that only "patriots" can govern Hong Kong is as repugnant to the world view of a figure like Eu as it is natural to the normative universe of the Chinese government. Ultimately, the nomos of pro-democracy figures is premised on a set of narratives that foreground "Two Systems" over "One Country." The conflict over Chief Executive elections reflects not only different interpretations of the relevant sections of the Basic Law, but divergences in deeply held "interpretive commitments" at the core of the two normative worlds in which those interpretations are situated.[34]

Cover posits that legal interpretation is an inherently violent act. As he famously argued in "Violence and the Word," "legal interpretation takes place in the field of pain and death."[35] This is true in several senses. An act of legal interpretation can obviously have tangible, concrete consequences on the person's life: it can cause someone to lose "his freedom, his property, his children, even his life," such that "when interpreters have finished their work, they frequently leave behind victims whose lives have been torn apart by these organized, social practices of violence." More subtly, the legal interpretations, even when they do not have any immediate physical impact on a person, are violent in the sense that they are embedded in an institutional framework which demands absolute obedience. In other words, there is no respite from the authority of law: the regime "of state authority" demands a "regime of obedience" and is synonymous with it.[36] Because their acts of interpretation take place within this institutional framework, officials who pronounce interpretations or judgments can impose their own *nomos* onto the subjects of the law through nothing more than the "superior brute force" of their own authority, and in doing so they delegitimize and extinguish alternative *nomoi* that may exist in other communities.[37] The violence inheres in the institutional force enabling law's eradication of other normative domains. For Cover, the seemingly straightforward principle that communities have to abide by the law as articulated by judges or other interpreters within a state-sanctioned system is indicative not only of the communities' duty to obey the law, but also the state's power to suppress or demolish any normative world that is not in line with its own. Cover coins the term "jurispathic" to describe how acts of legal interpretation can obliterate alternative or emergent *nomoi*.[38] Legal interpreters "do not create law, but kill it" in that by asserting that "*this*

---

[33] Audrey Eu Yuet-mee, "Down to Bare Essentials," *South China Morning Post*, April 17th, 2004.
[34] Cover, "Nomos and Narrative," *Essays*, p. 99.
[35] Cover, "Violence and the Word," *Essays*, p. 203.
[36] Cover, "Nomos and Narrative," *Essays*, p. 157.
[37] Cover, "Nomos and Narrative," *Essays*, p. 144.
[38] Cover, "Nomos and Narrative," *Essays*, p. 138.

one [their own interpretation] is law," they also "destroy or try to destroy the rest."[39] The choice of the word "kill" here is deliberate, and strikingly conveys Cover's contention that legal interpreters "are people of violence" because "theirs is the jurispathic office."

When considered in light of Cover's ideas about the violent nature of legal interpretation, it becomes evident that the NPCSC is a jurispathic organ: through its Interpretation and Decisions about the Chief Executive election, it imposes not only an electoral framework but an entire *nomos* on Hong Kong. In particular, the 2014 Decision, which in effect ensures that only candidates approved by China can run for office, forces the resolution over the election controversy in favor of considerations of political control and national security at the core of the Chinese government's normative world. Since the Decision is binding on Hong Kong, it also kills off the *nomos* associated with local aspirations towards a democratic political system. The local courts and community must obey the Decision and submit to the state's legally-endorsed superiority. It is this eradication of local narratives through a "structure of authority" within which Hong Kong has to adhere to NPCSC Interpretations and Decisions that constitutes the legal violence in this context.[40] One political commentator comes close to identifying the NPCSC's jurispathic nature when she notes that "by throwing down an election mechanism that is within the complete control of the central authorities, the Chinese government has brought the blade down on us (‘手起刀落’) [...] Beijing's ruthlessness sends shivers down my spine."[41] The metaphor of the blade, held by a ruthless ruler and slicing through the body politic of Hong Kong, echoes Cover's observation that "some interpretations are written in blood."[42]

Considered in relation to Cover's foregrounding of law's violence, the fights, the bloodshed, and the killings in *The Mobfathers* emerge as the visual expression of the insight that legal interpretation takes place in a field of pain and death, and more specifically, of the NPCSC's jurispathic nature. The final confrontation between Chuck, Wolf, and their gangs at the climax of the film provides a further instance of how cinema can make explicit the force of law that usually remains hidden or implicit in institutional legal and political processes. Chuck and Wolf kill each other in the fight, and the film again highlights the violent acts that lead to their mutual destruction. As they attack each other, Chuck delivers the final blow to Wolf by slicing his face open. The camera then zooms in on Wolf's face; it holds the shot for several seconds to show blood gushing out from an impossibly large wound, before presenting Wolf's collapse onto the ground in slow motion. Chuck also falls from his injuries. This moment is further accentuated through changes in the sounds of the sequence: as Chuck brings his blade across Wolf's face, the noise from the

---

[39] Cover, "Nomos and Narrative," *Essays*, p. 155.
[40] Cover, "Nomos and Narrative," *Essays*, p. 161.   [41] "Time to Wake Up."
[42] Cover, "Nomos and Narrative," *Essays*, p. 146.

skirmish in the background is replaced by slow music which creates an acoustic space setting the violence here apart from the rest of the narrative.

More importantly, their confrontation is juxtaposed with three scenes which make clear that the Mobfather is the mastermind behind the violence. In the midst of the fighting, there is a flashback to a conversation between the Mobfather and his confidante, in which he expresses his intention of inciting violence between Chuck and Wolf. That scene is then followed by a second flashback, this time of the murder of Chuck's wife. The murder scene is followed by a third flashback, of Chuck at a hospital where his son dies of an asthma attack triggered by the shock of witnessing his mother's brutal murder. The juxtaposition of these flashbacks, as well as their crosscutting with the gang fight, draws attention to the cause-and-effect relationship between Mobfather's moves and the unbridled violence at the heart of the final sequence: the Mobfather makes Chuck believe that Wolf is the culprit and seek vengeance against him, and this vengeance in turn leads to the bloody showdown. As Chuck himself declares: "If I cannot become triad leader, then my wife and my son will have died in vain," and from that moment on he vows to eliminate Wolf once and for all. Yau's editing makes plain that the Mobfather's decision to maintain a system giving him absolute control leads directly to the violence which eliminates the two candidates in the leadership race. The jurispathic violence arising from a legal decision imposing a statist *nomos* privileging order, stability, and unchallengeable sovereignty onto the local community is here given form in the physical violence, caused by the Mobfather's determination to maintain his grip on the triad community, that is inflicted on Chuck, the character pushing for democratic elections for the head of the crime syndicate.

The gang fight is also cross cut with scenes from a secret conversation between the Mobfather and the head of the police, in which the Mobfather convinces the police officer to instruct his men not to intervene in the fight to stop the violence. He tells the policeman that Chuck and Wolf are trouble-makers, and that there will be chaos in society if they are elected. The best outcome, he explains, is for the two of them to perish in the fight so that the Mobfather himself remains as triad leader. He promises the police officer that if he continues at the helm, the triad will not cause major disruptions in Hong Kong society so that there will be "order," "harmony," and "stability" – the very terms constituting the *nomos* of the Chinese authorities and in the name of which fully democratic Chief Executive elections are denied. The police officer is persuaded and orders his men to do nothing, and it is the absence of police interference that enables the rampant gang war to happen. Once again, there is a cause-and-effect relationship between the Mobfather's determination to maintain control and the violent acts. This point is further underscored by the camera work, and the enlarged images of the Mobfather visually indicate that he is at the center of the violence. The film's aesthetics of violence give form to the jurispathic brutality of the NPCSC's exercise of institutionalized power. With a nod to popular views of the kind of leader Hong Kong will have after Beijing's election framework is instituted, the Mobfather observes that "all we want is a puppet leader. We can find anyone to play that part."

Finally, the film underscores that the violence is inflicted not only on Chuck and Wolf, the two contenders in the leadership contest, but on the triad community more broadly. The sequence of the final confrontation opens with a shot of a large group of the syndicate's members; they are backing different candidates and are poised on opposite sides in the shot. When the fighting begins, the camera zooms in on two boxes of weapons: the triad members each pick up a weapon and start attacking one another. Like the institutionalized violence of legal hermeneutic acts, the violence here affects not only the people at the top but the community as a whole. The impact on the community is conveyed through multiple close-up shots of a particular member of the criminal organization, a newcomer who joins the triad just in time for the final confrontation. He is an unremarkable young man, and is virtually indistinguishable from the other triad members in dress, behavior, and demeanor. This utter ordinariness which defines him also establishes him as an archetype for the typical triad member. In the course of the confrontation, his hand is cut off by another gangster. The camera then zooms in on him: he shouts out in terror, with blood dripping from his gaping wound and a look of sheer panic on his face, and attempts to run away from his attacker before collapsing onto the ground. The final shot of this character shows him writhing on the ground, crying hysterically and screaming "It hurts! It really hurts!." It is not entirely clear that he will survive. The cinematographic focus on this unexceptional figure can be read as a visualization of the violence inflicted not on those whom one usually thinks of as being involved in the political process, such as candidates for office, politicians, or senior government officials, but on regular members of a group who are at the receiving end of the jurispathic violence that obliterates the ideas, values, and norms upon which they construct their normative worlds. By zooming in on this young man's injury and pain, the film articulates the idea that law's violence affects even the most commonplace or insignificant members of the community. They, no less than the more politically prominent figures, are caught in the field of pain and death in which the state's legal acts take place.

6.4 Conclusion

Like American gangster films, Hong Kong triad films constitute an iconic and popular cinematic tradition. Their tightly plotted narratives and their fast-paced fight scenes certainly contribute to their popularity, but the persistent engagement with key social, political, and, as this chapter has shown, constitutional controversies are a further reason for their enduring interest. By refracting the divisive and at times acrimonious disagreements about the

Chief Executive elections through a darker, more violent, but still recognizably similar process in the gangster world, post-handover triad films register the disappointment and outrage amongst many people in the territory towards this long-running constitutional saga. In his final voiceover in *The Mobfathers*, Chuck tells us that the Mobfather came to an ignoble end: "he pissed and shat himself" on the hospital bed in his final moments, and "died in a pool of his own piss and shit." This vivid description of abjection and degradation encapsulates the ire and resentment towards the normative universe which this figure represents. Yet it also intimates that one day its reign will self-implode and come to an end. The longstanding struggle for democracy in Hong Kong culminated in Occupy Central; this was the most significant civil disobedience movement since the retrocession, as well as the subject of some of the most captivating and socially engaged films in recent history. I will examine the cinematic engagements with the movement in the next chapter.

7

Scenes from a Traumatic Event:
Documenting Occupy Central (with Observations on Cinema and the Anti-extradition Bill Protests)

In the early hours of September 28, 2014, a legal scholar turned political activist named Benny Tai, who had been advocating for civil disobedience as a means to achieve universal suffrage in Hong Kong, made a dramatic announcement on stage to a cheering crowd: "Occupy Central . . . officially . . . commences!" What followed was a movement that lasted for seventy-nine days, during which protesters occupied the major thoroughfares in the city to express their opposition to the electoral system mandated by the 2014 Decision of the National People's Congress in Beijing, which I examined in the last chapter. The movement also aimed to pressure the local government into introducing democratic elections. Even though the participants congregated peacefully and showed no signs of immediate violence, the local police fired multiple rounds of teargas to disband them. Not only did this heavy-handed measure spark an outcry within the territory and abroad, but images of the demonstrators using umbrellas to shield themselves from the advancing police force were captured by the international media, which dubbed the movement the "Umbrella Revolution." The scale and duration of the movement surpassed even the 2003 protest against national security laws. As commentators recognized at the time, Occupy Central was a watershed moment in Hong Kong's constitutional history: just as 1997 inaugurated the postcolonial era, 2014 marked the beginning of the "post-Occupy era."[1]

Occupy Central was the result of the merging of two separate groups. The first is known as Occupy Central with Love and Peace. Founded by Tai, the sociologist Chan Kin-man, and the retired pastor Chu Yiu-ming, it advocated for genuine universal suffrage through acts of civil disobedience. The other was a coalition of student associations which organized a class boycott in response to the electoral reform package; key figures here include Alex Chow, Yvonne Leung, and Lester Shum, as well as then high school student Joshua Wong. Legal analyses of the movement have so far revolved around questions such as whether the movement was indeed a kind of civil disobedience, whether civil disobedience could constitute a defense for the actions of the Occupy leaders in

---

[1] Yeung Tin-shui, "The Post-Occupy Era," *Ming Pao Daily News*, December 5th, 2014.

a criminal trial, and whether the police used excessive force when dealing with the protesters. Yet these discussions, important as they are, do not quite get at the heart of what made the Occupy movement such a critical moment in the territory's legal, political, and cultural history. In this chapter, I argue that the event was triggered, and sustained, by pressures on the constitutive elements of Hong Kong identity: democratization, rights and freedoms, and the rule of law, all of which are supposedly unassailable under "One Country, Two Systems." As these pressures increased, there emerged a rift between those in Hong Kong who resigned themselves to the disappearance of the "Hong Konger" as they knew it, and those who refused to accept any further merging of identities between their city and the mainland. This fracturing occurred largely, though not exclusively, along generational lines: commentators have noted that the protestors on the streets tend to be relatively young, and that the different political stances between them and their parents led to intense conflict in many families.[2] The rift thus extended across the public and private spheres. During the fateful seventy-nine days, Occupy Central was most frequently described as an event that "tore apart" ("撕裂") Hong Kong.[3] It is not an exaggeration to describe Occupy as a *trauma* to Hong Kong society, a painful occurrence that ripped open the territory's body politic and from which it is still trying to heal itself.

A number of documentaries about Occupy have appeared in the wake of the movement. Like Tammy Cheung's *July* which sought to capture the 2003 protest directly on camera, these documentaries all seek to provide a historical record of the events of 2014, both for the participants themselves and for future generations. One of the protestors in Chan Tze-woon's *Yellowing* (亂世備忘; 2016) muses that after the movement ended, "everything returned to normal, as if nothing had happened," and all that was left were the "bits and bobs" he collected from the protest sites. These wistful reflections suggest that without the films, the movement could vanish, leaving behind little more than random, scattered objects. The project of documenting Occupy is especially urgent in light of the tightening control on political expression in China: the Central authorities have designated the movement as a lawless episode instigated by "foreign forces" to undermine Chinese sovereignty, and alternative depictions are censored in the mainland.[4] By providing first-hand accounts of the events of 2014, the documentaries constitute voices that speak back to this totalizing governmental discourse.

---

[2] Chris Lau and Shirley Zhao, "Hong Kong Families Split Over Support for Occupy Central Protest," *South China Morning Post*, November 17th, 2014.

[3] See, for instance, Mak Kwok-wah, "Real Heroes," *Hong Kong Economic Journal*, December 12th, 2014: "whether you support the movement or not, you cannot deny that society has been torn apart."

[4] Kristine Kwok and Teddy Ng, "Chinese Media Blames Foreigners Over Occupy Protests," *South China Morning Post*, October 2nd, 2014.

Yet the use of such documentaries as a window into the reality of Occupy Central raises important questions of its own. How does one document trauma? Trauma, by definition, is a form of *belated* knowledge, and one cannot fully *know* a traumatic event while one is in the midst of it: as the cultural and literary scholar Cathy Caruth points out, "events, insofar as they are traumatic, assume their force precisely in their temporal delay."[5] There is therefore a "fundamental dislocation" built into the making of an immediate filmic record of Occupy Central. With the urgency, but also the immense epistemological difficulty, of documenting the movement in mind, I will examine four different attempts to give a visual account of Occupy Central: Chan Tze-woon's *Yellowing*; Evans Chan's *Raise the Umbrellas* (撐傘; 2016); Nora Lam's *Road Not Taken* (未竟之路; 2016); and James Leong's *Umbrella Diaries: The First Umbrella* (傘上:遍地開花; 2018).[6] The fact that no fewer than four documentaries have appeared in the time since Occupy suggests that the films should be interpreted less as transparent windows into what happened in 2014 and more as belated, and ongoing, attempts to come to terms with the trauma that ushered in a new, and still unfolding, era in Hong Kong.[7]

In Section 7.1, I will draw on the work of cultural theorists of trauma, and in particular the work of Caruth, to think through what it might mean to approach Occupy Central as a traumatic event. My focus is less on the movement as a form of psychological trauma to any single individual – though there is certainly evidence of that – and more on the movement as a form of cultural trauma that struck at fundamental issues of identity. I therefore take my cue from Caruth's observation that trauma is not so much a symptom of any individual person's unconscious as it is "a symptom of history."[8] Section 7.2 examines the ways in which the films articulate, however imperfectly, the protestors' memories of confrontations with the police during the movement. Section 7.3 analyzes more specifically how the films are haunted by the memory of the Tiananmen Square Incident of 1989, and demonstrates that the Incident constitutes another trauma which shapes the way in which many of the protestors understand the twenty-first century protest in Hong Kong. Section 7.4 then discusses the ending of *Yellowing* to ask how a society might begin to heal itself in the aftermath of an event such as Occupy. In the conclusion, I consider the relationship between Occupy and the anti-extradition bill protests, and posit that the more recent events are a continuation of the process of coming to terms with the trauma of Occupy.

---

[5] Cathy Caruth, "Introduction," in *Trauma: Explorations in Memory*, edited by Cathy Caruth (Baltimore: Johns Hopkins University Press, 1995), pp. 3–13 (9).

[6] Leong's documentary was used as evidence in the case of *HKSAR* v. *Tai Yiu Ting and Others* [2019] HKDC 450.

[7] For an analysis of visual images from Occupy Central beyond documentary film, see my chapter entitled "The Artwork of Hong Kong's Occupy Central Movement," in *Civil Unrest and Governance in Hong Kong: Law and Order from Historical and Cultural Perspectives*, edited by Michael H. K. Ng and John D. Wong (Abingdon: Routledge, 2017), pp. 179–196.

[8] Caruth, *Trauma*, p. 5.

7.1 Occupy Central as Trauma

In *Unclaimed Experience: Trauma, Narrative, and History*, one of the seminal texts in the cultural study of trauma, Caruth defines trauma as a crisis or catastrophe which is not cognitively processed at the initial moment of occurrence: a traumatic experience is "not available to consciousness until it imposes itself again, repeatedly, in the nightmares and repetitive actions" of those who are affected by it.[9] In other words, trauma is characterized by belatedness; it should be located not in any "original event" but "in the way that its very unassimilated nature – the way it was precisely *not known* in the first instance – returns to haunt" a person or a community. As such, a traumatic experience "cannot be linked only to what is known, but also to what remains unknown in our very actions and our language." Film scholar Janet Walker makes a similar point about the relationship between trauma and knowledge when she underscores the need to address the "vicissitudes of memory" when interpreting records or testimony of a traumatic experience.[10] Caruth returns to the etymology of the term "trauma" and identifies it as a "wound" from which a society cannot easily recover.[11]

Several aspects of Caruth's analysis are worth highlighting here for the purposes of my discussion. First, a traumatic event poses particular challenges to those seeking to document it through film. On the one hand, a crisis which unsettles a society so profoundly means that there is an ethical imperative on the part of the documentary filmmaker to record, explain, and present it as faithfully as possible. On the other hand, the nature of trauma as a kind of "belated experience" means that filmmakers need to cultivate a different sensibility and develop a different set of cinematographic conventions to give visual form to it.[12] Second, trauma is marked by unconscious re-enactments of a crisis. The appearances, and reappearances, of scenes from Occupy Central in the documentaries I examine can be interpreted as precisely such a kind of re-enactment; their return onto our cinematic screens point to Hong Kong's continuing process of coming to terms with the unassimilated knowledge of the seventy-nine days. Third, traumatic memories can reappear as something that haunts, or ghostly presences which are at once keenly felt but difficult to describe. In Part III, I will address the question of how film might represent such hauntings.

Fourth, and most importantly, Caruth's description of trauma as a "wound" coincides precisely with the metaphor through which Hong Kong sought to conceptualize Occupy Central. Reflecting on the movement two days before Christmas in 2014, the Archbishop of the local Anglican Church famously

---

[9] Cathy Caruth, *Unclaimed Experience: Trauma, Narrative, and History* (Baltimore: Johns Hopkins University Press, 1996), p. 4.

[10] Janet Walker, "The Vicissitudes of Traumatic Memory and the Postmodern History Film," *Trauma and Cinema*, edited by E. Ann Kaplan and Ban Wang (Hong Kong: Hong Kong University Press, 2008), pp. 123–145.

[11] Caruth, *Unclaimed Experience*, p. 4.   [12] Caruth, *Unclaimed Experience*, p. 5.

described Hong Kong as a "wounded city" ("受傷的城市").[13] Archbishop Paul Kwong said that the city had been "wounded all over," and that its economy, livelihood, rule of law, and human relationships had all been "deeply injured." A newspaper columnist echoed Kwong's sentiment when he lamented that the atmosphere of the Christmas holidays cannot hide "the wound inflicted by political conflict" ("政治爭拗的創傷").[14] Variations of the same trope are commonplace in the broadsheets of the period. A commentator in the *Hong Kong Economic Journal* observed that Hong Kong had to "endure a wound which is very difficult to treat" ("難以治療的創傷"), and that society needed to "attend to its wounds" ("療傷") in the aftermath of Occupy.[15] Another commentator in the *Oriental Daily News* also believed that Hong Kong would take a long time to "heal this wound" ("治愈創傷").[16] In fact, the description of the movement as an event that "tore apart" ("撕裂") Hong Kong, a phrase used across the political schism by both supporters and opponents of Occupy, can be understood, in Cantonese as in English, not only in the sense of a tear to the social fabric, but also as an injury or even laceration in Hong Kong's body politic.[17] The city's wound manifested itself in multiple ways. On a psychological level, recent studies have identified Occupy as a significant mental health stress factor amongst Hong Kong residents.[18] In the first two weeks of the movement, the Red Cross received over six hundred calls for help from people who suffered from symptoms such as "insomnia, repeated nightmares, palpitations, and hand tremors" arising from being exposed to "those surreal images that were continuously disseminated on the television and on cell phones."[19] On a social level, signs of a society torn apart were visible everywhere. There were frequent confrontations between the anti-Occupy or "Blue Ribbon" faction and the pro-Occupy or "Yellow Ribbon" faction in the streets, and episodes of violence involving not only physical altercations but the tearing down of banners and the destruction of tents at the

---

[13] "Society Torn Apart, Paul Kwong and John Tong Hon Urge Mending Cracks," *Ming Pao Daily News*, December 23rd, 2014.

[14] "Christmas Bells Are Ringing, But How Many Are Happy and How Many Are Fretting?," *Oriental Daily News*, December 25th, 2014.

[15] Ai Ching-teen, "After Occupy, Society Should Attend to Its Wounds," *Hong Kong Economic Journal*, December 8th, 2014.

[16] Sung Lap-kung, "Society Torn Apart, Mutual Trust Gone," *Oriental Daily News*, December 27th, 2014.

[17] See, for instance, "Alan Leong: A Hardline Approach by the Central Authorities Will Not Lead a Positive Outcome,*Ming Pao Daily News*, November 19th, 2014 and "Holden Chow Criticizes Occupiers for Tearing Apart Society," *Ta Kung Pao*, December 24th, 2014

[18] Michael Y. Ni et al., "Longitudinal Patterns and Predictors of Depression Trajectories Related to the 2014 Occupy Central/Umbrella Movement in Hong Kong," 107(4) *APJH* (2017), 593–600 and Joseph T. F. Lau et al., "The Occupy Central (Umbrella) Movement and Mental Health Distress in the Hong Kong General Public: Political Movements and Concerns As Potential Structural Risk Factors of Population Mental Health," 52 *Social Psychiatry and Psychiatric Epidemiology* (2017), 525–536.

[19] Chan Po-wah and Chan Ah-kwun, "Occupy Leads Family Arguments – Cell Phone Messages Lead to Conflict," *Ming Pao Daily News*, November 10th, 2014.

protest sites were reported.[20] Family feuds developed as parents chided their children for their radical behavior, and the children responded with disdain towards their parents' political apathy. One student stopped speaking to his mother and blocked her on his mobile phone on the grounds that she was a Blue Ribbon, and his experience was by no means an uncommon one.[21] In *Raise the Umbrellas*, we are told that a student needed to rely on his fellow protestors for food to survive because his parents had cut him off since he joined the movement. In the same film, the singer and Occupy icon Denise Ho had to urge the protestors not to turn their backs on their families: "if you unfriended your mother on Facebook [...] please pretend you pressed the wrong button and re-friend her now."

These occurrences are psychological, social, and familial manifestations of a deeper trauma brought about by the pressures on Hong Kong identity. The NPCSC 2014 Decision, which in effect stipulates that Hong Kongers can only vote for candidates approved by Beijing, created an opposition between, on the one hand, those who accepted that the city's existence within an authoritarian regime meant it had to accept a truncated form of democracy, and on the other, those who insisted on genuinely democratic elections as a marker of difference between Hong Kong and mainland China. This was also the split between those who believed that an insistence on fundamental rights was impractical under Chinese rule, and those who insisted on the full protection of their right to vote and to stand for election as guaranteed by Article 26 of the Basic Law.

Moreover, the rule of law, so central to Hong Kongers' sense of themselves, came under profound stress as a pillar of identity during Occupy. The local government was insistent that the movement undermined the rule of law: in his speech at the Ceremonial Opening of the Legal Year in 2015, Rimsky Yuen, the city's top legal official, stated that Occupy Central brought about "blatant challenges to the rule of law."[22] His view echoed that of Chinese officials such as Wang Zhenmin, the Head of legal affairs at China's Liaison Office, who observed that the movement had "blatantly violated the rule of law in Hong Kong" and further noted that there would have been "nothing left of Hong Kong's rule of law" if the movement had continued beyond those seventy-nine days.[23] For officials such as Yuen and Wang, a movement which advocated breaking the law was necessarily undermining the rule of law.

Others, however, argued that it was the local government and the anti-Occupy camp that undermined the rule of law. Paul Shieh, the Chairman of the

[20] Liam Fitzpatrick, "Hong Kong Is Bracing Itself for More Anti-occupy Violence," *Time*, October 4th, 2014.

[21] Chris Lau and Shirley Zhao, "Hong Kong Families Split Over Support for Occupy Central Protest," *South China Morning Post*, November 17th, 2014.

[22] "Secretary of Justice's Speech at Ceremonial Opening of the Legal Year 2015," Hong Kong Government Press Release, January 12th, 2015.

[23] Wang Zhenmin, "'Occupy' Destroys Hong Kong's Rule of Law," *Wen Wei Po*, December 31st, 2014.

Hong Kong Bar Association, accused the Hong Kong government of "misleading the public" by confusing the rule of law with simply obeying the law.[24] Margaret Ng, a barrister and former legislator, angrily denounced the Hong Kong government for "importing Mainland China's understanding of the rule of law into Hong Kong, and turning the rule of law into 'rule by law'."[25] Benny Tai similarly noted that "perhaps he [C. Y. Leung, the Chief Executive at the time] only believes in the rule of law with Chinese characteristics."[26] The pro-Occupy camp therefore regarded the government as diluting the rule of law by smuggling in an alternative conception of it from across the border. Of course, the meaning of the rule of law is a matter of longstanding debate amongst legal and political philosophers: as Martin Krygier recently remarked, while it is possible to identify the traditions from which the rule of law derives or the problems it addresses, "no one [...] can dictate a uniquely correct meaning for the rule of law, or any uncontestable stipulation of the values it serves."[27] What I want to highlight here, however, is not so much the difficulty of defining the rule of law but the implications of that difficulty for Hong Kong identity: the fact that both sides, regardless of whether they supported the protestors or not, insistently claimed the rule of law as their own meant that one of the key elements of Hong Kongers' conception of selfhood was fracturing. The protestors' anxieties about the postcolonial administration's dilution of the rule of law, together with the government and the pro-establishment camp's deep-seated and intransigent belief that it was the protestors themselves who were trampling on the rule of law, together made a gash in the city's legal, political, and cultural imaginary.

Ultimately, Occupy Central wrenched apart that complex and delicate sense of affinity and alienation towards China that has long been constitutive of Hong Kongers' sense of themselves. To anti-Occupiers, the leaders of Occupy have led young Hong Kongers astray by arousing anti-China sentiments in them: as a commentator in the pro-Beijing *Ta Kung Pao* argued, instigators of the movement wronged these youngsters by burying their "love for China, which they inherited from generations before them" with "a thick layer of dust." According to him, the young protestors no longer felt the "honor and pride" which "every Chinese person should feel" towards the nation due to the pernicious influence of the instigators.[28] To supporters of Occupy, however, the 2014 Decision handed down by the NPCSC in Beijing was tantamount to an attack on the autonomy Hong Kongers were supposed to enjoy under the Basic Law: echoing the filial relationship with which this study began, one

---

[24] Stuart Lau, "Hong Kong's Legal Big Guns Tussle Over Rule of Law," *South China Morning Post*, January 13th, 2015.

[25] "'The Government Is Importing the Mainland's Framework into Hong Kong'," *Hong Kong Economic Journal*, December 24th, 2014.

[26] Benny Tai, "Rule of Law, C.Y. Leung-Style," *Ming Pao Daily News*, December 20th, 2014.

[27] Martin Krygier, "The Rule of Law: Pasts, Presents, and Two Possible Futures," 12 *Annual Review of Law and Social Science* (2016), 199–229 (202).

[28] Yu Ting, "End 'Occupy' and Let Hong Kong Shine Again," *Ta Kung Pao*, November 19th, 2014.

commentator angrily noted that Beijing treated Hong Kongers as "little children" and only wanted them to be obedient.[29] Another commentator lamented that "the day Hong Kong truly merges with the rest of China is coming" because "core Hong Kong values such as the rule of law, freedom, and fairness" were being destroyed.[30] This threat sparked localist sentiments: in one scene from *Umbrella Diaries*, we see a protestor shouting "Hong Kongers should not become second-class citizens of China!" while in another shot we see Alex Chow, one of the key figures in Occupy, declaring that Hong Kong is "our pad" to chants of "Hong Kongers! Hong Kongers!." E. Ann Kaplan has observed that trauma often leads to a "rupture" in political personas, and that rupture was apparent everywhere in Hong Kong during Occupy Central.[31]

7.2 Documenting Trauma

One of Caruth's most important insights is that the gash or wound of trauma *speaks*. Taking the story of Tancred and Clorinda, as told by Tasso in his sixteenth-century epic *Gerusalemme Liberata*, as a parable about trauma, Caruth explains the idea in this way: in the story, Tancred mistakenly kills his beloved Clorinda in a duel while she is disguised as an enemy knight. Later on, he wanders into a magical forest and slashes a tall tree with his sword. Unbeknownst to him, Clorinda's soul is trapped in the tree, and as blood flows from the cut he hears her bewail that he has wounded her yet again. For Caruth, the episode not only illustrates the repetition at work in trauma – he strikes her once with his sword, and inadvertently strikes her again – but also shows that a traumatic experience entails a "*voice* that cries out, a voice that is paradoxically released *through the wound*."[32] For Caruth, a core part of the cultural study of trauma is about listening to this voice that emerges. The documentaries that have appeared in the wake of the trauma that is Occupy Central can be understood as precisely voices speaking through the wound, voices that I will try to attend to.

A common, and striking, feature of the films is that events are often presented as memories, in the form of either the recollections of individuals who participated in the movement or as collective memories of Hong Kong society. In his recent book on Hong Kong cinema, Victor Fan identifies the films as part of "an archive of memories" about Occupy designed to engage spectators in political discussion.[33] I would argue that what the archive reveals

---

[29] Chan Wo-shun, "Hong Kongers, Don't Belittle Ourselves," *Hong Kong Economic Journal*, December 23rd, 2014.

[30] Leung Wai-see, "Still Want to Be a Hong Konger in the Future?," Ming Pao Daily News, December 26th, 2014.

[31] E. Ann Kaplan, *Trauma Culture: The Politics of Terror and Loss in Media and Literature* (New Brunswick: Rutgers University Press, 2005), p. 15.

[32] Caruth, *Unclaimed Experience*, p. 2 (original italics).

[33] Victor Fan, *Extraterritoriality: Locating Hong Kong Cinema and Media* (Edinburgh: Edinburgh University Press, 2019), p. 213.

is precisely the struggle to record or convey memories of an occurrence Hong Kong is still in the process of coming to know. The films therefore not so much perform the function of accurately storing, classifying, or documenting Occupy Central, but demonstrate the still evolving process of belatedly coming to terms with it. In other words, even though most of the footage comes from the place and time of the movement itself, what the films convey is less the facts or the objective reality of Occupy than the nature and texture of memories in the aftermath of experiencing it.

This is evident in a sequence from *Raise the Umbrellas*, in which the faces of two young protesters are superimposed onto footage of people being tear-gassed as they narrate their experience. This superimposition frames the background footage as the two protestors' memories, and the overall cinematography conveys the uncertainty and disorientation inherent in these memories. One of them says: "As we ran, we realized that we had inhaled the teargas. We coughed, and tears streamed from our eyes." The other remembers: "All of a sudden, I heard explosions. There was smoke, and total chaos around me. I couldn't breathe." As they speak, the scenes shift between extreme long shots, long shots, and point of view shots, and the varying distances between the unfolding events and the speakers' subjectivities point to an imprecision in their sense of exactly where and how they were positioned in relation to those events. Moreover, the images are at times blurred, suggesting the mental blocking or repression of moments that are too distressing to be brought to conscious memory. Finally, certain scenes are sped up, while others are presented in a jumpy slow motion, and such variations underscore the unreliability of the sense of time within their recollections of the traumatic experience.

Two other cinematic moments provide a sense of how intricately layered these memories can be. The opening montage of *Yellowing* alternates footage of protesters trying to escape the chaos of the teargas with scenes of celebratory fireworks on National Day. The film begins with a long shot of the fireworks. It is clear that the celebrations are taking place sometime after 2014, as evidenced by some of the artwork and slogans from the movement that remain on the street. The scene then fades into a sequence from the protest, and the sound of the fireworks merges with the sound of the teargas. As the sequence moves between the celebration and the protest, the blast of the fireworks continues to blend with the noise of the teargas, and sounds of the cheering crowd become indistinguishable with the protesters' shouts of panic. Fan argues that the sequence turns "memories into a stack of index cards" which we are "invited to flip back and forth," so that "what appears to be disorder and turmoil (the occupation)" can also be approached as "a form of hope and inspiration for different future."[34] However, the exact order of the scenes suggests a less optimistic reading: the sequence begins with the fireworks, and it is the

---

[34] Fan, *Extraterritoriality*, p. 228.

fireworks which trigger the memory of the traumatic teargas episode. The opening montage indicates that for those who have gone through Occupy, the sounds of celebration are inevitably inflected by the din of protest, cheers are tinged with sadness, and the embrace of the nation brings with it the memory of suppression. For them, the celebratory present is marked by the return of a painful and still palpable past.

In *Road Not Taken*, protestor and student leader Billy Fung recounts what he saw the night when the protestors stormed Civic Square, a public space outside the Hong Kong government headquarters. He remembers how he could not hand over necessary supplies to fellow protestors who had climbed over the barriers, and how the police refused to allow even those people with media passes into the square. He speaks of a protestor who had a heart attack, and how the police refused to allow a doctor to enter despite the fact that the person was evidently unable to leave the premises to obtain medical help. Finally, he recalls how police officers with riot shields forced the protestors to retreat the next morning. Fung's narration of these incidents is constantly interrupted by images from that night. The status of these images as part of his remembrance of things past is underscored by the title of the segment in which they appear: "In Retrospect." The first memory is of a scene of total chaos: the field of vision is unsteady and goes in and out of focus; we see protestors charging, policemen rushing forward, and people falling onto the ground; we hear whistles, shouts of anger, and cries of alarm; and incessant flashes from the cameras of reporters and other people present at the scene add to the disorder. The camera cuts back to Fung, but less than twenty seconds later, another scene disturbs the flow of his narrative: this time, we see the protestors with their hands held up in a gesture of surrender as they chant "Let us go! Let us go!." A third scene from the night is then inserted into the sequence: taken with a camera placed below eye level and possibly hidden from view of the police, it de-personalizes the law enforcement agents by cutting off their faces and enlarging their bodies on the screen. The multiple intrusions can be interpreted as unwitting mental re-enactments which disrupt Fung's attempt to provide a coherent, linear, factual account of what happened. They suggest that the need to articulate, to know, and to provide a record of trauma needs to contend with the ghosts of the past.

7.3 An Undying Spirit

One of the key characteristics of trauma is the way it "returns to haunt" those who have gone through it.[35] To be traumatized is to be in the "repeated *possession*" of an unassimilated experience; such uncanny repetition constitutes trauma's "haunting power."[36] In all the documentaries, one particular episode from the past returns to haunt the 2014 protest: the Tiananmen Square

[35] Caruth, *Unclaimed Experience*, p. 4.   [36] Caruth, *Trauma*, p. 4 (original italics).

Incident of June 4th, 1989. I have noted in previous chapters that the crackdown in Beijing scarred the people of Hong Kong: the anxious, even visceral, reactions at the time included mass emigration from the city; a stock market crash; widespread anger at the ruthlessness of the authoritarian regime; and the introduction of further local human rights safeguards which at best only partially succeeded in reassuring the inhabitants of the territory. The events of 1989 constantly return in the discourse of the protestors. In *Raise the Umbrellas*, Joshua Wong draws a comparison between 1989 and 2014 when he asks: "Students twenty years ago were willing to make such sacrifices. What are we, as students today, willing to give up?" In *Umbrella Diaries*, Alex Chow establishes an even more explicit parallel: speaking at the annual Hong Kong candlelight vigil that commemorates the crackdown, he declares:

> Hong Kongers today are just like the Chinese people of 1989: we both face a threat to our freedom and democracy. The students who occupied Tiananmen Square through acts of civil disobedience back then, and the Hong Kongers who advocate occupying Central today: are we not using the same methods, realizing the same ideals, and fighting against the same authoritarian regime?

Oscar Lai, another protestor in the same film, says starkly: "We don't want another 4th June crackdown."

The fear that a similarly brutal suppression of dissent could take place in Hong Kong is obviously one reason why the Tiananmen Square Incident is so prominent in the minds of the protestors. Yet the Beijing crackdown haunts Occupy Central because they are similar in a more fundamental and more troubling way: the events of 1989 remind us that all movements are in danger of being forgotten. In China, government censorship has meant that an entire generation grew up without any awareness of the atrocities.[37] To many young people in the mainland, what some have termed the "Tiananmen Square Massacre" – the tanks, the deaths, the injuries, the despair – never happened. The candlelight vigil in Hong Kong is an ongoing attempt to prevent, or to slow down, such forgetting: as Alex Chow notes on the same occasion: "We commemorate, because we refuse to forget." On the thirtieth anniversary of the crackdown, a woman who took part in the Beijing student protests declares at the Hong Kong vigil: "We refuse to forget. We refuse to believe the lies."[38] Yet can one really "refuse," as a matter of intent, to forget? How does one fight against time? The reality that the crackdown has become largely forgotten amongst the general public in mainland China, together with the awareness that the same could happen to Occupy Central in Hong Kong, can be said to be the real trauma of June 4th, 1989. The more insistent the calls to remember, the more they betray the awareness that time erodes and eventually washes away

---

[37] Louisa Lim and Llaria Maria Sala, "China Wants Us to Forget the Horrors of Tiananmen as It Rewrites Its History," *Guardian*, May 19th, 2019.

[38] "Tiananmen 30th Anniversary: Thousands Hold Huge Vigil in Hong Kong," BBC News, June 4th, 2019. www.bbc.com/news/world-asia-china-48516455

our memories. Yet the greater the fear of disappearance, the more likely the memories will return to haunt us as part of a repetition put in motion by that traumatic awareness. It is the same impulse to remember, to retain that which one knows will inevitably fade, that animates the films which I have so far been examining in this chapter. This impulse is perhaps best reflected in the motto of *Yellowing*, which itself written in Chinese characters that gradually fade away: "So that we might find again that which is about to disappear from us."

It is possible to probe the relationship between memory, forgetting, and these documentaries further. In what form might this ghost, this "possession" by the past, appear? Caruth argues that to be traumatized is more specifically to be "possessed by an *image* or event."[39] In the films, 1989 returns from the past as a series of images to remind us that everything fades. At the same time, it is the fear that everything fades that makes the images recur, again and again, thereby ensuring that they will not completely disappear. *Yellowing* and *Raise the Umbrellas* provide two fascinating examples of how Occupy Central is haunted by the ghost of 1989.

In *Yellowing*, 1989 returns as part of the narrator's personal history. The narrator begins the story of his life by remarking that, unlike "many people from previous generations who arrived in Hong Kong because they were fleeing atrocities elsewhere," his life is rooted to the city: "I, I was born here, and I grew up here." The sequence ends with a shot of the Legislative Council building in 2014, together with his observations that "I'm twenty-seven years old this year. Hong Kong still does not have democracy. Democratization has been delayed again and again, and the 'gradual and orderly progress' towards democracy [stipulated in the Basic Law] has morphed into 'without any kind of progress'. Our freedom and rule of law are being undermined." The year 1989 appears as a significant moment in his life history: "After the Tiananmen Square Massacre, a lot of our relatives decided to move abroad, but my family chose to stay." Significantly, this reference to the crackdown is made against the background of a number of homemade videos from this childhood. In the first video, we see the narrator as a child riding a toy car, and playing with two other children who are also on toy cars. This is followed by a clip of him watching television, and the final segment is of him singing karaoke at home with his sister. In an uncanny echo of the past and the present, in the third clip the narrator is singing a song by a local rock band called Beyond, whose "Boundless Oceans, Vast Skies" would many years later become the *de facto* anthem of the Occupy movement. From the dates on the videos, they were made around 1989. These images from his childhood capture a moment in history when Hong Kong was in turmoil, even if the narrator was unaware of what was happening at the time. There is a certain ghostliness to these images: their low definition inadvertently foregrounds their status as an outdated technological form, and the eerie background music is reminiscent of an

---

[39] Caruth, *Trauma*, pp. 4–5 (my italics).

Asian horror film. These episodes are a reminder that the narrator's childhood has irrevocably disappeared – he is now twenty-seven-years old, no longer a child, and deeply disillusioned with democratization. Yet their return also suggests that it does not completely fade away: the fact that Chan had these home videos in his mind when he made *Yellowing* suggests that they are not gathering dust in a corner but are watched at least periodically. These videos point not only to the inevitability of events fading away, but also to the paradox that the trauma of that inevitability means that those events always return, in the form of images that are watched and re-watched, reworked and incorporated into new films, and hence never forgotten.

In contrast to the return of an intensely personal past in the form of family videos in *Yellowing*, *Raise the Umbrellas* is possessed by some of the most iconic public images from the crackdown. The film's sequence on 1989 begins with the juxtaposition of two images: a shot of tents erected in Hong Kong is followed by a shot of tents that were set up in Beijing. Later on, pictures of the Goddess of Democracy, the symbol of June 4 movement, are followed by images of the statue known as the Umbrella Man, the artistic icon of Occupy. The juxtaposition of these images, with the blue color of the tents and the gestures of the statues echoing one another, establish an uncanny resemblance between the two movements. They also signal a traumatic repetition at work: we see the tents of Tiananmen Square reappear on the streets of Admiralty, and we recognize the flame of democracy which the goddess proudly holds up reincarnated in the instrument which the Umbrella Man proffers in outstretched hand. The film's arrangement of images make clear that the experience of June 4th is still very much with us, and has a role in shaping the direction and outlook of the current generation of protestors.

Moreover, many of the images from the crackdown appear in *Raise the Umbrellas* in an ephemeral, evanescent, and transient form: they are often superimposed onto other images, only to fade out on the screen to give way to other images. One famous picture by the Asian-American photojournalist Liu Heung-shing shows two students lying unconscious on stretchers as large blood stains spread on their respective white shirts. Also in the frame of the picture are three fellow protestors who are rushing them towards whatever medical aid they can find. This still image is superimposed onto the footage of a moving tank; the tank is bathed in red light, and from this footage we once again hear the screams of the fleeing protestors. Viewers can see through the bodies of the injured students to the tank beyond them. Both sets of images then fade away, to be replaced by another picture of a man on a stretcher. This man's face is covered in blood. These images appear as ghostly presences: they are only present as echoes, and vanish before we can make out their full contours.

Later in the sequence, two more images are merged with each other: a photo of a group of student protestors, and a photo of a group of soldiers from the People's Liberation Army. From the way the images are merged, the two groups appear to be locked in confrontation, as the students seem to advance towards the soldiers, who in turn seem to be pushing back. This spectral collage is only briefly visible on the screen, and its fading away can be read as a comment on how the confrontation is being erased from the nation's collective memory. The merged images are further superimposed onto a shot of the Umbrella Man; as they fade away, the Umbrella Man, which is presented in normal resolution, comes into sharper focus. By placing the Umbrella Man in the same complex collage as the photos of the student protestors and the PLA soldiers, the film seems to hint that the icon of Occupy, remembered in such solid colors and high definition in our own epoch, will similarly fade away as time passes. The return of these haunting scenes from 1989, once captured on camera with the same noble intention of bearing witness, suggests that all images lose their color over time, before eventually fading into nothingness. Yet their appearance in *Raise the Umbrellas* also suggests that the past is not the past, that images of the 1989 crackdown will haunt Occupy Central, just images of Occupy Central will haunt other movements, in a perpetual re-enactment of the trauma of disappearance which paradoxically means that these images will always return. The ghost or spirit that appears is an undying one; it returns as a symptom of trauma but also as testimony to a continuing past.

7.4 Healing

What role, then, might film play in the process of coming to terms with Occupy Central? In *Unclaimed Experience*, Caruth returns to the story of Tancred and Clorinda to think about how it might be possible for an individual or a community to start to heal. She points out that even though the story is about Tancred's trauma, the voice that calls out from the wound is that of another person. Clorinda, too, undergoes a trauma, the trauma of being killed her by loved one. Her voice, eerily emanating from the tree, is "enigmatic," yet it "demands a listening and a response."[40] For Caruth, the tale underscores the way in which "one's own trauma is tied up with the trauma of another, the way in which trauma may lead, therefore, to the encounter with the other, through the very possibility and surprise of *listening* to another's wound."[41] To listen to the voice of the other, to respond to one's own trauma by recognizing that it is also the trauma of the one who is calling out to you, is the crucial first step towards healing.

I would like to examine the ending of *Yellowing*, because it stages precisely such a scene of patient, thoughtful listening, a scene that is at once hopeful about the possibility of recovery in Hong Kong but demonstrative of the great hurdles that stand in the way. The scene involves a letter, written by the esteemed constitutional law scholar and Basic Law Committee member

[40] Caruth, *Unclaimed Experience*, p. 9.   [41] Caruth, *Unclaimed Experience*, p. 8 (my italics).

Albert Chen, to his students. In the letter, he makes a heartfelt plea to the students to desist from the Occupy movement; in his view, the protest will do nothing to change the electoral framework handed down by Beijing in the 2014 Decision and will put severe pressure both on the economy and on the viability of the "One Country, Two Systems" framework. The response is penned and read as a voiceover by a girl known only by her first name, Rachel; she is a student at the University of Hong Kong where Chen teaches, and an avid supporter of the movement. The voices are moving, and the intention to connect is undeniable, but the divide is deep, and it is uncertain whether the letters will reach their destinations. The Chinese title of one of the scenes of the exchange can be translated as "A Letter across the Generations": these are voices speaking across the two sides of a society torn apart by politics, age, conceptions of the Basic Law, visions of Hong Kong's future, and other factors, and they constitute attempts to articulate to each other the trauma which each has undergone.

Chen, who has been teaching at the university since 1984 – the year the Sino-British Joint Declaration was signed – and who has devoted his entire life to the study of Hong Kong constitutional law, tells his students that he is now approaching retirement age, and is writing "to share, with the utmost frankness and without reservation," his views on the future of "One Country, Two Systems" with them. Several terms are foregrounded in the letter. The first is "political reality": he urges the younger generation to accept the political reality that the mechanism for choosing the territory's leader must be acceptable to the Central government because Hong Kong is an integral part of China. Chen acknowledges that the electoral framework as stipulated by Beijing in the 2014 Decision does not correspond to conventional definitions of the democratic process, but he points out that Hong Kong's elections must be considered within the broader context of China's geopolitical concerns: they are part of a "fundamental national policy [. . .] built upon the need to maintain overall order and to prevent foreign forces from using Hong Kong as a means to subvert the People's Republic of China." The Chief Executive must therefore not only be acceptable to the people of Hong Kong, but must also be someone "the Central Government is willing to appoint." As a Special Administrative Region within China, Hong Kong elections can only be "democratic elections with characteristics of 'One Country, Two Systems'." He understands that "these are words that few Hong Kongers want to hear," but reiterates that "this is the political reality, just as foreign rule and a lack of democratic representation was the political reality in the colonial days."

Two other words frequently appear in the letter: "rational" and "pragmatic." Chen aligns these terms with the "Lion Rock Spirit": this phrase, which emerged in the 1970s and alludes to an iconic rock formation in the territory, is an amorphous one and generally connotes the sense of Hong Kongness which bound the inhabitants of the city together in a time of economic hardship.[42] Chen writes that to be "rational" and "pragmatic" in the post-Occupy era means knowing how to "find our way of life within the interstices of 'One Country, Two Systems'." Reflecting on the experience of his own generation, he tells his students that

> Hong Kong's achievements today are due to the rational mindset and pragmatic approach of the people of Hong Kong – these include your parents, and also the generation before them. They accepted the political reality, and worked away diligently within the limited space available to them. This was how they created one of the "Four Dragons of Asia," and how they turned Hong Kong into the "Pearl of the Orient".

For Chen, then, the idealism and uncompromising resistance of the Occupy movement goes against the longstanding mentality and work ethic behind Hong Kong's prosperity. Chen reiterates to his students: "You are young, and Hong Kong's future belongs to you." He therefore encourages them to "make the smart choice" about the territory's future by choosing to be "rational" and "pragmatic."

Rachel's response picks up on these terms which recur in her teacher's letter. There is therefore a process of repetition at work: the key phrases reappear in the discourse of the young Hong Konger. Yet the process of listening to the trauma of the other leads to a return that is very different from the traumatic repetition which I have discussed so far in this chapter: in her voice we hear a different inflection of the terms, an interpretation which provides glimpses of alternative political and constitutional worlds. Far from being a traumatic repetition, then, the terms come back in the student's response as the vocabulary for articulating the vision of the next generation.

Speaking in a slow, measured tone, Rachel questions why her generation needs to accept the political *status quo*: "Must we silently accept this 'political reality', and watch the Hong Kong we know gradually disappear?" Evoking the 1989 crackdown, she wonders: "You say that the national policy of China is premised on national security, order, and the prevention of subversion by foreign forces. But why are the Central Authorities so scared? [...] Perhaps a regime that maintains itself through tanks and bullets must live in constant fear of subversion." She further points out that the political reality in Hong Kong is characterized by longstanding social problems such as a lack of class mobility, unaffordable housing, and vast economic inequalities. Taking up his themes of rationality and pragmatism, she confesses to being unable to accept the "twisted" reality of a flawed democracy, and compares life within such a system to a form of confinement: "Must those who are born in a cage accept being in that cage for the rest of their lives? Is it not rational or pragmatic for the birds in the cage to want to fly?" Her response depicts

---

[42] The letter was also read on air in the Chinese language radio programme *Letter to Hong Kong*, on Radio Television Hong Kong (RTHK).

acceptance of the "political reality" as a form of inaction, and insists that "It is up to us to pave the very paths we walk upon."

When juxtaposed with the stoicism of the constitutional law scholar, the language of the response seems somewhat emotive and impassioned. Out of this language, however, emerges the picture of a utopian reality:

> For some reason, I found myself at the frontlines the night the students stormed Civic Square. We didn't have any supplies then, and could only rip up a couple plastic bags in a feeble attempt to cover our faces [...] and yet, as we stood there hand in hand, with nothing but our own bodies as shields, I felt a collective sense of determination [...] What I saw at the protest sites was a sea of faces, tired yet all the more determined for being so. What I saw was the re-emergence of the Lion Rock Spirit.
>
> Professor, I had never seen Hong Kong like this. Is this not what the older generation meant when they spoke of a Hong Kong where people stood side by side, and faced adversities together?

The articulation of the movement here echoes what Daniel Matthews posits, in a more academic register, as a "nomosphere" which enacts "a temporary exposure to a mode of living that might create powerful markers for future political projects," and which can also "conjure a sense – as the cliché has it – that another world is possible."[43] As Rachel speaks, images of other protestors appear on the screen. One of them looks up at the night sky while camping out on the thoroughfare, two others are lost in their thoughts as they lean against the barricades, and a fourth stares at the ground as she takes shelter under a yellow umbrella. Their pensive expressions, and Rachel's reading of the letter *a viva voce* as the voiceover to these images, together suggest that she is articulating their thoughts too, and that what we are hearing is both a personal and a collective voice. The response presents a vision of the Occupy movement not as a threat to the territory but as an embodiment of the very values upon which a different political reality for the territory can be found, values such as togetherness, solidarity, community, and speaking truth to power. Echoing Chen's emphasis on the responsibilities of the young to Hong Kong, the speaker admits that her response "may be overly naïve," but adds that "it is exactly because Hong Kong's future belongs to us that it breaks our hearts to see it go under. We do not want to wake up one day to find a Hong Kong we no longer recognize [...] We are young. We must resist to the end."

These two letters provide a rare instance of an attempt to reach across the schism which the movement opened up. There are no heroes or villains here, just two Hong Kongers who care deeply about the city, but who find themselves on opposite sides of an ever widening gulf. They have divergent views on

---

[43] Daniel Matthews, "Narrative, Space and Atmosphere: A Nomospheric Inquiry into Hong Kong's Pro-democracy 'Umbrella Movement'," 26 *Social & Legal Studies* (2017), 25–46 (40 and 41).

key issues such as the pace of democratization; the scope of autonomy; the impact of Occupy; and the nature of civil disobedience, and their exchange thus shows just how deep the wound still is. Yet the two letters also reflect a genuine attempt at listening to the voice of the other. They show that, despite the conflicting interpretations, a common vocabulary exists and may provide a foundation for the possibility of healing. At least, that was the case in 2014.

7.5 Conclusion: From Occupy Central to the Anti-extradition Bill Protests

Five years after Occupy Central, Hong Kong was again turned into a city of protest. Occupy ended in December of 2014, but it did little to change the electoral system or ease the worries about a fading identity. Discontent about the lack of democratic progress endured, as did anxieties about integration. In 2019, when the Hong Kong government attempted to introduce legislation that some people believed could lead to trial in the mainland even for people who committed crimes in Hong Kong, the simmering discontent and latent anxieties erupted and led to another round of protests. These protests quickly escalated into violence. The protestors of 2019 articulated five demands, including the implementation of genuine universal suffrage in Hong Kong and the withdrawal of the extradition bill.[44] The fact that continuing democratization is as important to them as the withdrawal of the bill itself indicates that the more recent events are a continuation of Occupy, though in a much more militant form. They can be understood as part of the traumatic repetitions I have discussed in this chapter, another symptom of the problems stemming from the cultural politics of disappearance which remain unresolved in contemporary Hong Kong. In the words of one commentator, the wound which Occupy Central opened up "continued to fester," even in the present.[45]

Like Occupy, the events that occurred in response to the anti-extradition bill are intensely visual: scenes of people dressed in black and marching on the streets, Molotov cocktails thrown at riot police, graffiti and slogans painted onto the surfaces of public arenas, and acts of arson at shops and subway stations are captured on camera and relayed to viewers through a variety of channels, including live coverage on television; news footage on announcement boards of local university campuses; videos uploaded onto YouTube; images streamed onto the pages of "Watch Parties" hosted by Facebook users; and updates on cellphones and other mobile devices. It may not be an exaggeration to call the protests the most watched event of 2019 in Hong Kong, and perhaps even globally. The circulation of these images constitute what film scholar Francesco Casetti calls a *relocation* of cinema in

---

[44] Alison Rourke, "What Do the Hong Kong Protestors Want?," *Guardian*, August 13th, 2019.
[45] Alice Wu, "After the Extradition Protests, Hong Kong Must Do What It Failed to Do after Occupy: Heal the Divisions," *South China Morning Post*, July 8th, 2019.

the twenty-first century, whereby the power of images to surprise us, provide us with knowledge of the world, and connect us to other spectators – in short, the cinematic experience – moves from the darkened halls of movie theatres to new digital environments.[46]

One of the most striking aspects of the 2019 protests is the references from popular culture, and from film in particular, that are used to characterize them in Hong Kong's political and cultural discourse. The movement of cinematic tropes into the real world began with Occupy, as reflected by the name of Joe Piscatella's Netflix documentary *Joshua Wong: Teenager vs. Superpower* (2017): as the subtitle indicates, the film is structured as a battle between good and evil, with Wong portrayed as a defender of Hong Kong and China cast as an invading power. The film's narrative premise is tellingly summed up in a line by student activist Derek Lam: "China is a rising darkness [. . .] If you want to defeat Darth Vader, then you have to train some Jedi." Journalist Jason Ng observes that in the aftermath of Occupy, Hong Kong society became "polarized" not only into "yellow versus blue," or pro-democracy versus pro-Beijing, but into "heroes versus villains," such that the act of protesting became conceived not only as the exercise of fundamental rights of freedom and assembly, but as a struggle for survival reminiscent of the intergalactic confrontations of *Star Wars*.[47] In Nora Lam's *Lost in the Fumes* (地厚天高; 2017), a documentary about Edward Leung, a localist politician arrested for rioting and banned from running in local elections due to what the government regards as his separatist stance, Leung speaks of popular perceptions of him as a "superman" and a "hero" fighting for Hong Kong, and the documentary interrogates this perception by contrasting Leung's public persona and his own views of himself. Film references multiplied in the 2019 protests. For instance, martial arts star Bruce Lee's advice to fighters to be as "formless" as water informs the guerilla tactics of the protestors, who aim to "flow" or "crash" depending on the responses of the police and the administration to their demands.[48] There are also memes and posters superimposing the face of Carrie Lam, the Chief Executive, onto the body of Gollum from the epic drama *Lord of the Rings*, whose obsession with the power bestowed upon him by a magical ring drives him to insanity.[49] Ng himself compares the anti-extradition bill protests to *Infinity War* (2018) and *Endgame* (2019) in

---

[46] Francesco Casetti, *The Lumière Galaxy: Seven Key Words for the Cinema to Come* (New York: Columbia University Press, 2015), p. 28. For discussions of new media in a jurisprudential context, see *West of Everything: Law and New Media*, edited by Christian Delage, Peter Goodrich, and Marco Wan (Edinburgh: Edinburgh University Press, 2019).

[47] Jason Y. Ng, "Hong Kong's End Game: Why the Extradition Bill Is an 'Infinity Stone' That Could Decimate Half of Society," *Hong Kong Free Press*, June 9th, 2019. www.hongkongfp.com /2019/06/09/hong-kongs-end-game-extradition-bill-infinity-stone-decimate-half-society/.

[48] Jeffie Lam, Naomi Ng, and Su Xinqi, "Be Water, My Friend: Hong Kong Protestors Take Bruce Lee's Wise Saying to Heart and Go with the Flow," *South China Morning Post*, June 22nd, 2019.

[49] Jerome Taylor and Elaine Yu, "Memes, Cartoons, and Caustic Cantonese: the Language of Hong Kong's Anti-Extradition Law Protests," *Hong Kong Free Press*, June 24th, 2019. www .hongkongfp.com/2019/06/24/memes-cartoons-caustic-cantonese-language-hong-kongs-anti-extradition-law-protests/.

Marvel Studios' *Avengers* franchise, in which a group of superheroes with special powers unite to fight against an alien named Thanos, who wants to restore balance in the universe by destroying half of its population. According to Ng's analogy, the Chief Executive's refusal to meaningfully acknowledge widespread concerns about the bill is akin to Thanos's stubborn insistence on his own moral righteousness, and the extradition bill itself, which "opens up a portal" connecting the legal systems of Hong Kong and mainland China, is the real-life equivalent of the Space Stone, which "opens up wormholes to teleport its users anywhere in the universe." Ng is not the first to draw a parallel between the events of 2019 Hong Kong and the *Avengers* movies; the English words "infinity war" and "endgame" stand out prominently in the protestors' own descriptions in the Chinese press and internet forums.[50]

Figures from other film genres and categories of popular culture made appearances in the 2019 protests, but Ng's observation about the polarization of Hong Kong society into "heroes versus villains" is worth probing in light of Caruth's discussion of trauma.[51] If the years since Occupy have been characterized by a wound that "continued to fester," then the tropes of the more recent protests bear witness to a deepening of the divisions, or the hardening of the wound into a scar that will not easily go away.[52] While the ending of a film like *Yellowing* points to a possibility of speaking across the rift, the more recent cinematic references point to a Hong Kong envisaged in terms of binary oppositions such as rebel versus invader, defender versus aggressor, and self versus other. When members of a society represent themselves in those terms, their interactions are likely to become increasingly combative, and opportunities for dialogue increasingly distant. The protests are ongoing at the time of writing, and as they continue to unfold, it becomes more urgent than ever to break out of this binary framework, to recognize that one's own trauma is tied to the trauma of another, and to heed Caruth's call to *listen* to the other's wound.

---

[50] "Frontline Protestors: Yesterday Was Not an Endgame, but We Should Treat It as One," *Ming Pao Daily News*, September 1st, 2019.

[51] For a discussion of the other figures, See Rachel Cheung, "Hong Kong Protest Art: Meeting the Student Leading the Defiant Design Team," *South China Morning Post Magazine*, August 28th, 2019. See also "Insects and In-Jokes: Hong Kongers Find Humor, Pathos Amid the Protests," Coconuts Hong Kong, June 20th, 2019. https://coconuts.co/hongkong/news/protest-art-jokes-and-memes/.

[52] Wu, "After the Extradition Protests," *South China Morning Post*, July 8th, 2019.

Coda:
Wong Kar-wai's *2046*

Since the 1980s, the major constitutional controversies that have arisen in Hong Kong have provoked anxieties about the erosion of rights, freedoms, and identity: the ambivalent local reactions towards the very idea of retrocession to China in the early 1980s; the sense of urgency in entrenching human rights protections, especially in the aftermath of the Tiananmen Square Incident; worries about the weakening of the common law in post-handover Hong Kong; suspicions about the scope and impact of national security laws; the struggle for universal suffrage; and the recent protests against an extradition bill that some believe would breach the ramparts of "One Country, Two Systems," all have as their impetus the yearning to prevent the liberties constitutive of Hong Kongers' sense of themselves from being erased or diluted under the authoritarian Chinese regime. Within the same period, Hong Kong cinema has given visual form to an idea of selfhood intertwined with law, and to the fears, agitations, unease, and sense of foreboding about its fading generated by the controversies. In this book, I have tried to show how film engages with a crucial dimension of the disputes that is often left unexamined in more doctrinal discussions.

It is befitting to consider here, in the coda, the cinematic reaction to another intriguing aspect of the Basic Law: its possible end date. The constitutional document stipulates that Hong Kong's "capitalist system and way of life" prior to the retrocession shall *"remain unchanged for 50 years"*, meaning that China's socialist system and policies will not be implemented in the territory until at least 2047.[1] It further states that unless they contravene provisions in the Basic Law itself, "the laws previously in force in Hong Kong [. . .] shall be maintained" during this period.[2] "Remain unchanged for fifty years" (五十年不變), first coined by Deng Xiaoping in the early 1980s, has since then become a talismanic phrase in Hong Kong's political, legal, and cultural discourse. Its codification as a constitutional mandate suggests that one of the aims of the Basic Law is to suspend time, to place the city in a capsule to ensure that it

---

[1] Article 5, *Basic Law of the Hong Kong Special Administrative Region of the People's Republic of China* (emphasis mine).

[2] *Basic Law*, Article 8.

remains the same not only as it moves from British governance to Chinese sovereignty in 1997, but also for the imaginable future beyond that date. This reading is bolstered by the language of the constitution itself: in addition to "remain," the words "maintain," "previous," and variations thereof are amongst those that appear the most frequently. For instance, the provisions of the international human rights covenants and labor conventions applicable before the handover "shall remain in force" (Article 39); "the principles previously applied in Hong Kong and the rights previously enjoyed by parties [. . .] shall be maintained" in all criminal and civil proceedings (Article 87); the government shall "maintain Hong Kong's previous systems of shipping management and shipping regulation" (Article 124); and it "shall maintain the policy previously practised" regarding subventions to non-governmental organizations (Article 144). Provisions such as these cumulatively point to an ambivalence about moving forward in time, and a concomitant reluctance to becoming unmoored from the past. As the writer Leung Man-tao noted in the final days of the colonial era, asking whether Hong Kong will change after 1997 – an anxious and ubiquitous question at the time – is tantamount to saying that "it's best that things do not change".[3] In this light, the Basic Law can be read as the cultural-legal product of what Ackbar Abbas identifies as the politics of disappearance, or the outcome of an attempt to prevent disappearance by giving temporal stasis the status of the territory's highest law.[4] If, as the legal anthropologist Carol Greenhouse has famously argued, linear time is the dominant temporal conception of both legal institutions and public life more generally, then part of the uniqueness of Hong Kong's Basic Law lies in the way it is predicted on freezing time, on guaranteeing a temporal hiatus for as long as it is in effect.[5] Yet how can anything – an economic system, a set of laws, a way of life, an identity – remain the same for fifty years? And what might it mean to aspire to a legal regime in which time comes to a standstill?

Wong Kar-wai's *2046* (2004) provides a fascinating, if somewhat oblique, way of thinking about these questions. *2046* centers around Chow Mo-wan, a dissolute, womanizing writer in 1960s Hong Kong, as well as the various women whom he encounters: his neighbor Bailing, a beautiful nightclub hostess; Jing-wen, his landlord's daughter; Lulu, a nightclub entertainer; and Su Lizhen, a professional gambler he meets in Singapore. There is also a brief but important flashback to So Lai-chun, the married woman with whom he falls in love in *In the Mood for Love* (花樣年華; 2000). The film's multi-layered

---

[3] Leung Man-tao, "Rose Garden," *Ming Pao Daily News*, June 27th, 1997.

[4] Ackbar Abbas, *Hong Kong: Culture and the Politics of Disappearance* (Minneapolis: University of Minnesota Press, 1997).

[5] Carol J. Greenhouse, "Just in Time: Temporality and the Cultural Legitimation of Law," 98 *Yale Law Journal* (1989), 1631–1652. On law and time, see also Emily Grabham, *Brewing Legal Times: Things, Form, and the Enactment of Law* (Toronto: University of Toronto Press, 2016); Nomi Claire Lazar, "Time Framing in the Rhetoric of Constitutional Preambles," *Law & Literature*, DOI: 10.1080/1535685X.2019.1688477; and Desmond Manderson, *Danse Macabre: Temporalities of Law in the Visual Arts* (Cambridge: Cambridge University Press, 2019).

narrative defies attempts at approaching it as a straightforward allegory of Hong Kong's legal or political situation, as does the deliberate ambiguity of its title: 2046 simultaneously refers to a room number, the title of a science fiction story which Chow is writing, and both the temporal and geographical settings within that sci-fi story. Nonetheless, it would be difficult not to hear in it at least an echo of the Basic Law's temporally demarcated existence, and Wong himself has underscored that the idea of legal time is an inspiration for the film: "Why did I pick the number 2046? It is because we all say it is very important for Hong Kong to remain unchanged before 2046."[6] For Wong, the Basic Law's guarantee that Hong Kong will "remain unchanged for fifty years" is a pledge for a city that exists in "changeless time."[7] *2046* constitutes an exploration of what such a temporal regime might mean.

"Is there anything in this world that does not change?" Jing-wen asks Chow. This question, so evocative of the constitution's promise of changeless time, is in fact a question about love: Jing-wen is love with a Japanese man named Tak, but cannot be with him because of her father, whose memories of the war cause him to harbor racist inclinations. Tak returns to Japan, but continues to write letters to her to express his devotion. Jing-wen's question to Chow arises because she is uncertain whether Tak's love for her can indeed remain constant in light of their uncertain future and the geographical distance between them. In *2046*, the constitutional guarantee of changelessness is evoked through the promise of unchanging love. Wong declares that, ultimately, "if we love something, of course we hope it will not change"; for him, that rings as true for one's city as it does for one's lover.[8] In moving from the time of the Sino-British Joint Declaration to the Basic Law's possible expiration, our analysis comes full circle: in Chapter 1, we saw how the cinematic exploration of affects arising from constitutional changes of the early 1980s took place through an allegory of love in *The Unwritten Law*. Here, *2046* articulates the question about the end of constitutional time by replacing the language of law and politics with another language: "not politics, but love."[9]

Chow's response to Jing-wen's question takes the form of a science fiction story which he eventually entitles "2047," a story intertwined with a popular serial, "2046," which he is writing for a newspaper. The characters, loosely based on Chow's real-life acquaintances, recur in both stories. When Jing-wen eventually decides to pursue Tak by moving to Japan, Chow gives her "2047" as a farewell present. Writing about Wong's early films, Abbas has astutely observed that each film "starts with the conventions of a popular genre – and deliberately loses its way in the genre."[10] If *As Tears Go By* (旺角卡門; 1988) is Wong's take on the gangster film, *Days of Being Wild* (阿飛正傳; 1990) his take on the youth rebellion tradition, *Chung King Express* (重慶森林; 1994) his

---

[6] *Wong Kar-wai: Interviews*, edited by Silver Wai-ming Lee and Micky Lee (Jackson: University of Mississippi Press, 2017), p. 109.

[7] Stephen Teo, *Wong Kar-wai: Auteur of Time* (London: British Film Institute, 2005), p. 142.

[8] *Wong Kar-wai: Interviews*, p. 109.   [9] *Wong Kar-wai: Interviews*, p. 109.   [10] Abbas, p. 50.

take on romantic drama, and *Ashes of Time* (東邪西毒; 1994) his take on the martial arts film, then, building on Abbas's argument, *2046* can be regarded as Wong's reworking of the science fiction genre. The actual science fiction that appears in the film, in the form of Chow's writings, therefore merits close analysis.

In Chow's science fiction universe, 2046 is a place where nothing changes, and people go there to recapture lost memories. The film begins with a sequence from this universe, in which a Japanese passenger is on a train leaving 2046. His motivation for going to 2046 in the first place is explained in the following way:

> I once fell in love with someone. After a while, she wasn't there anymore. I went to 2046. I thought she might be waiting for me there. But I couldn't find her. I could not stop wondering whether she loved me or not. But maybe there is no answer.

2046 evokes the promise of a city that remains unchanged by interweaving it with the idea of a love that does not fade. In doing so, it calls forth a sensibility associated with the experience of political and constitutional transition by articulating a sensibility associated with love. Even though Chow first conceived of the Japanese passenger as a stand-in for Tak, he confesses in a voiceover that as the writing progressed, the character gradually morphed into a stand-in for himself: "Perhaps I got too involved in the story . . . I began imagining myself as a Japanese man, on a train leaving 2046." At this point, the back story of *In the Mood for Love*, which Wong describes as the "missing chapter" to *2046*, becomes salient.[11] In the earlier film, Chow asks So to leave her husband and move to Singapore with him. Despite her feelings for Chow, So refuses to do so and leaves him heartbroken. When interpreted as part of Chow's own story, the Japanese passenger's quest to 2046 becomes Chow's own quest for an undying love, a quest fuelled by his desire to believe that the love between him and So will remain unchanged. The fact that the passenger leaves 2046 without finding his lover there suggests that Chow is disappointed by So's decision. Yet his own love for So remains steadfast. *In the Mood for Love* ends with a sequence in Angkor Wat, which Chow travels to in pursuit of a legend: "In the past, whenever people had a secret, they would climb a mountain, find a tree, carve a hole into a tree, whisper the secret into the hole, and cover it with mud. That way, no one would ever discover it." In Angkor Wat, Chow carves a hole not only to hide and bury his secret love for So, but also to preserve it, to make it eternal by placing it in the ancient temple. This hole reappears in *2046*, transformed into a mysterious dark opening surrounded by dramatic colors, and the Japanese passenger whispers his secret into it. Moreover, the story becomes the passenger's explanation for leaving 2046: he says that "whenever someone asks me why I left 2046, I would give

---

[11] *Wong Kar-wai: Interviews*, p. 102.

them the same vague answer," and he then repeats this legend. This "vague answer" about why he leaves can be interpreted literally: he goes to 2046 to preserve his love, to place it in an imaginary land where nothing changes, where his devotion to her will never fade. 2046 is the place that guarantees that his love will remain strong and unchanging despite the passage of time, like the rocks of Angkor Wat.

Yet the film seems to suggest that this obsession with unchangeability is, ultimately, an unhealthy one. As Jean Ma has observed, the characters in *2046* all share "a melancholic disposition that clings to the past and resists the necessity of moving on."[12] While Jing-wen arguably attains her happy ending because of the constancy of her love – she ends up marrying Tak in Japan – her removal to another country in the narrative suggests that her ideals ultimately do not have a place in Hong Kong. For Chow in particular, remembrance "assumes the form of repetition compulsion," whereby he is "doomed to repeat the failure of that relationship [with So] in an endless series of love affairs." In real life, Chow is unable to enter into a new relationship because of his unchanging, fixated feelings for So. For instance, Su Lizhen (whose name is identical to So Lai-chun, but pronounced differently in Mandarin), the gambler whom he meets in Singapore, rejects his advances because she intuits that Chow only sees in her a substitute for his former lover. Another example is Chow's dalliance with Bailing, his neighbor: despite her beauty and her advances, Chow is unable to love her because he is still devoted to So.

In the science fiction story, the Japanese passenger – still in the role of Chow's stand-in – searches for So's substitute in an android from the train's service staff: "I once fell in love with someone. I could not stop wondering whether she was in love with me or not. I feel that the android looks a lot like her. I started looking for answers from it." He even asks the question which Chow once asked So: "Will you leave with me?" The android does not answer. It transpires later in the sequence that this android is not the only one he falls in love with on the train. He has repeated the same question – "Will you leave with me?" – to another android, and has presumably been met with the same silence. At first, the passenger thinks that the lack of response is due to a mechanical fault in the androids' circuits which the conductor had told him about. Yet as time goes by, his reaction begins to echo Chow's own thoughts about So's feelings for him: "I slowly started to doubt myself. Perhaps the mechanical delay [in the android] is not the reason why she is not answering. It is possible that she simply does not love me. I finally understood that there are things that are beyond my control. The only thing I can do is give up". Chow's experience in real life, as well as the encounters of the Japanese passenger in his science fiction, suggests that those who insist on an undying love are doomed to repeat the cycle of disappointment and

---

[12] Jean Ma, *Melancholy Drift: Marking Time in Chinese Cinema* (Hong Kong: Hong Kong University Press, 2010), p. 143.

disillusionment over and over again as they search incessantly for a satisfactory substitute for their original love, a search that inevitably fails.

Ultimately, *2046* suggests that not only is the attempt to freeze the past likely to become a fixation that prevents one from moving on, but any promise of invariability, stasis, and unchangeability can only be an empty one: as Wong observes, "we want to emphasize Hong Kong will remain unchanged, but this is impossible because the world is changing. [...] You have to follow change."[13] The film, as well as Chow's science fiction, begins with the following description: "Everyone goes to 2046 to recapture lost memories, because nothing ever changes in 2046. Nobody knows if that is true, because nobody has ever returned ... except me." It is unclear that the place where things remain the same does exist, even in science fiction, and the passenger who claims to have been to 2046 does not shed any light on whether things there do indeed remain constant. The film ends with Chow terminating his affair with Bailing, and as he leaves her we hear the same description of 2046 as a terrain of sameness in the voiceover. Yet in this final iteration, the words "except me" are conspicuously omitted, implying that, by this point, Chow no longer has any foreknowledge of whether his own love for So will remain constant in real life. As the taxi speeds away, one wonders, along with Chow, how many more Bailings he can turn down, before So's image starts to fade in his mind and becomes replaced by that of one of the many women he will no doubt continue to meet. Has his love indeed been preserved in the hole in Angkor Wat, or does the hole contain nothing more than air which slowly dissipates over time?

A text appears in the final moments of the film: it states that Chow "felt as if he had boarded a very, very long train, one that is speeding through the night towards a hazy future." It is unclear whether any promise, in love or in law, to "remain unchanged" can be kept – the future is "hazy." Yet perhaps the images of 2046, the imaginary place where things supposedly remain constant, can provide a clue. In the film's opening sequence, we see a train moving through 2046. This is a cityscape constructed at least in part from buildings in Hong Kong, but so thoroughly transformed by color, resolution, superimpositions, and other digitally created additions that it is barely recognizable as Hong Kong anymore. This is a city that, despite the purported constitutional guarantee of temporal hiatus, is changed virtually beyond recognition. The images of 2046 seem to suggest that perhaps a viable legal promise to keep the city frozen in time, like a lover's commitment to preserving his love after a relationship ends, belongs more to the realm of science fiction than to reality.

[13] *Wong Kar-wai: Interviews*, p. 109.

Bibliography

Primary Sources

Key Constitutional and Legislative Documents

Basic Law of the Hong Kong Special Administrative Region of the People's Republic of China.

Deng Xiaoping, Deng Xiaoping on the Question of Hong Kong (Hong Kong: New Horizon Press, 1993).

Cap.392 Film Censorship Ordinance.

Cap. 383 Hong Kong Bill of Rights Ordinance.

Hong Kong Hansard.

Joint Declaration of the Government of the United Kingdom of Great Britain and Northern Ireland and the Government of the People's Republic of China on the Question of Hong Kong.

The Interpretation by the Standing Committee of the National People's Congress of Article 7 of Annex I and Article III of Annex II to the Basic Law of the Hong Kong Special Administrative Region of the People's Republic Of China (April 6th, 2004).

Decision of the Standing Committee of the National People's Congress on Issues Relating to the Methods for Selecting the Chief Executive of the Hong Kong Special Administrative Region in the Year 2007 and for Forming the Legislative Counsel of the Hong Kong Special Administrative Region in the Year 2008 (April 26th, 2004).

Decision of the Standing Committee of the National People's Congress on Issues Relating to the Selection of the Chief Executive of the Hong Kong Special Administrative Region by Universal Suffrage and on the Method for Forming the Legislative Council of the Hong Kong Special Administrative Region in the Year 2016 (August 31st, 2014).

Interpretation of Article 104 of the Basic Law of the Hong Kong Special Administrative Region of the People's Republic of China by the Standing Committee of the National People's Congress (November 7th, 2016).

The Practice of the "One Country, Two Systems" Policy in the Hong Kong Special Administrative Region, the Information Office, State Council (June 10th, 2014).

Explanations on the Draft Decision of the Standing Committee of the National People's Congress on Issues Relating to the Selection of the Chief Executive of the Hong Kong Special Administrative Region by Universal Suffrage and the Method for Forming the Legislative Council of the Hong Kong Special Administrative Region in the Year 2016 (August 27th, 2014).

Cases

Ng Ka Ling & Others and Director of Immigration [1999] CFA 72

Chan Kam Nga & Others and Director of Immigration [1999] HKCFA 16.

Lau Kong Yung v. *Director of Immigration* [1999] HKCFA 5.

Chief Executive of the HKSAR v. *President of the Legislative Council* [2016] HKEC 2487 (CFI).

Chief Executive of the HKSAR v. *President of the Legislative Council* [2017] HKLRD 460 (CA).

Chief Executive of the HKSAR v. *President of the Legislative Council* [2017] 4 HKLRD 115.

HKSAR v. *Tai Yiu Ting and Others* [2019] HKDC 450.

News Publications and Websites

Annual Review of Law and Social Science [141]

Asian Wall Street Journal

Atlantic

BBC News

Cardozo Law Review [21]

City Entertainment

CNN

Coconuts Hong Kong

Economist

ejinsight.com

Financial Times

Forbes

Fordham International Law Journal [10]

Guardian

Hong Kong Economic Journal

Hong Kong Free Press

hongkongfp.com [153]

Hong Kong Law Journal [17]

Hong Kong Standard

Hong Kong Top Ten Blogspot

Huffington Post

International Journal of Constitutional Law [16]

Law and Literature [21]

Ming Pao Daily News

Next Magazine

New Evening Post

New York Times

Nutshell Review

Oriental Daily News

Oxford Journal of Legal Studies [95]

Sing Tao Daily

Social and Legal Studies [151]

Social Psychiatry and Psychiatric Epidemiology [139]

South China Morning Post
Surveillance and Society [2]
Ta Kung Pao
Time
Wen Wei Po

Miscellaneous Primary Sources

"The Chinese University of Hong Kong Releases Survey Findings on Views on Hong Kong's Core Values," Communications and Public Relations Office, October 30th, 2014. www.cpr.cuhk.edu.hk/en/press_detail.php?id=1915&t=cuhk-releases-survey-findings-on-views-on-hong-kong-s-core-values.

Renu Daryanani, Renu (ed.), *Hong Kong 1994* (Hong Kong: Hong Kong Government Printer, 1994).

Human Rights Watch, *World Report 2019: China*. www.hrw.org/world-report/2019/country-chapters/china-and-tibet#eaa21f.

Human Rights Watch, "Tiger Chairs and Cell Bosses: Police Torture of Criminal Suspects in China," May 13th, 2015.

Report by the Hong Kong Council of Women on the Third Periodic Report by Hong Kong Under Article 40 of the International Covenant on Civil and Political Rights (1991).

"Secretary of Justice's Speech at Ceremonial Opening of the Legal Year 2015," Hong Kong Government, January 12th, 2015.

Shakespeare, William, *The Merchant of Venice* (first published 1598, Signet Classic 2004), New York.

Secondary Sources

Abbas, Ackbar, *Hong Kong: Culture and the Politics of Disappearance* (Hong Kong: Hong Kong University Press, 1997).

Ahmed, Aijaz, "Jameson's Rhetoric of Otherness and the 'National Allegory'," 17 *Social Text* (1987), 3–25.

Aitken, Ian and Michael Ingham, *Hong Kong Documentary Film* (Edinburgh: Edinburgh University Press, 2014).

Anderson, Ben, *Encountering Affect: Capacities, Apparatuses, Conditions* (Surrey: Ashgate, 2014).

Austin, Regina, "Documentation, Documentary, and the Law: What Should be Made of Victim Impact Videos?," 31 (4)*Cardozo Law Review* (2010), 979–1019.

Baker, Hugh D. R., "Life in the Cities: The Emergence of Hong Kong Man," 95 *China Quarterly* (1983), 469–479.

Bergson, Henri, *Laughter: An Essay on the Meaning of the Comic*, trans. by Cloudesley Brereton and Fred Rothwell (London: Macmillan, 1911).

Berry, Chris, "Hong Kong Watcher: Tammy Cheung and the Hong Kong Documentary," in *Hong Kong Culture: Word and Image*, edited by Kam Louie, pp. 213–229 (2010).

Bloom, Harold, *Shakespeare: The Invention of the Human* (New York: Riverhead Books, 1998).

Bordwell, David, *Planet Hong Kong: Popular Cinema and the Art of Entertainment*, 2nd ed. (Madison: Irvington Way Institute Press, 2011).

Bruzzi, Stella, *New Documentary: A Critical Introduction*, 2nd ed. (Abingdon: Routledge, 2006).

Carroll, John M., *A Concise History of Hong Kong* (Hong Kong: Hong Kong University Press, 2007).

Caruth, Cathy, *Unclaimed Experience: Trauma, Narrative, and History* (Baltimore: Johns Hopkins University Press, 1996).

"Introduction," in *Trauma: Explorations in Memory*, edited by Cathy Caruth (Baltimore: Johns Hopkins University Press, 1995), pp. 3–13.

Casetti, Francesco, *The Lumière Galaxy: Seven Key Words for the Cinema to Come* (New York: Columbia University Press, 2015).

Chan, Cora, "Demise of 'One Country, Two Systems'? Reflections on the Hong Kong Rendition Saga," 49 (2) *Hong Kong Law Journal*, 447–459.

Chan, Johannes, "A Storm of Unprecedented Ferocity: The Shrinking Space of the Right to Political Participation, Peaceful Demonstration, and Judicial Independence in Hong Kong," 16 (2) *International Journal of Constitutional Law* (2018), 373–388.

Chan, Johannes, *Human Rights in Hong Kong* (Hong Kong: Wide Angle Press, 1990).

Chan, Johannes, Hualing Fu and Yash Ghai (eds.), *Hong Kong's Constitutional Debate: Conflict over Interpretation* (Hong Kong: Hong Kong University Press, 2000).

Chan, Ming K., "The Legacy of the British Administration of Hong Kong: A View from Hong Kong," 151 *China Quarterly* (1997), 567–582.

Chen, Albert H. Y., *An Introduction to the Legal System of the People's Republic of China*, 5th ed. (Hong Kong: LexisNexis, 2019).

"A Perfect Storm: Hong Kong-Mainland Rendition of Fugitive Offenders," 49(2) *Hong Kong Law Journal* (2019), 419–431.

"Editorial," 20 *Hong Kong Law Journal* (1990), 145–150.

"Some Reflections on the Film Censorship Affair," 17 *Hong Kong Law Journal* (1987), 352–359.

"Further Aspects of the Autonomy of Hong Kong under the PRC Constitution," 14 (3) *Hong Kong Law Journal* (1984), 341–347.

Chen, Phillip M., *Law and Justice: The Legal System in China, 2400BC to 1960 AD* (New York and London: Dunellen Publishing Company, 1973).

Cheng, Jie, "The Story of a New Policy," 15 *Hong Kong Journal* (July 2009). www .hkbasiclaw.com/Hong%20Kong%20Journal/Cheng%20Jie%20article.htm

Cheng, Joseph Y. S. (ed.), *The July Protest Rally: Interpreting a Historic Event* (Hong Kong: City University of Hong Kong Press, 2005).

Cheung, Anne S. Y., "What Law Cannot Give: From the Queen to the Chief Executive," in *Law and Popular Culture*, edited by Michael Freeman (Oxford: Oxford University Press, 2005), pp. 425–447.

Cheung, Esther M. K., Nicole Kempton, and Amy Lee, "Documenting Hong Kong: Interview with Tammy Cheung," in *Hong Kong Screenscapes: From the New Wave to the Digital Frontier*, edited by Esther M. K. Cheung, Gina Marchetti, and Tan See-Kam (Hong Kong: Hong Kong University Press, 2011), pp. 151–165.

Choy, Howard Y. F., "Schizophrenic Hong Kong: Postcolonial Identity Crisis in the *Infernal Affairs Trilogy*," 3 *Transtext(e)s Transcultures* (2007), 52–66.

Chow, Rey, *Sentimental Fabulations: Contemporary Chinese Cinema* (New York: Columbia University Press, 2007).

Ethics after Idealism: Theory – Culture – Ethnicity – Reading (Bloomington:Indiana University Press, 1998).

Chu Yiu-wai, *Hong Kong Cantopop: A Concise History* (Hong Kong: Hong Kong University Press, 2017).

Lost in Transition: Hong Kong Culture in the Age of China (New York: SUNY Press, 2013).

Clarke, W. S., "Hong Kong under the Chinese Constitution," 14 (1) *Hong Kong Law Journal* (1984), 71–81.

Clover, Carol, "Law and the Order of Popular Culture" (1998), reprinted in *Trial Films on Trial: Law, Justice, and Popular Culture*, edited by Austin Sarat, Jessica Silbey, and Martha Merrill Umphrey (Tuscaloosa: Alabama University Press, 2019), pp. 17–39.

Conner, Alison, "Courtroom Drama, Chinese Style," 12 *Journal of Comparative Law* (2017), 437–461.

"Images of Justice (and Injustice): Trials in the Movies of Xie Jin," 35 *Hawaii Law Review* (2013), 805–882.

Creed, Barbara, *The Monstrous-Feminine: Film, Feminism, Psychoanalysis* (London: Routledge, 1993).

Creekmur, Corey K. and Mark Sidel (eds.), *Cinema, Law and the State in Asia*, (Basingstoke: Palgrave Macmillan, 2007).

Critchley, Simon, *On Humour* (Abingdon: Routledge, 2002).

Dapiran, Antony, *City of Protest: A Recent History of Dissent in Hong Kong* (Hawthorn: Penguin, 2017).

Davis, Darrell W. and Yeh Yueh-yu, "Warning! Category III," 54 *Film Quarterly* (2001), 12–27.

Delage Christian, Peter Goodrich, and Marco Wan (eds.), *West of Everything: Law and New Media* (Edinburgh: Edinburgh University Press, 2019).

Duxbury, Neil, *The Nature and Authority of Precedent* (Cambridge: Cambridge University Press, 2008).

Eagleton, Terry, *William Shakespeare* (Oxford: Blackwell, 1986).

Fan, Victor, *Extraterritoriality: Locating Hong Kong Cinema and Media* (Edinburgh: Edinburgh University Press, 2019).

Fang, Karen, "Cinema Censorship and Media Citizenship in the Hong Kong Film *Ten Years*," 16 (2) *Surveillance & Society* (2018), 142–157.

Farquhar, Mary and Chris Berry, "Speaking Bitterness: History, Media and Nation in Twentieth Century China," 2 (1) *Historiography East and West* (2004), 116–144.

Fonoroff, Paul, *Paul Fonoroff at the Hong Kong Movies* (Hong Kong: Film Biweekly Publishing House, 1998).

Freud, Sigmund, "Jokes and Their Relation of the Unconscious" (1905) in *The Standard Edition of the Complete Psychological Works of Sigmund Freud*, edited and trans. by James Strachey (London: Vintage, 1960), Volume 8.

Fu Hualing and Han Zhu, "After the July 9 (709) Crackdown: The Future of Human Rights Lawyering," 41 (5) *Fordham International Law Journal* (2018), 1135–1165.

Fung, Daniel R., "Paradoxes of Hong Kong's Reversion: The Legal Dimension," in *Hong Kong and the Super Paradox: Life after Return to China*, edited by James C. Hsiung (Basingstoke: Macmillan, 2000), pp. 105–125.

Ghai, Yash, *Hong Kong's New Constitutional Order: The Resumption of Chinese Sovereignty and the Basic Law*, 2nd ed. (Hong Kong: Hong Kong University Press, 1999).

Gilbert, Nora, *Better Left Unsaid: Victorian Novels, Hays Code, and the Benefits of Censorship* (Palo Alto: Stanford University Press, 2013).

Goldstein, Lawrence (ed.), *Precedent in Law* (Oxford: Clarendon Press, 1987).

Goodrich, Peter. "Proboscations: Excavations in Comedy and Law," 43 (2) *Critical Inquiry* (2017), 361–389.

"Screening Law," 21 (1) *Law & Literature* (2009), 1–23.

Law in the Courts of Love: Literature and Other Minor Jurisprudences (Abingdon: Routledge, 1996).

Grabham, Emily, *Brewing Legal Times: Things, Form, and the Enactment of Law* (Toronto: University of Toronto Press, 2016).

Greenfield, Steve, Guy Osborn, and Peter Robson, *Film and the Law*, 2nd ed. (Oxford: Hart, 2010).

Greenhouse, Carol J., "Just in Time: Temporality and the Cultural Legitimation of Law," 98 *Yale Law Journal* (1989), 1631–1652.

Ingham, Mike, "Hong Kong Cinema and the Film Essay: A Matter of Perception," in *Hong Kong Screenscapes: From the New Wave to the Digital Frontier*, edited by Esther M. K. Cheung, Gina Marchetti, and Tan See-Kam (Hong Kong: Hong Kong University Press, 2011), pp. 175–195.

Jacobsohn, Gary, *Constitutional Identity* (Cambridge: Harvard University Press, 2010).

Jameson, Fredric "Third-World Literature in the Era of Multinational Capitalism," 15 *Social Text* (1986), 65–88.

Jones, Carol A. G., *Lost in China?: Law, Culture and Identity in Post-1997 Hong Kong* (Cambridge, Cambridge University Press, 2015).

Kahn, Paul, *Finding Ourselves at the Movies: Philosophy for a New Generation* (New York: Columbia University Press, 2013).

Kamir, Orit, *Framed: Women in Law and Film* (Durham: Duke University Press, 2006).

Kaplan, E. Ann, *Trauma Culture: the Politics of Terror and Loss in Media and Literature* (New Brunswick: Rutgers University Press, 2005).

Krygier, Martin, "The Rule of Law: Pasts, Presents, and Two Possible Futures," 12 *Annual Review of Law and Social Science* (2016), 199–229.

Ku, Agnes, "Civil Society's Dual Impetus – Mobilizations, Representations and Contestations Over the July 1 March, 2003," in *Politics and Government in Hong Kong: Crisis under Chinese Sovereignty*, edited by Ming Sing (Abingdon: Routledge, 2009), pp. 38–58.

Lai, Linda Chiu-Han, "Nostalgia and Nonsense: Two Instances of Commemorative Practices in Hong Kong Cinema in the Early 1990s," in *Fifty Years of Electric Shadows*, edited by Law Kar and Stephen Teo (Hong Kong: Urban Council Publications, 1997), pp. 95–100.

Lau, Chi-kuen, *Hong Kong's Colonial Legacy* (Hong Kong: Chinese University Press, 1997).

Lau, Joseph T. F. et al., "The Occupy Central (Umbrella) Movement and Mental Health Distress in the Hong Kong General Public: Political Movements and Concerns as Potential Structural Risk Factors of Population Mental Health," 52 *Social Psychiatry and Psychiatric Epidemiology* (2017), 525–536.

Law, Kar, "Overview of Hong Kong's New Wave Cinema," in *At Full Speed: Hong King Cinema in a Borderless World*, edited by Esther C. M. Yau (Minneapolis: University of Minnesota Press, 2001), pp. 31–53.

Lee, Leo Ou-fan, *City between Worlds: My Hong Kong* (Cambridge: Harvard University Press, 2008).

Lee, Silver Wai-ming and Micky Lee (eds.), *Wong Kar-wai: Interviews* (Jackson: University of Mississippi Press, 2017).

Lo, Sonny, "The Mainlandization and Recolonization of Hong Kong: A Triumph of Convergence over Divergence with Mainland China," in *The Hong Kong Special Administrative Region in Its First Decade*, edited by Joseph Y. S. Cheng (Hong Kong: City University Press, 2007), pp. 179–232.

Lu, Sheldon H., "Filming Diaspora and Identity: Hong Kong and 1997," in *The Cinema of Hong Kong: History, Arts, Identity*, edited by Poshek Fu and David Desser (Cambridge: Cambridge University Press, 2000), pp. 273–289.

Ma, Jean, *Melancholy Drift: Marking Time in Chinese Cinema* (Hong Kong: Hong Kong University Press, 2010).

Macaulay, Melissa, *Social Power and Legal Culture: Litigation Masters in Late Imperial China* (Palo Alto: Stanford University Press, 1998).

MacKinnon, Catharine A., *Toward a Feminist Theory of the State* (Cambridge: Harvard University Press, 1989).

MacNeil, William P., *Lex Populi: The Jurisprudence of Popular Culture* (Palo Alto: Stanford University Press, 2007).

"Righting and Difference," in *Human Rights in Hong Kong*, edited by Raymond Wacks (Oxford: Oxford University Press, 1992), pp. 86–120.

Manderson, Desmond, *Danse Macabre: Temporalities of Law in the Visual Arts* (Cambridge: Cambridge University Press, 2019).

Marchetti, Gina, "Hong Kong as Feminist Method: Gender, Sexuality, and Democracy in Two Documentaries by Tammy Cheung," in *Hong Kong Society in the New Millennium: Hong Kong as Method*, edited by Chu Yiu-wai (Singapore: Springer, 2017), pp. 59–77.

Matthews, Daniel, "Narrative, Space and Atmosphere: A Nomospheric Inquiry into Hong Kong's Pro-democracy 'Umbrella Movement'", 26 *Social & Legal Studies* (2017), 25–46.

McCrudden, Christopher, "A Common Law of Human Rights? Transnational Judicial Conversations on Constitutional Rights," 20 (4) *Oxford Journal of Legal Studies* (2000), 499–532.

McIntyre, Stephen, "Courtroom Drama with Chinese Characteristics: A Comparative Approach to Legal Process in Chinese Cinema," 8 *University of Pennsylvania East Asia Law Review* (2013), 1–21.

Merry, Sally Engle and Rachel E. Stern, "The Female Inheritance Movement in Hong Kong: Theorizing the Local/Global Interface," 46 (3) *Current Anthropology*, 387–409.

Millett, Peter Julian, *Villainy in Venice* (Hong Kong: University of Hong Kong Occasional Publication, 2005).

Minow, Martha, Michael Ryan, and Austin Sarat (eds.), *Narrative, Violence, and the Law: the Essays of Robert Cover* (Ann Arbor: University of Michigan Press, 1993).

Mulvey, Laura, *Visual and Other Pleasures*, 2nd ed. (Basingstoke: Palgrave MacMillan, 2009).

Munby, Jonathan, *Public Enemies, Public Heroes: Screening the Gangster from Little Caesar to Touch of Evil* (Chicago: University Of Chicago Press, 1999).

Neoh, Joshua, "Law and Love in Abraham's Binding of Issac," 9 *Law and Humanities* (2015), 237–261.

Ng, Michael "When Silence Speaks: Press Censorship and Rule of Law in British Hong Kong, 1850s–1940s," 29 (3) *Law & Literature*, 425–456.

   "Fiftieth Anniversary of Chan Mon-kut's Trickery," 109 *Cup Magazine* (2011), 118–119.

Ni, Michael Y. et al., "Longitudinal Patterns and Predictors of Depression Trajectories Related to the 2014 Occupy Central/Umbrella Movement in Hong Kong," 107 (4) *American Journal of Public Health* (2017), 593–600.

Nichols, Bill, *Representing Reality* (Bloomington: Indiana University Press, 1991).

Nochimson, Martha, *Dying to Belong: Gangster Movies in Hollywood and Hong Kong* (Malden: Blackwell, 2007).

Petersen, Carole, J., "Introduction," in *National Security and Fundamental Freedoms: Hong Kong's Article 23 Under Scrutiny*, edited by Fu Hualing, Carole J. Petersen and Simon N. M. Young (Hong Kong: Hong Kong University Press, 2005), pp. 1–10 (p. 10).

   "Equality as a Human Right: The Development of Anti-Discrimination Law in Hong Kong," 34 *Columbia Journal of Transnational Law* (1996), 335–389.

Pils, Eva, *Human Rights in China: A Social Practice in the Shadows of Authoritarianism* (Cambridge: Polity Press, 2018).

Prince, Stephen (ed.), *Screening Violence* (New Brunswick: Rutgers University Press, 2000).

Raffield, Paul and Gary Watt (eds.), *Shakespeare and the Law* (Oxford: Hart, 2008).

Rosenfeld, Michel, *The Identity of the Constitutional Subject: Selfhood, Citizenship, Culture, and Community* (Abingdon: Routledge, 2010).

Samuels, Harriet, "Women and the Law in Hong Kong: A Feminist Analysis," in *Hong Kong, China, and 1997: Essays in Legal Theory*, edited by Raymond Wacks (Hong Kong: Hong Kong University Press, 1993), pp. 61–86.

Saw, Tiong-guan, *Film Censorship in the Asia-Pacific Region: Malaysia, Hong Kong and Australia Compared* (Abingdon: Routledge, 2013).

Shapiro, James, *Shakespeare and the Jews* (New York: Columbia University Press, 1996).

Sherwin, Richard K., *Visualizing Law in the Age of the Digital Baroque* (Abingdon: Routledge, 2011).

   When Law Goes Pop: The Vanishing Law between Law and Popular Culture (Chicago: University of Chicago Press, 2000).

Shih, Shu-mei, *Visuality and Identity: Sinophone Articulations across the Pacific* (Berkeley: University of California Press, 2007).

Silbey, Jessica, "Filmmaking in the Precinct House and the Genre of Documentary Film," 29 *Columbia Journal of Law & the Arts* (2005), 107–180.

Slocum, David J. (ed.), *Violence and American Cinema,* (New York: Routledge, 2001).

Smart, Carol, *Feminism and the Power of Law* (London: Routledge, 1989).

Smoodin, Eric, "'Compulsory' Viewing for every Citizen: 'Mr Smith' and the Rhetoric of Reception," 35(2) *Cinema Journal* (1996), 3–23.

Sobchack, Vivian, *Carnal Thoughts: Embodiment and Moving Image Culture* (Berkeley: University of California Press, 2004).

Spencer, Herbert. "The Physiology of Laughter," in *Essays: Scientific, Political, and Speculative* (London: Williams and Norgate, 1891), Volume II, pp. 452–467.

Tan, See-kam, "Ban(g)! Ban(g)! Dangerous Encounter – 1st Kind: Writing with Censorship," 8 (1) *Asian Cinema* (1996), 83–109.

Teo, Stephen, *Wong Kar-wai: Auteur of Time* (London: British Film Institute, 2005).

Todd, Janet, *Sensibility: An Introduction* (London: Methuen, 1986).

Tsang, Steve, *A Modern History of Hong Kong* (Hong Kong: Hong Kong University Press, 2004).

Wall, Illan Rua, "The Law of Crowds," 36 *Legal Studies* (2016), 395–414.

Walker, Janet, "The Vicissitudes of Traumatic Memory and the Postmodern History Film," in *Trauma and Cinema*, edited by E. Ann Kaplan and Ban Wang (Hong Kong: Hong Kong University Press, 2018), pp. 123–145.

Wan, Marco, "Gay Visibility and the Law in Hong Kong," 32 (3) *International Journal for the Semiotics of Law* (2019), 699–713.

"A Ghost Story: Electoral Reform and Hong Kong Popular Theatre," in *Administering Interpretation: Derrida, Agamben, and the Political Theology of Law*, edited by Peter Goodrich and Michel Rosenfeld (New York: Fordham University Press, 2019), pp. 272–290.

"The Artwork of Hong Kong's Occupy Central Movement," in *Civil Unrest and Governance in Hong Kong: Law and Order from Historical and Cultural Perspectives*, edited by Michael H. K. Ng and John D. Wong (Abingdon: Routledge, 2017), pp. 179–196.

Watt, Gary, *Equity Stirring* (Oxford: Hart, 2009).

Weisberg, Richard, *Poethics and Other Strategies of Law and Literature* (New York: Columbia University Press, 1992).

Wesley-Smith, Peter, *An Introduction to the Hong Kong Legal System*, 3rd ed. (Hong Kong: Oxford University Press, 1998).

"Anti-Chinese Legislation in Hong Kong," in *Precarious Balance: Hong Kong between China and Britain, 1842–1992*, edited by Ming K. Chan (Armonk: M. E. Sharpe, 1994), pp. 91–107.

"The Common Law of England in the Special Administrative Region," in *Hong Kong, China and 1997: Essays in Legal Theory*, edited by Raymond Wacks (Hong Kong: Hong Kong University Press, 1993), pp. 5–41.

Wilson, Ron, *The Gangster Film: Fatal Success in American Cinema* (New York: Wallflower Press, 2015).

Wood, Miles, *Cine East: Hong Kong Cinema through The Looking Glass* (Guildford: FAB Press, 1998).

Yoshino, Kenji, *A Thousand Times More Fair* (New York: HarperCollins, 2011).

Young, Alison, *The Scene of Violence: Cinema, Crime, Affect* (Abingdon: Routledge, 2010).

Filmography

All films are listed by English titles with Chinese titles and directors' names provided in traditional Chinese characters.

2046 (directed by Wong Kar-wai 王家衛, 2004)

A Simple Life (桃姐; directed by Ann Hui 許鞍華, 2011)

As Tears Go By (旺角卡門; directed by Wong Kar-wai 王家衛, 1988)

Ashes of Time (東邪西毒; directed by Wong Kar-wai 王家衛, 1994)

Avengers: Infinity War (directed by Anthony Russo and Joe Russo, 2018)

Avengers: Endgame (directed by Anthony Russo and Joe Russo, 2019)

Chung King Express (重慶森林; directed by Wong Kar-wai 王家衛, 1994)

Comrades, Almost a Love Story (甜蜜蜜; directed by Peter Chan 陳可辛, 1996)

Days of Being Wild (阿飛正傳; directed by Wong Kar-wai 王家衛, 1990)

Dr Lamb (羔羊醫生; directed by Danny Lee 李修賢 and Billy Tang 鄧衍成, 1992)

Election (黑社會; directed by Johnnie To 杜琪峯, 2005)

Election 2 (黑社會: 以和爲貴; directed by Johnnie To 杜琪峯, 2006)

Father and Son (父子情; directed by Allen Fong 方育平, 1981)

From the Queen to the Chief Executive (等候董建華發落; directed by Herman Yau 邱禮濤, 2001)

Hail the Judge (九品芝麻官; directed by Wong Jing 王晶, 1994)

Happy Together (春光乍洩; directed by Wong Kar-wai 王家衛, 1997)

In the Mood for Love (花樣年華; directed by Wong Kar-wai 王家衛, 2000)

Joshua Wong: Teenager vs. Superpower (directed by Joe Piscatella, 2017, released on Netflix)

July (七月; directed by Tammy Cheung 張虹, 2004)

Justice, My Foot! (審死官; directed by Johnnie To 杜琪峯, 1992)

Lawyer Lawyer (算死草; directed by Joe Ma 馬偉豪, 1997)

Legal Innocence (溶屍奇案; directed by Cha Chuen-yee 查傳誼, 1993)

Little Caesar (directed by Mervyn LeRoy, 1930)

Lord of the Rings (film series; directed by Peter Jackson)

Lost in the Fumes (地厚天高; directed by Nora Lam 林子穎, 2017),

No Justice for All (真相; directed by Herman Yau 邱禮濤, 1995)

Portrait of a Serial Rapist (香港奇案之屯門色魔; directed by Wong Gam-Din 黃錦鈿, 1994)

Raise the Umbrellas (撐傘; directed by Evans Chan 陳耀成, 2016)

Raped by an Angel (香港奇案之強姦; directed by Andrew Lau 劉偉強, 1993)

Red to Kill (弱殺; directed by Billy Tang 鄧衍成, 1994)

Remains of a Woman (郎心如鐵; directed by Clarence Fok 霍耀良, 1993)

Road Not Taken (未竟之路; directed by Nora Lam 林子穎, 2016)

Scarface (directed by Howard Hawks, 1932)

Sentenced to Hang (三狼奇案; directed by Taylor Wong 黃泰來, 1989)

Star Wars (film series, multiple directors)

Story of a War Vet [19]

Ten Years (十年, anthology of five short films, 2015):

- *Extras* (浮瓜; directed by Kwok Zune 郭臻)
- *Season of the End* (冬蟬; directed by Wong Fei-Pang 黃飛鵬)
- *Dialect* (方言; directed by Jevons Au 歐文傑)
- *Self-Immolator* (自焚者; directed by Chow Kwun-wai 周冠威)
- *Local Egg* (本地蛋; directed by Ng Ka-leung 伍嘉良)

The Final Judgment (紙盒藏屍之公審; directed by Norman Chan 陳奧圖, 1993)

The Judge Goes to Pieces (審死官; directed by Yeung Kung-leong 楊工良, 1948)

The Mobfathers (選老頂; directed by Herman Yau 邱禮濤, 2016)

The Piano (directed by Jane Campion, 1993)

The Public Enemy (directed by William A. Wellman, 1931)

The Rapist (屯門色魔; directed by Cha Chuen-yee 查傳誼, 1994)

The Secret (瘋劫; directed by Ann Hui 許鞍華, 1979)

The Story of Woo Viet (胡越的故事; directed by Ann Hui 許鞍華, 1981)

The Three Wolves Murders [70]

The Untold Story (八仙飯店之人肉叉燒包; directed by Herman Yau 邱禮濤, 1993)

The Unwritten Law (法外情; directed by Ng See-yuen 吳思遠, 1985)

Triad (紮職; directed by Daniel Chan 陳翊恆, 2012)

Umbrella Diaries: The First Umbrellas (傘上: 遍地開花; directed by James Leong 梁思眾, 2018)

Unclaimed Experince [149]

Yellowing (亂世備忘; directed by Chan Tze-woon 陳梓桓, 2016)

Index

Made in the USA
Las Vegas, NV
12 February 2022

43695745R00109